SETTLER

Identity and Colonialism

SETTLER

Identity and Colonialism

2ND EDITION

WRITTEN BY

Emma Battell Lowman & Adam J. Barker

Fernwood Publishing
Halifax & Winnipeg

Copyright 2025 © Emma Battell Lowman and Adam J. Barker

All rights reserved. No part of this book may be reproduced or transmitted in any form by any means without permission in writing from the publisher, except by a reviewer, who may quote brief passages in a review.

Development editor: Fazeela Jiwa
Copyediting: Amber Riaz
Text design: Lauren Jeanneau
Cover design: ALL CAPS Design
Printed and bound in the UK

Published by Fernwood Publishing
Halifax and Winnipeg
2970 Oxford Street, Halifax, Nova Scotia, B3L 2W4
www.fernwoodpublishing.ca

Fernwood Publishing Company Limited gratefully acknowledges the financial support of the Government of Canada through the Canada Book Fund and the Canada Council for the Arts. We acknowledge the Province of Manitoba for support through the Manitoba Publishers Marketing Assistance Program and the Book Publishing Tax Credit. We acknowledge the Nova Scotia Department of Communities, Culture and Heritage for support through the Publishers Assistance Fund. We also acknowledge the Urban Studies Foundation for publishing support.

Library and Archives Canada Cataloguing in Publication
Title: Settler : identity and colonialism / written by Emma Battell Lowman & Adam J. Barker.
Names: Battell Lowman, Emma, 1980- author | Barker, Adam J., 1980- author.
Description: 2nd edition. | Includes bibliographical references and index.
Identifiers: Canadiana 20250113465 | ISBN 9781773637341 (softcover)
Subjects: LCSH: Settler colonialism—Canada. | LCSH: Colonists—Canada. | LCSH: Identity (Psychology)—Canada. | LCSH: Social change—Canada. | LCSH: Indigenous peoples—Canada—Colonization. | LCSH: Canada—Ethnic relations.
Classification: LCC E78.C2 B368 2025 | DDC 305.897/071—dc23

Contents

Preface to the Second Edition ix

Forever *(a poem by January Rogers)* 1

1 ≈ Why Say Settler? 6
    Understanding and Avoidance 7
    Asserting the Settler Identity 27
    On Being and Knowing: Notes on Ontology and Relationship ... 38
    Toward Decolonization 42
    Notes 44

2 ≈ Canada and Settler Colonialism 52
    Beyond Binaries 58
    Spaces, Systems, Stories: Structures of Invasion
    at Work in Canada 63
    Whiteness and Capitalism 70
    Settler Colonization and the Settler Identity 74
    Being Settler Canadian 76
    Looking to the Land 87
    Notes 88

3 ≈ It's Always All About the Land 95
    Identity and the Land 96
    Settler Colonialism, Identity, and the Land 105
    Belonging Through Treaty? 115
    Notes 121

4 ≈ "Settling" Our Differences 125
Settler Colonial Complicity 126
Becoming Settler People 137
Settler Benefits: Mobility and Comfortable Ignorance 144
Notes 150

5 ≈ Fear, Complicity, and Productive Discomfort 154
Settler Fear 154
Moves to Comfort 164
Beyond Settler Certainty 174
Notes 177

6 ≈ Decolonization and Dangerous Freedom 179
Decolonization: From Awareness to Responsibility 182
Always in Relationship 190
Entering the Space of Dangerous Freedom 196
Notes 200

Bibliography 202

Index 217

Acknowledgements

We first want to thank January Rogers, whose work, art, and expertise continue to animate and shape our understandings. We first heard her poem, "Forever," as a live performance at the Indigenous Leadership Forum (Victoria, 2013), and we are grateful to January for permission to reprint her work again. That "Forever" begins this book is very important to us, and we hope it also helps readers find and feel their way into the work we need to do.

We next want to thank Chaw-win-is Ogilvie, Trish Rosborough, Audra Tseianenhawi Taillefer, and Paulette Regan for allowing us to share stories of our experiences and relationships, and Vanessa Watts for giving permission to reproduce an illustration from her important work. We also wish to thank Adam Gaudry for sharing his expertise on Métis history and nationhood, Damien Lee for his perspectives on identity and relationships, and Daniel Coleman for insights into Settler belonging. A much wider community has contributed support and critical conversations, including Christine O'Bonsawin and Alan Kerr, Bonnie Whitlow, Terri Monture, Shauneen Pete, Kirsten Mikkelsen, and many more who we hope will see their influence in this work. It is also important to acknowledge those knowledge holders who have passed, whose memory and contributions we hold close. If we continue to write of them in the present tense, it is because their impact and work are still very much alive for us.

Next, we thank Lorenzo Veracini for his generosity with his time and critical attention to the first edition. We also want to thank Candida Hadley, editor of the original book and whose guidance and patience, insight, humour, and genuine care and expertise were key to its success. We wrote the first edition of *Settler* in the Crystal Beach home of Donna Polgar, whose generosity made every difference and who gave us time, space, and warmth near Lake Erie to immerse ourselves in this work in early 2015. Judith St. Denis hosted us with great love and kindness during the opening and closing stages of writing the first edition, and her fierce love and support got us through difficult moments. And importantly, our current editor Fazeela Jiwa, who commissioned the second edition and whose expertise and experience have had a strong positive influence. We also appreciate her patience with us as the twists and turns of life threw off our plans to hit deadlines, and the support of the whole team at Fernwood Publishing.

Finally, our warm thanks to our loving community of family and friends who have and continue to support us. We especially acknowledge the patience and kindness of our parents — Melanie, Joe, Kathy, Robert, and Mary — who have given us space, time, love, inspiration, and houseroom on occasions too diverse and numerous to fully recount. We also thank our parents' friends, especially our radical aunties, including Anne Hoelscher, Margie Hadley, Jane Moon, and Nora Quinn, for lessons in life-long learning and the power of friendship. We thank James for always actively supporting our work. We remain grateful for the unwavering support and love of our Leicester family: Jo, Tim, Ben, Harry and Amelia Smith, Tine Julhert, Lorna and Alex White, Jody, Kevin, William, and Olivia Shields, Jen Ratcliff, Mandy and Jo Braves, Jane Kelly, and Lou Brown. Over the past few years, we have also benefitted from working with organizers and activists in England, and we want to recognize the trade union activists and radical educators whose comradeship in struggle continues to teach and inspire, in particular David Harvie, the inCommons collective, and the regulars of the Goose & Picket.

We also want to thank our non-human friends and family, who bring so much to our lives and whose love and learnings have made us better people every day. Huge love to Xena and Andy, Yoshi and Zelda, Darcy and Chica, Griffin and Skylar, Jimmy, Rio, Teddy, Poppy, George, and Winston, and Gabrielle who did her best to make us smile when things were tough.

The original book was primarily written on the lands of the Haudenosaunee, Anishinaabe, and Coast Salish. We have mostly lived away from these territories over the past decade but remain connected and accountable to the peoples whose lands we call "home." It is our hope that this book contributes to people taking action towards decolonization and Indigenous resurgence in those territories and across Turtle Island.

Preface to the Second Edition

CANADIAN SETTLER COLONIALISM HAS NOT ENDED. Indigenous People and Nations continue to challenge genocide, deprivation, and disregard of Indigenous rights. Why? Because settlers continue to colonize, governments continue to ignore or actively oppose Indigenous struggles for decolonization, and corporations continue to assault Indigenous lands. This situation remains unchanged since the publication of *Settler* in 2015.

But some things have changed in the past decade. We see hope in the ways people are using the calls to action in the Final Report of the Truth and Reconciliation Commission (TRC) of Canada to push positive change in workplaces and spaces of learning. We see hope in the Missing and Murdered Indigenous Women (MMIW) Inquiry's admission that Canada is founded on historic and ongoing genocide because it makes the historic and ongoing realities of Canadian colonialism clear at home and internationally. We see hope in Indigenous communities reclaiming lands from 1492 Landback Lane to the Wet'suwet'en gateway camps, and that there are some Settler Canadians supporting these efforts. We see hope in changes to the way these issues are discussed by people in classrooms, in the media, and in social discourses in Canada.

We, Settler Canadians, need to do more of this work and, to do it, we need to understand ourselves. As authors, *Settler* is part of our contribution. In this book, we seek to communicate and amplify what we have learned from Indigenous scholars and experts through teaching, deep critical reflection, and personal experience and growth. Our goal is to provide effective and accessible ways for other Settler Canadians to build their capacities for understanding and action.

We are energized by people taking up these challenges. We've heard from folks who have used *Settler* in book clubs, classrooms, professional training, faith groups, podcasts, living rooms, and more, and we appreciate hearing that it has been serving its purpose: helping people change the conversation and the scope for action.

We have updated this book to support its usefulness as a tool and learning resource, and we hope the changes help more people see themselves in these issues and their solutions. We also hope we have clarified how important it is for Settler Canadians to take up the reciprocal work of creating opportunities for truly just Indigenous–Settler relations, and how we can develop capacity to do so. There is no single path to meaningful settler decolonization; similarly, there are a multitude of excellent resources — books, articles, videos, poetry, research — available today to support this effort. This book contains tools, stories, and calls to action that we hope you will read in connection with your wider experience and learning.

Where we are insufficient in this book, we ask others to go further. Because that's the point. We need to support each other to progress in decolonization with courage and compassion. And to progress, we need to use the tools we have and build new tools to take on challenges that arise as we work. We need to do this together, with compassion, criticality, and strength.

In this new edition, in addition to streamlining the text, we have made changes in three main areas:

- We updated some stories and illustrative examples in light of events since the first publication. We kept stories or examples that had particular significance (historical, political, social, etc.) or that were meaningfully connected with our experience and learning journey.

- We have updated references to expert work in light of developments since first publication, including new works by Indigenous scholars such as Leanne Simpson, advocates like Cindy Blackstock, and reporters like Jorge Barrera, among others. We have kept references that speak to how we came to engage with concepts or ideas. Work in connected areas has expanded significantly over the past decade — a positive development — and we hope readers will seek out and engage widely with these excellent resources.

- We have nuanced our attention to regional and other differences in how settler colonialism is perceived and practiced, signposting specific resources in these areas including discussions of French Canada and Québécois nationalism, settlers abroad, and Black and People of Colour in Canada.

The original version of *Settler* was born out of a decade of work and discussions and our desire to share what we learned. The national conversation about settler colonialism in Canada has advanced significantly since that time. However, a decade later, the need for a book like this remains. We would like to thank and signal the importance of Fernwood Publishing and our editor, Fazeela Jiwa, in pursuing this updated edition. They, like us, recognize that progress has been made. They, like us, know that progress is not nearly enough. We are still confronting many of the same issues and problems, and most importantly, the same underlying inequalities and violences of settler colonization at the core of Canadian identity, politics, and society. We know things can change, but only if — or when — people from all ages, classes, cultures, and other markers of difference join in the struggle.

Forever

by January Rogers

as long as the sun shines upon the earth
as long as the water still flows
as long as the grass grows at a certain time each year
Forever
as long as Mother Earth is still in motion
still in motion, still in motion

It's hard work to maintain the middle row
one line makes I separating sides
they navigate a boat down a similar river
we paddle a canoe packing values
never touching, forever separate
maintaining the course
step by step laws of RESPECT
intended to protect sacred relationships

Words from good minds
Guswenta, Two Row Wampum
not treaty like it was told but a non-apology
canoe and Boat Ever Flowing Large Water River
buoyancy beyond democracy
boundaries not borders
the law was not authored in an angry house
of disputes but rather inspired from witness
to cause and effect of free will resulting in greed
and corruption and un-lawful things

Protection of our relationship to our mother
not better than the other but something necessary
to exercise caution
Careful!
Steady!
Carry on ....
Your side
Our side
Maintaining the middle
is most difficult

I is for Indian Affairs
I is for Indigenous
I is for Imperialism
I is for Identity
I is for Iroquois/Haudenosaunee
I is for Incident
I is for Initiation

A league of nations
corresponding by beads on a belt
and anyone thinking beads to be insignificant
should try getting them back from a museum
Crime Minister/Prime Minister
simultaneous colonization and decolonization
relational trade quasi-kin two sides kept equal
This is Women's work

Those mountains didn't build themselves

Forever
As long as the sun shines upon the earth
As long as the water still flows
As long as the grass grows at a certain time each year
Forever
as long as Mother Earth is still in motion
still in motion, still in motion

It's about balance and focus
it's about commitment and loyalty
hard things, put in place
speaking the language of agreement
being included from a distance
peace and respect and prosperity

Do NOT Cross that Line
we said
DO NOT CROSS THAT LINE

Disruption results in consequences
remember Kanenhstaton Caladonia
remember Gustafen Lake
remember Ipperwash
remember Oka
remember Alcatraz and Eagle Bay
remember Wounded Knee
everyday is remembrance day
everyday

Ongwehonwe Original
a national fabric forming
blessing and protecting
something spiritual
not material but a difficult journey
staying the course better or worse
leaving nothing to debate
constitutional consensus overflowing with intelligence
Peacemaker would be proud

Forever
As long as the sun shines upon the earth
as long as the water still flows
as long as the grass grows at a certain time each year
Forever
as long as Mother Earth is still in motion
still in motion, still in motion
Forever

— From *Peace in Duress*, 2014. Reprinted here with permission.

January Marie Rogers

January is a Mohawk/Tuscarora poet, media producer, and performance and sound artist. She lives on her home territory of Six Nations of the Grand River where she operates Ojistoh Publishing and Productions. She has seven published poetry titles and wrote and produced a comedy web series, *NDNs on the Airwaves* (2022) and a play published as *Blood Sport* (Turtle's Back Publishing 2023).

January combines her literary talents with her passion for media making to produce audio and video poetry. Her video poem "Ego of a Nation" won Best Music Video at the American Indian Film Festival in 2020 and her sound piece "The Battle Within" won the Best Experimental Sound prize at the imagineNATIVE Film and Media Festival in 2021. She was Western University's Writer in Residence (2022/23) and is one of Audible Indigenous Writers Circle mentors for 2022, 2023, and 2024. January is also lead mentor with the Indigenous Story Sharing Residency at the Banff Centre for the Arts 2024.

Why Say Settler?

THE WORDS WE USE TO NAME OURSELVES ARE IMPORTANT. How we conceive of ourselves collectively is a part of wider, more complicated discussions about who is included and who is excluded from our society. In Canada, we like to think of ourselves as having a fairly inclusive society; we pride ourselves on being open and accepting of difference. We talk about being polite and respectful and peace loving. And we lie by omission, because we do not talk about our country being built on the attempted destruction of many other nations — or if we do, we discuss it in terms of past wrongs, not present-day realities. We do not talk about the questionable legal and political basis of our country or our history of profiting from invasion and dispossession. "Canadian" — a notoriously hard-to-pin-down concept — may not have a clear definition, but for some it refers to an invasive people, a nation that violently displaces others for its own wants and desires, a state that breaks treaties and uses police and starvation to clear the land. We need a name that can help us see ourselves for who we are, not just who we claim to be. For that, we need a term that shifts the frame of reference away from popular ideas of the Canadian nation and its geography and on to our relationships with systems of power, land, and the peoples on whose territory our country exists.

In recent decades, something has begun to shift. Alongside the 2008 official apology to Indigenous People from the federal government for the residential school era, Indigenous activism forced a deep reckoning to begin within Canadian society. The sweeping nationwide and globe-spanning protests under the banner of Idle No More in 2012–2013 pushed contemporary issues to the forefront of national news. The release of the final report of the Truth and Reconciliation Commission (TRC) in 2015 on residential schools and its finding of cultural genocide had ripple effects throughout Canadian government, business, and education. The ongoing and increasingly high-profile occupations of territory in resistance to development by the Unist'ot'en of the Wet'suwet'en and others in the Interior of British Columbia have laid bare ongoing violence against Indigenous Peoples and lands. All these events have contributed to major shifts in social discourse. That is to say, the terms people used to describe Canada and its relationships to Indigenous People have changed. We heard more and more people using the term "settler" to refer to non-Indigenous Peoples, communities, states, and governments. Some were Indigenous People, referring to "settler states" or "would-be settler allies"; others were Canadians claiming the term as an identifier, baggage and all. The term is often challenged; some claim the term is racist. Others reject it as divisive. Some argue about whether "settler" is the "right" word and turn to dictionary definitions for confirmation or clarification. However, this debated and debatable term — all but unknown and unused in Canada outside of a small circle of academics and activists prior to 2005 — stuck.

Settler. This word voices relationships to structures and processes in Canada today, to the histories of our peoples on this land, to Indigenous Peoples, and to our own day-to-day choices and actions. Settler. This word turns us toward uncomfortable realizations, difficult subjects, and potential complicity in systems of dispossession and violence. Settler. This word represents a tool, a way of understanding and an acknowledgement that we can choose to act differently. It is a tool we can use to confront the fundamental problems and injustices in Canada today. Settler. It is analytical, personal, and uncomfortable. It can be an identity that we claim or deny but that we inevitably live and embody. It is who we are, as a people, on these lands.

We are Settler Canadians. And this is a book about us.

Understanding and Avoidance

This book is an examination of the Settler identity in Canada, an identity that is shared by growing numbers but is still unclear to many. This Settler Canadian identity is entangled both historically and in the present with the process of settler colonization, the means through which our state and nation have wrested their land base and legitimacy from Indigenous Peoples. In this book, our construction of "Settler" as an identity mirrors the construction of "Indigenous" in contemporary terms: a broad collective of peoples with commonalities through particular connections to land and place. Settler is an analytic, that is, a tool that describes particular sets of relationships to land and place and to those identified as "like us" versus "Other," rooted in histories of the colonization of the lands we now call Canada. For Settler people, however, those connections are forged through violence, displacement, and assimilation of Indigenous communities and nations. In this book, we examine what it means to be a Settler person in Canada, how we constitute our national narratives and social structures, why Settler Canadians react in certain ways to Indigenous communities in resistance, and how we can each work toward finding more ethical, just ways of being together on the lands we call home.

Part of the reason that there has been an increase in attention to and use of the term "settler" is because of a curious double vision in Canada today. There is at least some willingness to admit that colonization happened, that it had devastating impacts on Indigenous Nations and communities, and that a colonial legacy persists into the present in the form of socioeconomic inequality, racism and discrimination, and political marginalization of Indigenous People and communities. There are nods to Indigenous histories in the territory acknowledgements of city councils and university conferences. While it took court battles waged over decades, governments have begun to engage in forms of "reconciliation" that speak to prior harms. However, colonialism continues. Today, Indigenous Nations are still losing their land bases to "development" or industrial pollution, facing infringement from resource extraction and mining companies, property developers, and the pressures of urbanization. Many government commissions, from the 1996 Royal Commission on Aboriginal People to the 2015 final report of the TRC, have made clear and unambiguous recommendations for what Canada and Canadians should do to address Indigenous Peoples' concerns, but there has been precious little action to implement these, especially by governments. Do territory acknowledgements mean anything if what follows is business as usual? What has truly been "reconciled" with Indigenous Nations? These nations struggle for self-determination against governments seemingly bound to the notion that Indigenous Peoples should be constantly monitored and managed. And Indigenous Peoples face constant racism and violence: from the epidemic of Missing and Murdered Indigenous Women and Girls (MMIWG) to discrimination by social services, to incidents of brutality at the hands of police, Indigenous People confront the reality every single day that colonialism is far from a legacy. Attempting to make Canadian governments take these issues seriously has required constant pressure from Indigenous communities. Until recently, the vast majority of investigation and research into MMIWG has been led by family members of victims and community activists. A tremendous amount of work has been done to uncover systemic violence against Indigenous women, girls, and femme people for decades but only gained popular political purchase with the creation of the 2016–2019 National Inquiry into Missing and Murdered Indigenous Women and Girls. The final report of the Inquiry states:

> The violence the National Inquiry heard amounts to a race-based genocide of Indigenous Peoples, including First Nations, Inuit and Métis, which especially targets women, girls, and 2SLGBTQQIA people. This genocide has been empowered by colonial structures evidenced notably by the Indian Act, the Sixties Scoop, residential schools and breaches of human and Indigenous rights, leading directly to the current increased rates of violence, death, and suicide in Indigenous populations.[1]

Sadly, none of this is really news to most Canadians. The knowledge of what has been done and is being done to Indigenous Peoples already exists, and there is no reasonable justification for Canadians to claim ignorance.

A high-profile public example is that of the Royal Commission on Aboriginal Peoples, which, in 1996, clearly identified ways that Canadian society remains colonial — dishonouring treaties, systemically discriminating against Indigenous Peoples, maintaining reserves as economically marginalized and politically disempowered, and not doing nearly enough to address the present-day effects of historical warfare, murder, and policies of assimilation. The final report of the TRC echoed these findings. These research-intensive, investigative and analytical undertakings demonstrate not only the problems, but also how little effort Canada and Canadians have made to address the causes and our own complicity in ongoing colonialism. The problems affecting Indigenous communities are not unknown; their causes are in fact well understood through decades of research including that funded by the federal government itself. These results have been publicly available, summarized into easily readable formats, and presented in a myriad of forms and formats freely accessible online. Yet most Canadians refuse to engage with these sources or believe the arguments that they support, regardless of the evidence to the contrary.[2]

The refusal to see colonization as occurring in the present is connected to being unable and/or unwilling to perceive how the colonial state makes use of Canadians to target Indigenous Peoples. Colonialism is commonly understood as an attempt to control territory or resources beyond the official boundaries of a state or empire. Colonies are founded in unsecured territories as a foothold for trade, military excursions, diplomatic contact, and to otherwise serve as an extension of the central power. However, in twenty-first-century Canada there are no distant footholds because it is the country's land base itself that has been and continues to be the target of colonial power. Canada, as a nation and a state, is dependent on the land taken from Indigenous Nations, land that those nations still contest, and colonialism is about the need to secure those lands and justify the legitimacy of those claims at all costs. This positions Canada and Canadians directly at odds with Indigenous Peoples, who have not just prior, but competing claims to the land. Canada essentially has no legal grounds for its own sovereignty, which is to say, no reason in law as to why Canadian territory should be Canada's to govern.[3] It should be no wonder why Indigenous claims to land — especially when asserted with confidence — cause great concern for political leaders and many other Canadians: Indigenous enactment of land responsibilities and stewardship, protest against incursion and forms of disruption, community- and land-based teach-ins must all be understood as acts of resistance against the ongoing efforts of Settler Canada, as a collective entity, to eliminate Indigenous Peoples' claims to the land and permanently end any question about Canada's legitimacy.

The colonial history and the ways the legacies of colonial institutions and practices continue to disadvantage Indigenous People are not uncontested or unknown. The TRC may have tabled its final report in 2015, but new and horrific information about Canada's Indian Residential School system continues to be unearthed.[4] In a literal sense, since the discovery of dozens of children's graves around the Kamloops residential school in 2021, First Nations across Canada have begun deploying ground-penetrating radar to identify further unmarked graves around former residential schools.[5] More than that, extensive research shows that Indigenous People continue to face prejudice and racism from police, media, and public servants.[6] Yet, some Canadians continue to argue that the harms experienced by Indigenous children in the schools or by Indigenous People experiencing police brutality were the fault of "a few bad apples," not a systemic and accepted part of a system created and supported by Canadians. Or they contend that the intent of systems like the residential schools — meaning, in some sense, education — was good even if, in reality, it failed. But intent does not displace impact, and government systems and services across the country demonstrate that the supposed "bad" apples far outnumber the good. Consider the striking poverty and lack of infrastructure in Indigenous communities, specifically the reserve communities situated on tiny fractions of their traditional homelands. It is this that has led to economic devastation, with some families waiting nearly a decade for on-reserve housing. In 2023 alone, the federal government contributed only $4 billion of the estimated $44 billion it would take to adequately provide on-reserve housing. This level of systemic denial of a fundamental necessity of life is not, and cannot be, accidental. But Canadians often insist on seeing these crises as the fault of negligent band governments or inadequate economic development.

Finally, even when Indigenous Peoples' concerns are acknowledged as legitimate, there is very little public impetus to act. When Québec Liberal Member of Parliament (MP) Marc Miller spoke Mohawk in Parliament in 2017, many applauded — but the performance of concern for Indigenous languages seems insignificant when the same government condoned the use of heavily armed Royal Canadian Mounted Police (RCMP) to arrest and displace Indigenous People protecting disputed lands, as they did in Wet'suwet'en territory in British Columbia in 2019. And there is very little chance of limiting or preventing these harms through established methods of political engagement, like voting. Establishment politics in Canada may seem built on intractable conflict between progressive and conservative positions — especially after the polarizing effects of the COVID19 pandemic and resulting lockdowns and counter-protests — but in reality, on the key issue of Indigenous Peoples' rights, there is a significant consensus at the core of Canadian politics. Broadly, Canadian discourses on Indigenous Peoples, rights, and concerns tend to fall into two camps that align roughly with Canadian politics: the conservative and the liberal.

Popular works by scholar and political advisor Tom Flanagan and media mogul Conrad Black have been formative to the conservative discourse on Indigenous Peoples in Canada. Flanagan's work, in particular *First Nations? Second Thoughts*, while dated, still holds a powerful sway over the conservative imagination. His ideas are predicated on the assertion that Indigenous cultures and societies before the arrival of Europeans were primitive, undeveloped, and lacking significant culture. According to Flanagan, colonization was essentially inevitable: Indigenous Peoples formed small, backward tribes occupying vast spaces; they were bound to be replaced by more advanced, organized, and numerous migrants. Black's re-telling of the story of Canada's past, *Rise to Greatness*, does not focus on Indigenous Peoples at all. Rather, it reinforces Flanagan's story by repeating old refrains of European explorers, pioneers, and fortune-seekers as "great men" hacking a new, civilized country out of a hostile and largely empty wilderness. Perhaps the most well-known and demonstrative example of this occurred in 2009, when Conservative Prime Minister Stephen Harper, at a meeting of the G20 in Pittsburgh, declared that Canada has "no history of colonialism." A few years later, Governor General David Johnston's Speech from the Throne that opened Parliament in October 2013 lauded the history of pioneers bravely venturing into empty wilderness and the enduring spirit of adventure and hard work that this has instilled in Canadian society. All of this reinforces a belief that colonization was an inevitable process, tied to the march of progress and civilization; that settlers and colonizers were doing unquestionably good things by reshaping the land; and that even if colonial crimes were committed, they were both inevitable and in the past, and so do not merit redress. Furthermore, in the time since Harper and the Conservatives lost federal power, these attitudes have spread and hardened among the far right. Prior to his election as the current Conservative Party leader, Pierre Poilievre had already established a history of making anti-Indigenous assertions that have only solidified his popularity among right-wing populists. His assertions date back to 2008 when he was forced to apologize for stating that residential school survivors needed "a stronger work ethic." Showing how little he has learned, in 2024, Poilievre was "sharply criticized" by many First Nations chiefs after he spoke to the Assembly of First Nations annual general assembly. He "failed to mention missing and murdered Indigenous women and girls, inherent Indigenous rights, the climate crisis, residential school survivors and whether he would support a proposed $47.8 billion child welfare settlement."[7] Among the so-called Freedom Convoy that descended on Ottawa in 2022, and which was actively supported by Poilievre, racist and white supremacist attitudes were prevalent from the outset.[8] Later, Convoy leaders began appropriating Indigenous symbols, both traditional ceremonial objects like peace pipes, and also more contemporary symbols like the Orange Shirt Day originally organized to commemorate Indigenous children who lost their lives in residential schools.[9] As Dene author Amy Ede wrote in *The Tyee*:

> A frightening element of the convoy's appropriation of Indigenous ceremony, activism, protest and acts of resistance is its alignment with a desire to feel oppressed and victimized ... I believe this desire to be seen as oppressed comes from a racist misconception that Indigenous communities and other marginalized communities are playing the victim, and that our hard-won and insufficient rights are in fact privileges.[10]

But this is not a partisan critique — it is simply a description of how settler colonialism manifests at one end of the political spectrum. Toward the centre and moderate left, it appears in different forms.

The liberal discourse tends to acknowledge Canada's colonial past, portrays Indigenous Peoples as possessing sophisticated, vibrant societies and cultures, and recognizes that early settlers and Canadian society in general could not have become established without the aid of Indigenous Peoples. Books like John Ralston Saul's *A Fair Country* tend to focus on the technological achievement and cultural complexity of Indigenous Peoples, applauding the "contributions" that Indigenous People(s) have made to Canadian society. Saul calls Canada a "Métis nation," not formed of conquest like the United States and not a distillation of European traditions, but rather a mix of Indigenous, European, and more recently, global cultures. Former Governor General Adrienne Clarkson's book, *Belonging: The Paradox of Citizenship*, is an examination of the struggles of diverse communities to find belonging in Canada — linked to legal recognition of status — especially for new immigrant communities that frequently experience racism, inequality, or face loss of identity and culture in joining a new society. Clarkson, an immigrant born in Hong Kong, whose family fled the Japanese invasion in 1942, speaks from experience, which is important because her views are widely held among many immigrant communities, both recent and well-established. Paralleling Black's book, Clarkson's subject is a Canadian society that focuses less on Indigenous Peoples and more on the project of imagining a unified narrative of what it means — or could mean — to be Canadian. In this case, Clarkson identifies the negotiation of immigrant roots and Canadian "belonging" as a common experience that can bind Canadians together. Clarkson constructs this social inclusion as following from Indigenous ideas of welcoming newcomers, one of the many "gifts" of Indigenous Peoples to Canadians. Such popular ideas are backed by work by well-known liberal academics like Will Kymlicka, who ultimately argue for a kind of Canadian exceptionalism based on liberalism, pluralism, and multicultural values. In his work, Kymlicka constructs Indigenous People as a "minority nation" present at the founding of the Canadian state, and therefore deserving of some special rights and treatments in the name of cultural preservation, which are balanced by the universal nature of human rights and the Canadian Constitution.[11] However, when push comes to shove, he says that Indigenous Nations have to reconcile to the reality of Canadian sovereignty, that is, reconcile to being subsumed within the Canadian state. These attitudes have been borne out in the actions of the Justin Trudeau–led federal Liberal Party that came to power in 2015 — a government that was generally seen as progressive and justice-minded — especially when compared with the United States' election of convicted fraudster Donald Trump and the United Kingdom's xenophobic vote to leave the European Union in 2016.

The election of Trudeau and defeat of Harper was accompanied by a great deal of fanfare, even by those who are generally more cynical with respect to electoral politics, in part because of the nature of the election discourse. The Conservatives under Harper ran on a platform of fear, division, nationalism, and isolation, while Trudeau ran on more traditionally liberal principles like equality and the importance of fixing public services. And given the election of Trump close on the heels of Trudeau, the gap between the policy and ideology of these two broad groups seemed wide. However, the Trudeau government's commonsensical approach to equity — well-illustrated by the prime minister's famous response to the question of why his first cabinet had an equal number of men and women: "Because it's 2015"[12] — has not extended to Indigenous People. While making gestures to Indigenous Nations, such as the appointment of Mary Simon, who is Inuk, to the role of governor general in 2021,[13] the Trudeau–led Liberals also dragged their feet on addressing mercury poisoning in Grassy Narrows.[14] They underfunded Indigenous community services — including those directly impacting children[15] — and fought court-ordered compensation, and perhaps most infamously, purchased the Trans Mountain Pipeline project in 2018 "to ensure the expansion proceeded despite opposition."[16] That opposition has long been led and sustained by Indigenous communities, such as the Stk'emlupsemc Te Secwepemc Nation, who object to the project's approval both due to their ongoing contestation for land rights and the potential for the destruction of sacred spaces by construction or pollution.[17] Even the recommendations of the TRC, released just prior to

Trudeau's election and much touted by his government as a priority, seem to have been shelved: a 2023 report by the Yellowhead Institute indicated that only thirteen of ninety-four calls to action have been implemented, with none in 2023.[18]

Some differences between these two broadly sketched positions are easy to spot. The conservative discourse is rooted in assertions of primitive Indigenous under-development, the inevitability of European conquest, and the fiction that Indigenous lands were empty and therefore free to be claimed by newcomers as Indigenous Peoples gave way to naturally superior groups. Overwhelming evidence and research has demonstrated that each of those ideas is both false and deeply racist, and they have all been rejected by international organizations like the United Nations. The conservative camp's belief that Canada is an unproblematic improvement over whatever Indigenous societies existed requires that we ignore massive depopulation accomplished through disease, warfare, starvation, and other tactics of removal, and ongoing policies of marginalization and forced dependence. The conservative view also demands that we ignore the complexity of Indigenous politics, economics, international relationships, kinship and social structures, technologies and traditional knowledges, and oral and written histories and cultures both in the past and today.

The liberal approach to Indigenous rights and issues, however, is based on appreciation and recognition. Indigenous Peoples are held up as key national contributors — as a part of what makes Canada such a distinct, successful, and special country. The liberal view sees the wrongs of the past and is shamed by the stain on Canadian "honour." It proposes that the harms suffered by Indigenous People and communities because of colonial pasts should be addressed by striving to fully include Indigenous communities in the benefits of citizenship in the multicultural state of Canada, perhaps as "citizens plus" or through economic development partnerships. Identifying Indigenous Peoples as deserving of "recognition," appreciation, and special rights, the liberal position seems to confront the ignorance and racism of the conservative discourse.[19]

There is much dividing these two approaches, but they share common ground. Both are concerned with understanding and improving Canadian society, and both draw on deeply held ideas about freedom, equality, and fairness. Both also centre Canada as a special place, home to a special people. Both assert a Canadian exceptionalism that is ahistorical and rooted in racist and colonial perceptions regardless of contemporary political allegiance.

Both require Indigenous People to come under the control of the Canadian nation state or to disappear. Fundamentally, the liberal and conservative positions rely on the same fundamental assumption: Indigenous Peoples pose a "problem" to Canada, one to be managed, accounted for, and ultimately dealt with — be it with regret and uplift or racism and assimilation — so that Canadians can get on with the business of being Canadian.

Historically, one of the ways that Canada has been forged is through assertions of the right to control Indigenous People's lives: making them wards of the state, attempting to "civilize" Indigenous individuals through enfranchisement, residential schools, and coercive socioeconomic programs,[20] and more recently, through the breakup of reserve land into fee simple private property. For Canada to exist as it does, the disciplining and control of Indigenous lives is required to open and preserve space for newcomer people. This has left a legacy of attempts to fix what Canada called the "Indian problem"[21] through the twentieth century, but our Canadian gaze is so rarely turned back on ourselves that we do not see that problems facing Indigenous communities originate with us.

While there will always be those who disagree, there is now a clear research consensus and growing social understanding that colonial ideologies underpin much of the social, political, and cultural life of Canadians. As Yellowknives Dene political theorist Glen Coulthard has described, Canada uses the "recognition" of Indigenous People to perniciously assimilate Indigenous People into Canadian society as "minorities." On a political level, this includes the "recognition" of bodies like the Assembly of First Nations or individual band governments, but not the rights of people to self-determination with respect to their traditional lands as sources of both physical and spiritual strength.[7] This is a part of larger strategies that have evolved over time, designed to deny self-governance to Indigenous Nations, and often to deny basic freedoms to Indigenous People. When Indigenous Peoples protest colonial domination, media, policy makers, and other activists lecture Indigenous protesters about how they should stop angering average Canadians with their roadblocks and militant language. Indigenous resistance — to environmental destruction, to police violence and mass imprisonment, to the murder or disappearance of thousands of women, to the lack of basic services, to an unequal education system, systemic discrimination, and so many other ills — is constructed as the problem. Conveniently, this evades engaging with the actual issue of inequity baked into Canadian systems and society.

A useful contrast can be drawn here with the way that authorities have dealt with nationalist protests, including the Freedom Convoy and other protests foregrounding public health measures during the COVID-19 pandemic. Many politicians, including Poilievre, actively supported the majority white protesters, and used their occupation of Ottawa — which terrorized residents and largely paralyzed the city — as photo opportunities. When Trudeau eventually invoked the Emergency Measures Act to disperse the occupation, it became a lightning-rod issue for right-wing protesters and politicians alike. While several organizers of the Convoy were eventually arrested and then stood trial, others are still active. An RCMP report from after the protests indicates that the federal police as a whole could not enforce the law with respect to the Convoy protesters because too many of their own officers were sympathetic to or compromised by association with the protesters.[22] Historian Audra Diptee shows the stark difference between the ways the Canadian state has violently and with little tolerance attacked Black protesters on a variety of civil rights issues across the decades and the response to the Convoy protesters, and concludes that it is because the Convoy protesters saught to reinforce normative, racist attitudes rather than actually trying to make change. She states that "it is these historically accepted Canadian practices that have guaranteed participants in the 'freedom convoy' minimal police and state interference, as they assume the right to occupy public space while displaying racist symbols and simultaneously claiming to fight for freedom."[23] Ultimately, these far-right protests have spread, including the strange encampments of Ramona Didulo, the self-styled "Queen of Canada" and her cult-like followers, and new Convoy-type protests under the banner of "axe the tax," a Pierre Poilievre–led attack on Liberal and New Democratic Party attempts to introduce a carbon tax. They have become flashpoints for unscrupulous leaders and media figures to increase their profile, while increasingly shifting Canadian political discourse toward a more hostile, individualistic tone.

Contrast this with the response to a relatively small and isolated Indigenous protest effort around the same time. The RCMP were called in to raid encampments of Wet'suwet'en and allied protesters on their own lands in central British Columbia. These raids — that have continued since, resulting in the charging and criminalization of many community leaders and members — were conducted despite the protest posing no active threat to anyone, despite the recent passing of legislation endorsing the United Nations Declaration on the Rights of Indigenous People in British

Columbia, and despite the fact that the legal title to the lands remains in question due to the absence of Treaty. Moreover, RCMP commanders argued:

> ... that "lethal overwatch is req'd" — a term for deploying an officer who is prepared to use lethal force. The RCMP commanders also instructed officers to "use as much violence toward the gate as you want" ahead of the operation to remove a roadblock which had been erected by Wet'suwet'en people to control access to their territories and stop construction of the proposed 670km (416mile) Coastal GasLink pipeline (CGL). In a separate document, an RCMP officer states that arrests would be necessary for "sterilizing [the] site."[24]

To be sure, many Canadians opposed the truckers and their convoy and have opposed the use of extreme violence by state forces against Indigenous protesters. A lasting legacy of these events is the connection between the Canadian flag and violence, white supremacy, and fascism, which upsets those who valued the flag as a symbol of hope and pride. As mentioned earlier, the use of the flag to reinforce norms and values that were and are a part of Canada's past — and, obviously, present — makes many people uncomfortable but also confused as to what to do. How can people who believe in liberal multiculturalism and people who believe in racism and white nationalism both claim to be proud of the Canadian nation and expect others to know what it means when they hang a flag outside their house?

Institutions and individuals seem unable to respond to the evidence of persistent colonialism, racism, and violence as accepted rather than exceptional, but Indigenous Peoples are and have been vocal in the halls of power in Canada and overseas, in the media, in the streets, and in engagements and negotiations with officials throughout Canada's history. These efforts are not about dredging up past conflict; they are often centred on continuing conflicts over land, governmental authority, economic disparities, and legal and Treaty obligations. So why do Canadians insist on treating colonialism as a thing of the past? Be it conservative or liberal, the denial and obfuscation of Canada's colonial present and the unwillingness to even consider the involvement of everyday Canadians in creating or perpetuating harm against Indigenous Peoples is a problem. But it is also a feature of the particular kind of colonialism at work in Canada today.

It is in trying to come to grips with the historical legacy and present-day impacts of this form of colonialism — settler colonialism — that the use of "settler" as a term to refer to many non-Indigenous Canadians has gained traction.

The rise in the use of the term "settler" is best understood through the rise of Indigenous resurgence. As we have summarized in *The Handbook of Indigenous Public Policy* (2024):

> Resurgence is an identifier applied to particular land-based, self-determining, political and material practices (or movements). These are performed by Indigenous individuals, collectives and communities intended to generate decolonial spaces and futurities for Indigenous Nations and Peoples. It is simultaneously a strategy and an ethos predicated on prefiguration and ethical consistency between goals and the means deployed to pursue them, the necessity of mutually sustaining relations between humans, the land and the more-than-human world, and the incommensurability of Indigenous autonomy and settler colonial sovereignty. That incommensurability is practically understood to mean that challenges facing Indigenous Nations and communities cannot be "solved" by state policies because, regardless of the part in power, the state structure itself is colonial and requires the ongoing elimination of Indigenous nationhood and sovereign capacity. As such Indigenous resurgence is most commonly articulated as the embrace of Indigenous nationhood, including recognising the incredible diversity of national identities and ambitions among Indigenous societies in place of (or against) settler colonial nationalisms.[25]

These movements reveal most clearly the pernicious colonial dynamics at work in Canada because they challenge illusions that Indigenous Peoples are or have been "vanishing" by insisting on present-day vibrancy, and Indigenous futures.

As recently as the late twentieth century, the pronouncements of many early anthropologists, ethnologists, and political authorities who confidently predicted that Indigenous Peoples were destined to disappear, left behind by the modern world, rang true for many Canadians. The possibility of Indigenous Peoples existing as distinct nations — which early European powers understood and which motivated the initial "peace and friendship" treaties between Indigenous and European nations — had disappeared from the imaginations of most Canadians by the 1960s and 1970s. The 1969 "White Paper," a statement of intent of the federal government to legally terminate financial and legal obligations to "Indians," was a clear signal that Indigenous politics held little meaning or import for Canadian political leaders except as an obstacle to be cleared. Following this, the drive to ameliorate the rift between Anglo and French Canadians (the "two solitudes") dominated the political stage leading up to the 1982 patriation of the Constitution.[26] Indigenous leaders had to fight to make their voices heard in the negotiations. To be sure, there were Canadians who were aware that Indigenous People existed, but they rarely saw them as peoples, that is, as nations with sovereignty and territory, self-determining communities, and as distinct, living cultures. Indigenous histories were not generally taught in schools, Indigenous cultures and languages were viewed as anachronisms or "quaint" in the minds of most Canadians. For newcomers, Indigenous cultures were fascinations that existed outside of modern Canada. In all cases, "Indians" were exiled to the past and excluded from the future. For most Canadians, then, the highly publicized events of 1990 came as a rude awakening.

The Oka "Crisis" or "Standoff" of 1990 — the label applied by Canadians to the conflict between Mohawks attempting to defend a cemetery from destruction so the area could be used to expand a 9-hole golf course to 18 holes, and provincial police and the Canadian military who were deployed to subdue them — was not nearly so surprising for Indigenous communities. While many Canadians might have been shocked to see tanks, helicopters, and armed soldiers protecting a leisure site for the relatively wealthy, Mohawks and other Indigenous People were not. Their struggles with Canadian people, police, and governments had never ended, so the direct violence of colonialism was ever-present, from police harassment to attacks by everyday Canadians. But the wider perception of Canada as a successful postcolonial society was badly shaken by the conflicts at Kahnawake and Kanesatake. The government and police response to the occupation of a small road in rural Québec and the blockade of the Mercier Bridge in Montréal — which eventually included the deployment of armoured vehicles and military helicopters against Mohawk community members — was a shambles. It was clear to everyone that no government officials expected that the Mohawk, or any Indigenous Nation, could or would be able to disrupt the will of Canadian property developers or defy the combined force of the police and military. But the Mohawks of Kahnawake and Kanesatake did resist and they did defy the incursions into their lands. While Canadians were shocked by the events at Oka, it was just the most recent moment in over two centuries of Mohawk resistance to settler colonialism. Over the next decade, Oka ceased being seen as an isolated incident and instead became understood as being the most well-known of an increasingly powerful phenomena: Indigenous People standing up for nationhood, defying colonial erasure, and demanding that Canada — and Canadians — account for their actions.[27]

The responses of Canadians to such actions have been striking. During the Oka Crisis, over five hundred "average" citizens lined up on berms either side of the road leading out of Oka and pelted cars carrying Mohawk community members with rocks — cars that were leaving the conflict site, many with children and elders. This act resulted in the death of Mohawk elder, Joe Armstrong, who was hit in the chest with a large rock and who died of heart failure a week later. Famed Abenaki filmmaker, Alanis Obomsawin, chillingly recounted these events in her 2000 documentary *Rocks at Whiskey Trench*, demonstrating a "visceral display of hatred and violence, rarely seen so publicly in Canada, [which] shocked the nation."[28] However, while shocking in its visibility, this was not an isolated incident, and, as we discuss in Chapter 2, it is important to see that when Indigenous People refuse to be marginalized and displaced on their own lands and take action in unavoidably visible ways, Canadians have responded with both anger and violence. This is, in part, a contest over sovereignty, and when Indigenous Peoples contend for control of their own lands, it is seen as a threat to the very foundation of Canadian society.

The Idle No More movement of 2012–13, characterized by peaceful marches and flash-mob round dances, was dogged by acts of violence perpetrated by otherwise "average" Canadians. Two white men abducted, beat, brutalized, raped, and strangled an Anishinaabe woman in Thunder Bay, Ontario. During the attack, the men invoked racial slurs, telling the victim: "You Indians don't deserve Treaty Rights." At a protest on a highway near Edmonton, a man drove a truck through a line of Idle No More demonstrators, deliberately endangering the lives of several people. And a video went viral on the internet showing a woman in London, Ontario, calmly walking out of an apartment building, up to an Idle No More convoy travelling slowly down an urban street, and then attacking one of the cars with a hammer before just as calmly turning and walking back inside.[29]

The cause of these marches and protests does not matter — for Canadians, the simple assertion of Indigenous presence is enough to trigger such severe discomfort and dissonance that they choose to try and resolve those feelings with extreme violence. And it continues. In 2022, a March for Recognition of Residential Schools near Mission, BC, with participants decked out in orange shirts and waving "every child matters" orange flags, was disrupted when a white man in a truck sped through, hitting four participants. Even though Kwantlen journalist Robert Jago, who was in attendance, provided video of the incident and the driver turned himself in to the police within a day, it took six months of activism and advocacy by Indigenous community leaders before charges were filed.[30]

The hostility shown by individual Canadians and in government responses to Indigenous People's calls for justice and redress speaks to a limit to society's recognition of Indigenous People. Indigenous People can exist in Canada, can even be elected premier of a province like Wab Kinew or made governor general like Mary Simon. However, they cannot exert sovereignty or demand a right to self-determination as Indigenous Peoples, that is, as collective and independent political entities. When the attempt occurs, the state has shown a willingness to respond with increasingly militarized violence, and Canadians more broadly have demonstrated that anti-Indigenous racism remains a persistent feature of our society. Events and moments when Indigenous Peoples have insisted on protecting their lands, cultures, histories, and bodies against incursion, elimination, or theft are not the cause of these conflicts. It is the society that takes domination of Indigenous Peoples for granted that is the root issue.

All across the continent, Indigenous Peoples have a long history of encountering newcomers. Indigenous Peoples moved around their own territories and into each other's long before European imperial colonization. These new relationships were not accidental or haphazard and ranged from individual adoptions into Indigenous Nations, to the incorporation of whole societies into political confederacies.[31] In many situations, some of these "foreigners" stayed, settling and living either with or alongside the local Indigenous communities. Protocols for engagement with outsiders were extended to the odd arrivals from Europe who began to appear in what would become Canada in the late sixteenth and early seventeenth centuries.[32]

What changed from an arrangement where Indigenous Nations held the balance of power, and small newcomer settlements were reliant on multiple alliances just to sustain themselves to what we see now? The first important shift was the withdrawal or expulsion of competing European powers who needed the knowledge, labour, and skills of Indigenous traders and warriors. In the mid-seventeenth century, the British Empire took New Netherlands, effectively ending Dutch influence on the continent, followed by the conquest of New France and signing of the Treaty of Paris to end the Seven Years' War and French ambitions in the Americas.

The second important shift took place between 1763 and 1813. Wary of the growing size, power, and independent attitude of settlers in the Thirteen Colonies, the British Crown issued a Royal Proclamation (1763) that drew a line — one of the many imaginary colonial and imperial lines drawn to divide Turtle Island — that separated "New England" from "Indian Territory." No colonist was allowed to occupy or purchase land in Indian Territory without the consent of the Crown, and the Crown would only purchase lands it deemed necessary to support its own interests. The ambitions of land-hungry colonial settlers in the Thirteen Colonies increasingly did not correspond to those of the British Crown.[33] They understood this limit to their territorial expansion as an unfair restriction on their natural economic and political growth. Following American independence, major changes began to occur in settlement patterns and pace. The emergent American state, reluctant to raise taxes and incite rebellion, but wanting funds, turned to Indigenous lands. Ignoring the Proclamation, the American government made huge pre-emptive claims on whole territories, then sold them in pieces to land speculators. Settlers pushed westward, attracted by the opportunity to raise their socioeconomic status through access to land available to them at low cost.

In the Canadian colonies, settlement and expansion remained restrained by the British Crown, now even warier than before about uncontrolled growth of settlement colonies. By the early 1800s, in Upper Canada, settlement was also slowed by the economic monopolies of several merchant families, mostly of Scottish origin, who tightly held the reins of patronage and used bureaucratic and economic clout to stifle the growth of potential rivals. The future city of Toronto remained a relatively small port; the Niagara peninsula was covered by scattered farms and homesteads; the largest power in the area remained the Haudenosaunee Confederacy community that had relocated to the Grand River having been forced to abandon their homelands in New York State because of their alliance with the British against the Americans in the War of Independence. So it was that by 1812, the population of the United States of America — spurred by the westward race for land, money, and power and its associated immigration boom — was much larger than in the settlements on the north of the Great Lakes and St. Lawrence River.[34]

The United States attacked Britain's northern American colonies in 1812 and it was widely assumed that between the small number of British troops defending the settlements, and the settlers themselves rising up against "Imperial tyranny" and throwing in with their American "brothers," the fighting would be short and the British driven out within weeks. The war of 1812 was not, as it turned out, either short or particularly decisive for Britain or America. The Americans took Detroit and shattered the military strength of the Shawnee Confederacy under Tecumseh, destroying key resistance to westward colonization. But they were unable to gain a foothold across the Niagara River, and unwilling to attempt another push northward to try and claim Montréal and the Québec settlements. Warriors from the Haudenosaunee Confederacy community on the Grand River, who fought alongside the British, terrified American troops with surprise attacks and a reputation for ferocity in battle, and, despite small numbers, loomed large in many engagements. In the end, the result of the war was mainly a hardening and formalizing of imperial borders that had already existed: the British north of the Great Lakes and the 49th parallel, Americans to the south.

This period, though, also marks the end of restraint upon settlement and the rapid rise of settler colonization as the predominant form of colonialism on the continent. Before this, European colonial powers were operating in a complex geopolitical terrain — calculating their moves in the Americas not so much against Indigenous Peoples, but against other competing European empires — and Indigenous Nations held great power to tip the scales of inter-imperial conflicts. However, as the British expelled France from Canada, and with Spanish power crumbling leading to both the Mexican War of Independence and later massive territorial annexations by the United States, the geometry shifted. With the normalization of relations between Britain and America, Indigenous People and their territorial claims took on greater importance. The setting of an agreed imperial boundary — the present-day Canada–US border — limited the potential for northward or southward expansion, prompting increased and more energetic interest in expanding across the continent. America turned to an even more aggressive program of westward expansion. The "Indian Wars" followed, as even Indigenous Nations that signed treaties were eventually confined within their own homelands to "reservations" so their lands could be sold to wave after wave of settlers chasing the next boom commodity or looking to stake out their own plot of "free land." The British were fearful that the westward thrust of American settlement might turn northward, into territories still largely populated by Indigenous People, including the Cree and Métis, and pose a threat to their Canadian colonies. They began to relax restrictions in what was then still called "the Northwest" so that settlement, farmsteading, and industry would secure their lands and borders against possible American encroachment.

By the 1850s, this pattern of competitive settlement had taken on a life of its own. In the Pacific Northwest, an exemplary form of this drama played out. James Douglas, a Hudson's Bay Company man, founded the colony of Fort Victoria on what is today known as Vancouver Island. Not long afterward, settlers were encouraged — in a massive change from British policy of the previous century — to simply claim fertile lands in the Cowichan Valley, just north of Fort Victoria, as their own. Predictably, the Cowichan objected, and their expulsion of several homesteaders prompted the reaction of the Royal Navy, attacking a number of villages, threatening violence, and even hanging local Indigenous men after show trials. Then, gold was discovered in the interior: huge numbers of American miners, bouncing from one gold rush to the next, flooded north of the 49th parallel, warring with the Nla7kápmx and other local Indigenous Nations, and — worst of all for the British — forming their own camp counsels, which acted as ad hoc governments. In a move calculated to preempt potential American annexation, the Crown simply laid claim to the entirety of what is today mainland British Columbia, declaring it a colony in 1858.

This brought an end to what vestiges of respect remained in the British Crown for Indigenous tenure on the land. Far from the policy of 1763 that actively restrained settlement, the Crown (which referred to the government of Canada after Confederation in 1867) now undertook to sign a series of "treaties" with Indigenous Peoples ostensibly to agree to rights and responsibilities. However, both elected officials and Treaty negotiators approached Treaty negotiations as land-purchase agreements, designed to provide certainty of title for mass settlement and resource exploitation. The burgeoning Canadian government began openly targeting Indigenous Peoples for posing even a conceptual threat to settlement and sovereignty now that they were no longer needed to maintain a balance of power among other empires. Among the earliest policies of the Dominion of Canada were the starvation and forced confinement of Indigenous Nations across the prairies, the military invasion of Indigenous communities beginning with the Red River Métis, who were attacked by the Northwest Mounted Police, and the increasing confinement of Indigenous communities to "reserve land." Larger tracts of land claimed by or even recognized as belonging to Indigenous communities — such as the Haldimand Grant to the Confederacy of the Grand River — were sold off piecemeal. The government partnered with churches to encourage the spread of residential schools, designed to eliminate Indigenous languages and cultures and facilitate the assimilation of Indigenous individuals into the developing Canadian nation state. They became a key mechanism in settler colonial dispossession in that they served as factories for "disappearing" Indigenous Peoples from the land. Many administrators and teachers are known to have used their positions of almost unquestioned power over the children to abuse and degrade them, preying on the constructed absence of parental oversight within a system that saw Indigenous students as less than human. Many schools "disciplined" students for the most banal infractions or perceived misconduct with severe beatings, starvation, isolation, and enforced labour. Meanwhile, reserve communities were put under increasing surveillance by government agents (known as "Indian Agents"), and Indigenous Peoples living off-reserve were increasingly criminalized. Violent race-based attacks by members of settler communities became more common and less punished. Disease and malnutrition racked Indigenous communities, forcing even further breakup and dispersal of social structures and increasing dependence on a hostile government.[35] By the beginning of the twentieth century, the last of the "numbered treaties" were being signed, formalizing what was already reality in the minds of many: virtually all land north of the Rio Grande was claimed by either the United States of America or the Dominion of Canada.

From then until now, across the whole of the twentieth century and continuing in the twenty-first, Indigenous Peoples have challenged colonial claims in a variety of ways, including court and legal challenges to international diplomacy, direct action occupations of land, protest marches and sit-ins, among others. The contemporary conflicts between Canadian society and Indigenous Peoples that we have mentioned are evidence that the process of land theft and Indigenous dispossession has not ended yet. Settler colonialism was not "over" in 1969 when the Trudeau government attempted to abolish the Indian Act, and Indigenous resistance that prevented it from occurring is just one of many pieces of historical evidence that colonization was and is occurring, and continues to need addressing. This is where we depart from the conservative or liberal positions on Indigenous Peoples: there is no "Indian problem" in Canada, and in fact there has never been one. In asserting the need to discuss and understand who and what Canadians really are, we are looking into the very fabric of Canadian society, culture, and everyday life to understand the reality: we have a Settler problem.

Asserting the Settler Identity

Identities are complex, shifting, and multiple. To speak of identity is to speak of the point at which we make assumptions and pre-cognitive decisions about others and ourselves. It is to speak of the part of ourselves where the individual meets society and says, "I belong here," while internalizing and deploying important lessons for how to belong. Because identities are shifting and multiple, it is important to investigate some of the common ways the Settler identity[36] functions in order to very intentionally try to shift how we think about ourselves and our relationships with our wider worlds. For example, even Settler Canadians from the same family, place, class, and ethnic background may experience very different social relationships on the grounds of gender or sexuality; this does not mean that they occupy separate worlds; rather, that their experiences of the same world are themselves variable. We often discuss the "Settler identity" in the singular. But we are aware that Settler identities are in fact multiple and shifting, and always plural. Ours is a calculated rhetorical move to allow us to make use of a "Settler" identity in the same way that "Indigenous" identity has become an important point of negotiation, debate, and discourse in discussions of international rights and law. It is a term that can provide a way of connecting, of understanding commonalities and ultimately providing a platform for investigating all the ways we can be something other than colonizers.

These debates help clarify the uses of the term and its connections to a sense of identity, group belonging, and culture of place, as well as emphasizing discontinuities between different colonial histories. For example, Mahmood Mamdani, the well-known Indian-born, Ugandan-raised academic, has consistently rejected the term "settler" and the perceived "Indigenous–settler binary" that he sees implied in settler colonial analyses.[37] Mamdani deals specifically with the legacies of British colonialism that brought "indentured" labour from places like India to British colonies in Africa in huge numbers from the 1860s until the end of the empire following the Second World War.[38] National revolutions in the twentieth century, often under the auspices of decolonization, resulted in many cases of Indians, either previously indentured labourers or their children and families — sometimes several generations — being persecuted, facing violence and even expulsion. This has led Mamdani to argue that nationalisms — even for example, the resurgent nationalism of Indigenous Nations like the Mohawks — and colonialism always share roots, and that the only way out of oppressive governance is for Indigenous and Settler people to have full and identical equality in a shared nation state. We had the opportunity to discuss his critiques with him at a conference in Montréal, in 2021, and came away convinced that our disagreements were based on miscommunications or assumptions about the sameness or uniqueness of settler colonial contexts around the world. Certainly, we cannot apply the same concepts and same definitions of terms to the Canadian and Ugandan situations, given the very different racial and class dynamics around "settler" populations imported as labour from India by British colonial administrators in Uganda, and the ways this played out in the nationalist expulsions of Indian and other minority populations under Idi Amin in 1972, but we disagree with the implication that the term does not have use. Instead, we believe the term must be used carefully, in specific contexts, and with willingness to understand the "fuzzy" and indeterminate boundaries of the terms. These boundary areas include the role of racial and ethnic identities, the impacts on identity of "transiting" through different imperial spaces, and the role of concepts like citizenship in uniting (or dividing) people.[39]

In academic literature, it is perhaps more common to discuss settler "subjectivities"; that is, the way people think and act as settlers in relationship with a pre-existing settler colonial society. We prefer to position our work with respect to Settler identities to foreground issues of agency, responsibility, and accountability with respect to Indigenous Nations that is in part pursued through how we identify. Further, this parallels important work on "Indigenous" as a lived and embodied identity, which has fuelled much of our work. We also encourage people to identify with and as Settler people as part of a process of transformative change. We want to focus on identity as something lived and embodied every day, and simultaneously something that can be mobilized to shape everything from states to systems of capital, for better or for worse.

Internationally, Indigenous identity (collective and individual) has gained traction as a way of strategically articulating commonalities between a vast number of Peoples and Nations whose cultural, geographical, and historical differences might seem to defy collective terms. Especially with the rise of international forums, such as the United Nations Permanent Forum on Indigenous Issues, communities that identify and are identified as Indigenous have recognized common features that form the core of a broad group identification. Deep relational attachments to particular places, ecological knowledge and environmental technologies, and territorial politics that do not form state structures are among the key articulated features of Indigenous identity. Mobilization around Indigenous identity has proven useful in the international arena in providing a platform for many stateless peoples to help communities that face common challenges and struggles come together in collective action and to generate a critical mass of visibility, making Indigenous challenges to contemporary nation states that much harder to ignore. For example, the work done by Indigenous People from around the world over many years to craft and successfully ratify the United Nations Declaration on the Rights of Indigenous People (UNDRIP) brought a great deal of attention to countries like Canada and Australia, in no small part because they resisted adopting it for many years (Canada signed the UNDRIP in 2021, fourteen years after it was introduced).

Indigenous People are far from homogenous, and what it means to any individual to identify as "Indigenous" will be widely varied. However, for many identifying as Indigenous is a rejection of the right of a government or others to define and limit who counts as "Aboriginal" — that is, who is officially "recognized" as an Indian, Métis, or Inuit by the Canadian government. In contrast to these practices of official identification and recognition under the state, Indigenous identity is based on the experience of being the primary targets of colonization, and being Indigenous means being oppositional to colonization (see Chapter 3). Indigenous Peoples comprise many nations and cultural traditions, and identifying as Indigenous does not replace an identification with a specific nation or community. Rather, it is a deliberate way of evoking commonalities between different peoples, underscoring the significant differences between Indigenous and settler colonizer societies, and an understanding of the specific political and land-based issues in Canada today.

It may be useful here to have a clearer definition of, and contrast between, identity and subjectivity as intertwined terms. Loosely, identity refers to our concept of "who we are," with an emphasis on the "we." Identification with or as part of a group is often a shorthand for cultural practices, group experiences, social conventions, and modes of expression. However, identities do not emerge in a vacuum. Subjectivities refers to ways of understanding how people are "grouped." This means that identities are as often formed by what "we" are not — disidentification — than with what we are, and this is especially true in settler colonial contexts. Settlers, however they identify their collective "self," in part define themselves based on what they are not, which has involved exercising the power to "group" other people, including Indigenous People. This involves both social and cultural racism, and the power of the state to create identities like "Status Indian." Indigenous Peoples have worked to assert a collective identity in part based on the common experience of being subjectivized by colonizers as subhuman, exploitable, or inevitably disappearing. This does not mean that those things are at the core of being Indigenous, but Indigenous identities share the impact of colonization.

To clarify some of the murkiness around identities and subjectivities, we need a connected conversation around who the "we" is that is doing the colonizing. There are terms that have been used as stand-ins — more or less accurate — for colonizers in this context. "White," "newcomer," "non-Aboriginal," "non-Indigenous," or simply "Canadian." We also have terms that create or imply divisions based on nationality or history on the land: "Québécois," "immigrant," "westerner." Some of these terms describe some of us, but not all. If we try these on, some are uncomfortable and the fit is poor. Some are too comfortable, and tell us little we do not already know. We are not homogeneously "white"; many of our families have been on the lands called Canada for generations so we are not "new," and describing us by what we are not says little about what we are. Even our regional differences are often seen as part of the diversity that makes the essential something that we call "us."

Throughout this book, our terms of choice and analysis are "Settler Canadians" and "Settler people." First, we discuss "Settler Canadians" specifically, not because there is a vast difference between the structures of various settler colonial states, but because many people in these states *feel, perceive, or believe* that they are unique from each other. We are attempting here to engage with other settler colonial people who would see themselves as intrinsically "like us." For us as authors, that means working from our experiences and analyses that are closely enmeshed with the places we have called home and their systems, structures, and stories. We use "being Canadian" — for many, still a point of pride or aspiration — to connect it specifically with understanding and taking action, and to work from points of connection and comfort toward unsettling and action. We recognize that many people experience being Canadian differently; some may have other national identities and heritages that shape how they see Canada and others may not be citizens but aspire to be one day. We hope for many of the readers of this book to see themselves in the term, to further read into the term with their own experiences and meanings, and their own vital questions.

It might be surprising to some to see Settler — with a capital "S" — deployed in this way. In this book, we are using the capitalized term to refer specifically to an identity that connects a group of people with common practices, a group to which people have affinity, and can belong either through individual identification or recognition by the group (or some combination). We use capitalization of this term in this book because it disrupts some of the ways we seek to distance ourselves from the difficult understandings and work we need to do. Our intent is to open space to rethink things we think we understand or that we take for granted so we can turn this word into a tool we can use to make change.

The first person either of us ever heard use the word "Settler" in a personal, present-day sense was historian Paulette Regan, a white Canadian academic who went on to be the Director of Research for the Truth and Reconciliation Commission (TRC) on residential schools. When we heard Paulette refer to herself as a Settler person, the term resonated. This sparked us to rethink how we understood colonization in Canada. Given conclusive evidence that colonization had not ended, then, logically, colonizers persisted. If colonization had changed form, then maybe what a colonizer looked like was different now, too. If Canada remained a nation in the act of colonizing, then we ourselves were implicated. This book is an attempt to articulate our efforts to understand ourselves as Settler Canadians, as colonizers, and as people with deep moral and ethical responsibilities to change our relationships to the lands that we call home. It is also an invitation to other Settler Canadians to see themselves in these responsibilities, and hopefully to provide them with tools to begin remaking their relationships with Indigenous Peoples and their lands.

We develop the Settler identity as situated, process-based, and pervasive in Canada but also in the United States, Australia, and other settler societies worldwide. Our focus is, then, on the community to which we most closely belong, that of being Settler people whose identities intersect with Canadian cultural traditions, histories, and territories. When we say that the Settler identity is situated, we mean that Settler identity is based on location-specific relationships to the lands we occupy and in relation to Indigenous Peoples. Settler people, as we shall discuss, live on lands that have a pre-existing and undisputable claim upon them. When we say that the Settler identity is process-based, we acknowledge that Settler people do not strictly identify with one set of cultural practices, political or economic institutions, or even particular languages or religions: Settler Canadians are diverse. But Settler people do come to identify with each other through common ways of doing things — particular processes — that root them to the lands on which they intend to stay, and which, while evolving over time, maintain that goal of claiming and asserting belonging on the land. As we show in Chapter 2, this aspect of the Settler identity is rooted in the processes and practices of settler colonialism.

As we have already mentioned, there is significant resistance and reluctance to meaningful acknowledgement of Canada's colonial present. In addition to being situated and process-based, the Settler identity is often disavowed. The specific type of colonialism at work in Canada that structures relationships between Indigenous Peoples and others on these lands specifically seeks invisibility in order to achieve its end goals (see Chapter 2). As such, disavowal is a key part of the Settler identity and marks Settler people as benefitting from the dispossession and destruction of Indigenous Peoples while at the same time vehemently denying complicity in the events and processes that make that happen. In this, Settler identity operates differently to Indigenous identity. Indigenous Peoples struggled for many years to develop a way of identifying that was both collective and not controlled by any particular state, which has been a key defence against attempts to eliminate Indigenous practices, communities, and people. Settler identity, by contrast, is denied even as people attach themselves to the processes of becoming and being Settler.

We build on Paulette Regan's use of the term to construct Settler as an identity that, when claimed, articulated for what it is, and examined with a self-critical eye can bring to light the effects of the relationships that Canadians forge with the territories on which we live and the Indigenous Peoples who hold prior and continuing claims to (and relationships with) those lands. Settler Canadian identity, as we will show, is reliant on the ongoing exercise of colonial power to provide attachment to and legitimacy on the land; however, we also argue that while most Settler people in Canada participate in colonial domination, their involvement is not guaranteed. Theoretically, there are many different ways to be a Settler. However, they are often foreclosed by powerful structures and systems, be they officially recognized powers of the capitalist state or more diffuse structures like whiteness and individualism.

While we focus on the individual level, we are not suggesting any individual Settler Canadian could successfully transcend these structures on their own.[40] Rather, our individual choices and efforts are necessary as a first step toward building collective action that is required to create change. All the same, systems and structures should never be abstracted from society. All these systems and structures are occupied and operated by people, and they function because of many people operating in concert, agreeing actively or passively on certain principles (such as who owns the land and as such who has the right to make decisions about what kind of society should exist on the land). No one — including us — can simply step outside of these structures and systems. However, building on the critiques and insights developed by generations of Indigenous academics and scholars (under the umbrella of what we currently refer to as Critical Indigenous Studies), as well as Indigenous authors and artists, activists and spokespeople, and community leaders, we can begin to become aware of our own surroundings and our own complicity, and to make choices about how and why we will struggle to change them (or not).

We position Indigenous and Settler as identities "always in relationship." We articulate this relationship through a concept philosopher Anne Waters has drawn from Indigenous linguistic traditions. Indigenous languages often define concepts and meanings by establishing relationships and relationality between people, places, objects, concepts and so on. Waters draws from these understandings to create a conceptual framework for how we can understand entities in relationship through "non-discrete, non-binary dualism."[41] Indigenous and Settler, as identities, function in this relational way. What this means is that Indigenous and Settler identities exist in tension with each other, even as these identities overlap with each other, and with other identities that cannot be accounted for within the Indigenous–Settler construct. The groups are nondiscrete in the sense that they overlap with each other and there are many people caught between Settler and Indigenous identities, and therefore pressured by conflicting social treatment based on how they are subjectively perceived and/or claimed by other

Settler or Indigenous People(s). They are also nonbinary in a number of ways. First and most obvious, is the existence of people living on the lands of Indigenous Nations, but not doing so as settler colonizers or in a way recognizable to the Settler identity, and most importantly, not in opposition to Indigeneity.[42] As we discuss throughout the book, Indigenous and Settler peoples are not defined by their distances and differences, but rather their relationships to each other and to the land.

Unpacking the meaning of Waters' concept is worthwhile because it helps confront the possibility of sliding into essentialism or the establishment of "Manichean duals" or "master-slave dialectics."[43] In other words, the concept helps us with the misunderstanding that identity groups are bounded by rigid behavioural or familial structures, never to meet or interact. So, "Indigenous People" is an extremely heterogeneous and diverse group, as is "Settler people." There are many people who have a foot in both worlds, and more besides, because Indigenous and Settler identities do not account for all peoples living in Canada, nor the massive diversity of peoples around the world that Indigenous or Settler peoples might encounter, interact with, and relate to. We might also think about people with Indigenous ancestry seeking (re)connection with their Indigenous communities and the complexities that settler colonialism has caused and is causing for these folks. So, we use this philosophical construct to provide a glimpse of the multiple possible alternatives and variations.

By positioning Indigenous and Settler identities as nondiscrete, we are first acknowledging that Indigenous and Settler peoples interact constantly with each other, and that all cultures and communities within those broad identity categories are affected by the actions of the others. For example, consider the Métis people of the Red River: while undoubtedly an Indigenous People, their heritage includes both Settlers and colonial sojourners, traders, and explorers. The Métis languages draw from several different languages, but are much more than simply bits and pieces of the others. The Métis, in their history and development as peoples, cultures, and communities, are a demonstration of how Settler and Indigenous intercourse and interaction can create change without assimilation or one identity disappearing into the other.[44] This is part of what it means to position these identities as nondiscrete: they overlap in frequent and often surprising ways.

To say that Indigenous and Settler identities are nonbinary is to take into account the complexity around these identities. Canada does not exist as a container, with Indigenous and Settler Canadians within and the world without. There are many people who do not quite fit either category. For example, Canada accepts refugees, driven to Canada by forces beyond their control, who would return to a distant home if they could, and who are often marginalized or are living precariously within Canadian society. These recent arrivals are certainly not Indigenous, but are they Settler? What about the many visitors who come to Canada temporarily, for work, for recreation, or for family or personal reasons? What of enslaved people and indentured workers brought to Canada but prevented from accessing education and having the right to safe working conditions, not allowed to choose to remain or not — in the past and also today? And if these people are not Settlers, what of their children and descendants? There has been an enormous amount of discussion around this, in both public and academic spheres. When Eve Tuck and K. Wayne Yang famously argued, in the landmark 2012 article "Decolonization is Not a Metaphor," that settler colonialism is underpinned by a triad of Indigenous-settler-chattel (meaning enslaved people), they introduced a useful way of discussing settler colonialism beyond a simplistic and unworkable Settler-Indigenous binary that did not take into account race or differences in power among non-Indigenous populations. It also provoked a major discussion on their third category specifically, as the article was criticized for reducing the non-Indigenous and non-settler part of the population to simply forced labour.[45] One alternative proposition comes from Chickasaw scholar, Jodi Byrd, who uses the term "arrivants" to refer to people impelled to come to and stay in settler colonies through a variety of means, emphasizing the role of movement in producing different identities and relationships to place.[46] However, neither of these critiques can — or should — tackle the question of when or how people move between these categories because this is simultaneously an intensely personal and widely systemic question.

In 2016, we were having a conversation with two of our oldest friends about our family histories and how we felt about Canada, especially as we had been living in the United Kingdom for several years. Emanuel and Karen DaCosta are Black and have experienced racism in Canada, but have also frequently expressed that they would choose to live there over anywhere else. Their personal connection to historical colonization is important. They carry a Portuguese surname, because their ancestors were trafficked from Africa and enslaved. Their families came to Canada from the Caribbean at times with the intention of returning, at times with the intention of staying, and never all at once. As individuals, they are proud of being Canadian and identify with Canada's positive values and narratives. They later said of their family history: "We made our homes here. We had no other options. For generations we did not even know Alkebulan existed."[47] This made us think of how different and similar our own experiences were. Emma's family experienced a privileged amount of mobility between the United Kingdom and Canada through the twentieth century. Adam's family made a one-way trip, investing what little they had into an opportunity to permanently move to Canada, with the implication that return was unlikely if not impossible. But Adam, at least, knew what England was and had heard stories of it from his grandparents.

We will never share our friends' experiences of racism and white supremacy, but as differently racialized yet still Settler Canadians, we do share a great deal of other things, and these differences and similarities are worth trying to understand. Everyone's origin story of becoming Canadian involves differing levels of mobility, as do our contemporary lived experiences, but these differences still overlap, are still nondiscrete (meaning, Canadians can share some aspects of their experience of mobility) and nonbinary (meaning not simply divided into settler and non-settler). It is in this recognition of similarity — not sameness — that we group most people in Canada as Settler Canadians because an exclusive focus on our differences risks erasing the patterns of settler colonization that we all contribute to generating. Again, who is or should be considered a settler colonizer is less important than what settler colonial collectives do, and most Canadians — willfully or unwittingly — are part of those collectives. All of this is to say that Indigenous and Settler identities are not exclusive or exclusionary. There remains a tremendous and changing variety of other peoples who will pass through these lands and come into contact with Indigenous and Settler communities, and all of them relate to both Indigenous and Settler peoples in multiple and dynamic ways.

So what, then, does it mean to position Indigenous and Settler as dualistic? Overwhelmingly, these two identities coalesce around an observable, general, and crucial difference: relationship to the land. Often, these relationships to the land have brought Indigenous and Settler peoples into conflict — a conflict that has played out as colonization, dispossession, and domination of Indigenous Peoples by Settler colonizers — but we remain hopeful that there are other possibilities, other ways that this flexible and malleable duality can play out. We return to this theme in Chapter 3.

Let us also be clear that "Settler" should not be assumed to be pejorative or an insult. When we say Settler, we recognize that being a Settler Canadian in the present is inherently bound up with the settler colonization of these lands. However, we also recognize that settler colonialism is collective in nature. We identify ourselves as Settler Canadians and understand that, in so doing, we are declaring that we benefit from and are complicit with settler colonialism and therefore are responsible, as individuals and in collectives, for its continued functioning. Though it would be unproductive and incorrect to hold any individual Settler Canadian solely responsible, recognizing that settler colonialism is a shared burden means that it is only through collective action that we can make the choice to be colonizers, or to be something else. This choice can only be made if we start from a position of honesty about who we are, collectively, how we think about and live on the lands we call Canada, and how else we might do these things.

So, if the Settler identity is not derogatory, then what is it? Consider Settler instead as an *interrogative* or questioning identity. When people identify as Indigenous, we will often hear them discuss not just a broad cultural heritage but specific places of importance, clan lineages and familial connections, and people from whom they have learned. To identify as Indigenous is to identify with entire histories and creation stories of how Peoples belong on certain lands, with cultural, spiritual, and political practices that are embodied in those stories that connect them to those lands. When we say we are Settler people, we are recognizing that our stories are different, and when we ask others to identify as Settler people, we are likewise asking them: How do you come to be here? How do you claim belonging here? And, most importantly, can we belong in a way that does not rely on colonial dispossession and harm?

Our hope is that, by addressing individual complicity and responsibility in this book, Settler people will come to see opportunities for making positive and decolonizing change. When colonialism and oppression are understood only as distant structures, it can be difficult to perceive how any one of us can make a difference, leading to apathy and cynicism and disengagement. There has been a noted tendency among some researchers to treat settler colonialism as inevitable, a trend we wish to avoid.[48] Instead, we hope to provoke and energize — we want people to understand that things are how they are only because we do not collectively organize to challenge and change them.

We take instruction from some of the lessons learned from studies of social movements, both their successes and failures, as well as the deeper considerations of what it means to be successful. As anthropologist, Alex Khasnabish, and historian, Max Haiven, have shown in their study of progressive and radical leftist organizing in Halifax, movements that aim to change society in broad and drastic ways rarely see their "goals" come to fruition as such.[49] This does not mean that they have failed, however. Often the relationships built through common struggle, the lessons learned from confrontations with powerful structures of oppression, or the creative tactics generated on the fly or in the context of an energized and vibrant challenge to power that opens up space for the "radical imagination," are all more valuable — and more realistic — successes than what activists envision might be possible.

On Being and Knowing:
Notes on Ontology and Relationship

In conjunction with our reasons for focusing on identity rather than subjectivity, in this book we also take a different tack for approaching conflicts between Indigenous and Settler peoples. We engage with economic inequality, structural racism, state violence, and other material effects of settler colonialism, and their effects on the conditions and aspirations of both Indigenous and Settler communities. We also take up the metaphysical or ontological questions of what it means to be Settler because, as Vanessa Watts argues and as we discuss in Chapter 3, the ways that we think about where we are, who we are, and how we are related to all of the things around us make enormous differences for what we are able to accomplish. How we think about the world and our place in it must change as part of our efforts to change our material conditions and cultural conditioning.

By "ontology" we mean ways of knowing and being in the world. Ontology is a way of referring to a worldview, and within that particular worldview, what it is possible to know. Epistemologies are related to ontologies, meaning approaches to going about creating knowledge. As such, epistemologies (ways of knowing) are limited by the ontological framework — the beliefs about what it is possible to know — that they are embedded in. Ontologies are often linked to cultural practices, and for Indigenous Peoples, to particular relationships to place. Nêhiyaw and Saulteaux scholar, Margaret Kovach, describing Indigenous research methods, says: "Within research, epistemology means a system of knowledge that references within it the social relations of knowledge production. It is different from ontology, in that ontology is concerned with the nature of being and relating. In referencing Indigenous ways of knowing ... I consistently use the term epistemology."[50] It has long been argued, especially by critical Indigenous scholars, that Indigenous and Western (newcomer or Settler) peoples have vastly different ontological frameworks and philosophies. It is extremely important to understand that Indigenous epistemologies are rooted in particular social practices in relation to particular places at particular times. Settler epistemologies tend to draw from abstracted knowledge, with unacknowledged influences from cultural narratives. As such Indigenous and Settler Canadians literally "know" the land differently in that they produce knowledge about it in very different ways. As geographer Sarah Hunt has identified, these ontological differences "are difficult to explain yet that is where their power lies — in the spaces between intellectual and lived expressions of Indigeneity." As such, Hunt proposes that "these gaps in regimes of knowledge provide sites where ontological shifts are possible."[51] We must grapple with things that we do not understand, perhaps things that we cannot understand, as part of challenging taken-for-granted colonial "truths."

This is more than an effort to understand or respect "difference." Rather, Indigenous Peoples' relationships to land as alive (powerfully expressed in what Dan Wildcat and Vine Deloria have called "personality of place"[52]) need to be taken seriously, and the political, economic, social, cultural, and spiritual aspects of those relationships all matter. We cannot start from the material and work outward or we risk reading our own biases into Indigenous ways of being. For centuries, Indigenous People have had to learn to understand the Settler world and how Settler people think as a matter of survival. In order to find new ways of living together respectfully on this land, Settler people need to take up the responsibility of learning about Indigenous Peoples — including both broad-based understandings of Indigenous worldviews, and also the ways of knowing and being specific to the peoples on whose lands Settlers live — and then finding complementary ways of co-existing. This is a starting point for creating respectful spaces to begin connecting, and as Settlers, for learning how we might relate in non-dominating, non-colonial ways.

Meaningful understanding of the disjuncture between Indigenous and Settler worldviews is not simple. It is also unlikely to be achievable alone. After twenty years, we continue to struggle with concepts and unpack ideas that challenge and change how we think. Our work is informed by our experiences with and learning from Indigenous communities and, especially, critical Indigenous experts and academics who have made important inroads into challenging the innate colonialism of educational and social care systems.[53] We have had the privilege of working with Indigenous academics in Haudenosaunee territories, especially around Six Nations in southern Ontario and in Coast Salish territories on Vancouver Island. Our academic mentors have come from diverse traditions and backgrounds, from anthropologists to political scientists to historians, all under the broad umbrella of what is probably best described as Critical Indigenous Studies. We are heavily influenced by scholarship on Indigenous resistance to colonization going back to the mid-twentieth century: luminaries like Vine Deloria Jr., Philip Deloria, Patricia Monture, Leroy Little Bear, Haunani Kay Trask, and Harold Cardinal, among others. We also are deeply indebted to the works of political and social activists like the Manuels (George, Arthur, and Kanahus), Howard Adams, and Ellen Gabriel, who shaped the idea of resurgence through their efforts, leading into the contemporary work of scholars like Glen Coulthard and author and artist Leanne Betasamosake Simpson. We are also indebted to a wider community of Indigenous activists, educators, practitioners, and community leaders whose articulations of Indigenous thought and social change have been foundational to our understanding and analysis. Among these are the people who hold us to account, and our responsibilities in those relationships are key to the work that led to the creation of this book, its shape and expression.

In locating responsibility at the level of the individual and in terms of settler collective identity, we are not really saying anything new. Indigenous People have been saying this for a long time. For example, when the chiefs of the Shuswap, Okanagan, and Couteau or Thompson tribes wrote their "Memorial" petition to Sir Wilfrid Laurier in 1910, they ultimately appealed to him to act on their behalf not as the prime minister of Canada, but as a person with morals and empathy. They said:

> We want you to be interested in us, and to understand more fully the conditions under which we live. We expect much of you as the head of this great Canadian Nation, and feel confident that you will see that we receive fair and honorable treatment … We speak to you the more freely because you are a member of the white race with whom we first became acquainted, and which we call in our tongue "real whites."[54]

These chiefs understood that, while it mattered that Laurier was the prime minister, their appeal was to his "real" and individual humanity rather than to his position within a hostile government.

We seek to do the same. This book is a holding of ourselves and of each other to account, not as subjects of empire or citizens of a state, but as individuals, families, and communities. It matters that we are Canadian citizens or residents, even if it is not something under our control. However, how we discuss this with others, how we use it to interrogate our own complicity with colonization, and how our entanglements with imperialism and colonialism both limit and provide opportunities for change in our own lives and communities matters as much or more, and these are within our power to engage. This is not likely to be an easy or comfortable process. By making moral and ethical arguments, we are inherently asking Settler people to see that they are personally and collectively involved and responsible for indefensible acts of cruelty and greed, even if these acts usually occur at such a remove that most of us are never troubled by them. When we ask Settler people to understand Indigenous Peoples' resistance and resurgence movements, we are asking them to connect intellectually and emotionally with deep historical interconnections with particular environments and resources, a responsibility to relate to and care for these lands enshrined in ceremony and protocols of governance, and a very valid anger toward the systems and people that have actively or passively targeted them for generations.[55] This book takes up difficult subjects, and the resulting discomfort is both individual and shared — as are the wide range of reactions and emotions involved. It is a powerful and productive decision to engage in this education and transformation. Understanding isn't action, but it is a necessary condition for action, and we recognize the effort and energy it takes to change ourselves in the pursuit of broader positive changes. We see this book as a resource for creating your own journey toward authentic and respectful relationships with Indigenous Peoples and their lands, whether that is taking away useful information and tools or identifying and addressing its shortcomings. Both drive the work we need to do.

Reading this book may provoke unsettling reactions including feelings of guilt, shame, anger and outrage, or fear and despair. Encountering and working through these are key to unpicking embedded colonialism, making them valuable learning guides. In this book, we approach understanding settler colonialism both at the level of structures and individuals, and this is why we refuse to exempt ourselves from any of the critiques we make here.

If we learn to see ourselves and our roles in the systems and structures of settler colonialism — to "identify" with the kinds of settler colonial thought and action we describe — then we create an incredible opportunity because, then, we have a place from which we can make change.

Our motivation to act and to write in this way comes from our understanding of our responsibilities to the Indigenous communities to whom we are accountable, and the learnings we have received. First and foremost, we must take responsibility for ourselves as Settlers and for engaging in uncomfortable and difficult conversations and the wider Settler Canadian community. As Jana-Rae Yerxa (Anishinaabe) has written, Settler comfort cannot be a burden that Indigenous Peoples must carry.[56] We ourselves have learned — and continue to learn — from discomfort, failure, and serious self-reflection, often generated from our direct relationships with Indigenous Peoples and communities, and we acknowledge that one of our greatest failures has been the extent to which our friends and mentors have had to carry our discomfort. We have struggled to correct this balance over many years, and in the process have come to value the discomfort that comes with facing settler colonialism head-on. We are inspired by Siku Allooloo's exhortation that we must personally and collectively move from struggles based in "outrage" to "radical love."[57] In the spirit of radical love for all we could be, we need to unsettle, to destabilize our assumptions about what it means to be Canadian by revealing and engaging with the settler colonial reality of our nation. Discomfort in this process is not action, but we can use it to create space for new and better understandings. We can use it to understand both the necessity and the possibility for positive change.

Toward Decolonization

In this book, we draw out what it means to identify as a Settler person in twenty-first-century Canada, to expose the internal process of understanding and reconciling our identities as Settler Canadians. This involves understanding the nature of settler colonialism as an ideology, as a political project that implicates and requires the participation of large populations, and as a historical current that shapes present political economies, cultural norms, and social institutions. It also means that our differences as Canadians — anglophone and francophone, eastern, western, central, and northern, our many ethnicities and heritages, families that recently arrived and those that have been here for centuries — cannot distract us from our common implication in settler colonization. But this book is more than technical descriptions; it is our attempt to clarify what it means to identify with the systems and societies created through settler colonialism.

In the chapters that follow, we build the concept of the Settler identity, and its specific articulation in Canada: the Settler Canadian identity. We begin in Chapter 2 with settler colonialism, with how it functions and how it manifests as a set of processes in Canada today. We consider its deep entanglement with Canadian social spaces, political systems, and cultural stories. In Chapter 3, the focus is on relationships to land and their foundational role for both Indigenous and Settler identities. In particular, we examine Settler "belonging" on the land and some specific ways that Settler Canadians "root" themselves in Canada. We also investigate the existence of possible alternative ways that Settler people in Canada could relate to and identify with the places they think of as home, considering treaties and historical examples of living on the land outside settler colonial contexts. We turn, in Chapter 4, to complex questions of who identifies as and is identified as a Settler Canadian given that the "Settler" part of the construct is often explicitly disavowed. We expose how Settler Canadian society disciplines, absorbs, and assimilates problematic "Others" across differences such as race and class, and how multiculturalism and anti-capitalism can be used to serve settler colonial agendas. We then briefly discuss the purported "benefits" of belonging in Settler society. Chapter 5 carries on this discussion, focusing on the fear of confronting one's own status as a settler colonizer and what it might mean for belonging on the land. Finally, in Chapter 6, we look to the future to discuss the possible ways that Settler people could become other than settler colonizers, and what the costs of such a transformation might be. This chapter centres on personal responsibility, building relationships with Indigenous communities, and envisioning political identities beyond the framework of Canadian citizenship and nationhood.

We intend in this book to offer possibilities, approaches, and ways of thinking differently. We do not intend it to be exhaustive — it is highly encouraging that there are many more excellent resources available today to support this work than are referenced in this book. The people and works mentioned here are, in a way, a map of the paths we have taken, and there are certainly many more that can be explored. To support individuals and groups seeking to make change, we want to share tools for Settler people to develop understandings and skills that can underpin effective anti-colonial action. While we engage allyship and understanding the "Settler problem," at no point do we offer a simplistic antidote to the fundamental problems in Canada and facing Canadians today. That is something we will find together. This work is possible because of the excellent research, education, and advocacy of Indigenous scholars, leaders, activists, and accomplices.[58]

In this book, we speak as and to Settler Canadians, and hope others will see their own lives and experiences reflected in the arguments we make and the stories we tell. Most importantly, we make space to understand ourselves and to begin to hold ourselves accountable through action so we can start thinking — and building — beyond this present colonial conflict, to a future defined by reciprocity, responsibility, and restitution.

Notes

1 *The Final Report of the National Inquiry into Missing and Murdered Indigenous Women and Girls* is available at https://www.mmiwg-ffada.ca/final-report/. We encourage everyone to read the report.

2 For more on Canadian colonialism, see: Adam J. Barker, "The Contemporary Reality of Canadian Imperialism: Settler Colonialism and the Hybrid Imperial State," *American Indian Quarterly* 33, 3 (2009); Glen Coulthard, *Red Skin, White Masks: Rejecting the Colonial Politics of Recognition* (Minneapolis: University of Minnesota Press, 2014); Victoria Freeman, "'Toronto Has No History!': Indigeneity, Settler Colonialism, and Historical Memory in Canada's Largest City," *Urban History Review* 38, 2 (2010); Scott Morgensen, "The Biopolitics of Settler Colonialism: Right Here, Right Now," *Settler Colonial Studies* 1, 1 (2011).

3 Michael Asch, *On Being Here to Stay: Treaties and Aboriginal Rights in Canada* (University of Toronto Press, 2014); James Tully, *Strange Multiplicity: Constitutionalism in an Age of Diversity* (Cambridge University Press, 1995).

4 The residential school system has been the subject of intense scrutiny and scholarship. Most importantly, we recommend everyone read the *Final Report of the Truth and Reconciliation Commission on Indian Residential Schools*, which is available here: https://nctr.ca/records/reports/#trc-reports. For general overviews of this system, see: J.R. Miller, *Shingwauk's Vision* (University of Toronto Press, 1996); John Milloy, *A National Crime: The Canadian Government and the Residential School System, 1879–1986* (Winnipeg: University of Manitoba Press, 1999); and Paulette Regan, *Unsettling the Settler Within: Indian Residential Schools, Truth Telling, and Reconciliation in Canada* (Vancouver: UBC Press, 2010).

5 BBC News, "Dozens More Graves Found at Former Residential School Sites," February 16, 2022. bbc.co.uk/news/world-us-canada-60395242.

6 On anti-Indigenous bias in policing, see: Pamela Palmater, "Shining Light on the Dark Places: Addressing Police Racism and Sexualized Violence against Indigenous Women and Girls in the National Inquiry," *Canadian Journal of Women and the Law* 28, 2 (2016); Andrew Crosby and Jeffrey Monaghan, *Policing Indigenous Movements: Dissent and the Security State* (Halifax: Fernwood Publishing, 2018). On

anti-Indigenous media bias, see: Brian Budd, *News Framing of Indigenous Politics in Canada: Representation in the Era of Reconciliation* (New York: Springer, 2024); Daniel Johnson, "From the Tomahawk Chop to the Road Block: Discourses of Savagism in Whitestream Media," *American Indian Quarterly* 35, 1 (2011). Anti-Indigenous bias in the public service appears in a number of seemingly disparate fields, including health care, social service provision, and policy making. Broadly, see: Margo Greenwood, "An Open Invitation to Address Anti-Indigenous Systemic Racism," *The Lancet* 397.10293 (2021); Jane Bailey, "Confronting 'Cognitive Imperialism': What Reconstructing a Contracts Law School Course is Teaching Me about Law," in *Royally Wronged: The Royal Society of Canada and Indigenous People*, eds. Constance Backhouse, Cynthia E. Milton, Margaret Kovach, and Adele Perry (Montreal: MQUP, 2021); Kyle Wilmott and Alec Skillings, "Anti-Indigenous Policy Formation: Settler Colonialism and Neoliberal Political Advocacy," *Canadian Review of Sociology/Revue canadienne de sociologie* 58, 4 (2021).

7   CBC News, "Conservative MP Apologizes for 'Hurtful' Comments on Aboriginal People," June 12, 2008. cbc.ca/news/canada/conservative-mp-apologizes-for-hurtful-comments-on-aboriginal-people-1.712106; Joy SpearChief-Morris, "Pierre Poilievre Sharply Criticized after Speech to First Nations: 'You have a Lot of Education to Do'," *Toronto Star*, July 11, 2024. thestar.com/politics/federal/pierre-poilievre-sharply-criticized-after-speech-to-first-nations-you-have-a-lot-of-education/article_c1869ba6-3e1e-11ef-8112-2ba3b757030b.html.

8   Kayla Preston, "'Freedom Convoy' Rolls through Ottawa Encouraging the Participation of Canada's Far-Right," *The Conversation*, February 1, 2022. theconversation.com/freedom-convoy-rolls-through-ottawa-encouraging-the-participation-of-canadas-far-right-175902.

9   CBC News, "Indigenous Leaders Condemn Misappropriation of Orange Shirt Day by Protest Convoy," February 12, 2022. cbc.ca/news/canada/british-columbia/indigenous-leaders-condemn-misappropriation-of-orange-shirt-day-by-protest-convoy-1.6349344.

10 Amy Ede, "The Convoy's Appropriations are an Attack on Indigenous People", *The Tyee*, February 18, 2022. thetyee.ca/Opinion/2022/02/18/Convoy-Appropriations-Attack-Indigenous-People/.

11 Will Kymlicka, *Politics in the Vernacular* (Oxford: Oxford University Press, 2001).

12 The Canadian Press, "Meeting between B.C. RCMP, Indigenous Group Got 'Out of Hand' After Hit-and-Run at Memorial March". *CTV News*, June 9, 2022. bc.ctvnews.ca/indigenous-group-meets-with-rcmp-after-memorial-marchers-allegedly-hit-by-truck-driver.

13 Even this move has been opposed, however. A Québecois group filed a motion in court to have Mary Simon dismissed as Governor General on the grounds that she is not fluent in French. According to the Canadian Constitution, government representatives must be bilingual in English and French. Mary Simon is bilingual in English and Inuktitut. She speaks English as a result of attending an English-language day school in northern Québec. See: Tracey Lindeman, "Quebecers Take Legal Route to Remove Indigenous Governor General over Lack

14 Brett Forester, "Grassy Narrows Chief Questions Federal Commitment to Mercury Care Home amid Delays, Soaring Costs". *CBC News*, June 20, 2023. cbc.ca/news/indigenous/grassy-narrows-delays-mercury-care-home-1.6882699#:~:text=The%20federal%20government%20and%20Grassy,centre%20to%20nearly%20%2490%20million.

15 Cindy Blackstock, "The Case for an Inquiry into Canada's Treatment of First Nations Children". *Maclean's*, January 21, 2022. macleans.ca/opinion/canadian-government-first-nations-cindy-blackstock/.

16 Nia Williams and Rod Nickel, "Trans Mountain Oil Pipeline Change Approved by Canadian Regulator". *Reuters*, January 12, 2024. reuters.com/world/americas/canada-regulator-wraps-up-trans-mountain-pipeline-variance-hearing-2024-01-12/.

17 Kamya Razavi, "Indigenous Rights Collide with $35B Western Canada Pipeline Expansion". *Global News*, November 22, 2023. globalnews.ca/news/10103531/indigenous-rights-collide-with-35b-western-canada-pipeline-expansion/.

18 Eva Jewell and Ian Mosby, *Call to Action Accountability: A 2023 Status Update on Reconciliation* (Toronto: Yellowhead Institute, 2023). yellowheadinstitute.org/trc/.

19 However, as is discussed in greater detail throughout this book, the "politics of recognition" are not in the interests of Indigenous Peoples, but rather, they support the settler colonial-neoliberal capitalist state. Research in this area has been led by political theorist Glen Coulthard in works such as "Subjects of Empire: Indigenous Peoples and the 'Politics of Recognition' in Canada," *Contemporary Political Theory* 6, 4 (2007); and *Red Skin, White Masks*.

20 Many of these concepts are commonly discussed in relation to Indigenous Peoples and colonialism in Canada, but we are also aware that, especially for some concepts relating to more historical practices, not everyone may be aware of the details. For example, enfranchisement was a strategy of forcibly assimilating Indigenous People by removing their Status, right to live on reserve, and any other legal and political markers defined by the state. This was often seen as a "reward" or recognition that an individual had become sufficiently "civilized" — it was applied to Indigenous People who earned degrees or served in the military, for example. To learn more about this and many other foundational concepts, we encourage participating in University of Alberta's free online course, "Indigenous Canada": https://www.ualberta.ca/admissions-programs/online-courses/indigenous-canada/index.html.

21 The phrase "Indian problem" is largely associated with Duncan Campbell Scott, former Superintendent of Indian Affairs during the height of the residential school era (1913–32) and architect of assimilation-based policies, although he more frequently referred obliquely to the "Indian question." On Scott's impact and legacy, see: Brian Titley, *A Narrow Vision: Duncan Campbell Scott and the Administration of Indian Affairs in Canada*, (Vancouver: UBC Press, 1992).

22 Catharine Tunney and Guy Quenneville, "RCMP Feared that Mounties Might Leak Operational Plans to Convoy Protesters: Documents," *CBC News*, November 16, 2022, cbc.ca/news/politics/rcmp-insider-threats-convoy-covid-pandemic-ottawa-1.6569502.

23 Audra Diptee, "Black and Indigenous Protesters are Treated Differently than the 'Convoy' because of Canada's Ongoing Racism," *The Conversation*, February 17, 2022. theconversation.com/black-and-indigenous-protesters-are-treated-differently-than-the-convoy-because-of-canadas-ongoing-racism-176653.

24 Jaskiran Dhillon and Will Parrish, "Canada Police Prepared to Shoot Indigenous Activists, Documents Show," *The Guardian*, 20 December, 2019. theguardian.com/world/2019/dec/20/canada-indigenous-land-defenders-police-documents [Paragraph breaks removed].

25 Adam J. Barker and Emma Battell Lowman, "Indigenous Resurgence," *The Handbook of Indigenous Public Policy*, eds. Sheryl Lightfood and Sarah Maddisson (Cheltenham: Edward Elgar Publishing, 2024).

26 For more, see: Joel Hebert, "'Sacred Trust': Rethinking Late British Decolonization in Indigenous Canada," *Journal of British Studies* 58 (July 2019); Maurice Bulbuliam, "Dancing Around the Table, Part 1," National Film Board of Canada (documentary film), 1987. nfb.ca/film/dancing_around_the_table_1/.

27 For more on Oka, see: Leanne Simpson and Kira Ladner, *This Is an Honour Song: Twenty Years Since the Blockades* (Winnipeg: Arbeiter Ring Press, 2010); and the following National Film Board of Canada documentaries: Alec MacLeod, *Acts of Defiance*, National Film Board of Canada (documentary film, 1992), nfb.ca/film/acts_of_defiance; Alanis Obomsawin, *Kanehsatake: 270 Years of Resistance*, National Film Board of Canada (documentary film, 1993), nfb.ca/film/kanehsatake_270_years_of_resistance (both available to stream online at www.nfb.ca).

28 Alanis Obomsawin, *Rocks at Whiskey Trench*, National Film Board of Canada (documentary film, 2000), nfb.ca/film/rocks_at_whiskey_trench/.

29 For more on these and similar incidents that occurred during Idle No More, see, Adam J. Barker, "'A Direct Act of Resurgence, a Direct Act of Sovereignty': Reflections on Idle No More, Indigenous Activism, and Canadian Settler Colonialism," *Globalizations* 12, 1 (2014); Jeff Denis, "A Four Directions Model: Understanding the Rise and Resonance of an Indigenous Self-Determination Movement," in *More Will Sing Their Way to Freedom: Indigenous Resistance and Resurgence*, ed. Elaine Coburn (Halifax: Fernwood Publishing, 2015). For a comprehensive history of Idle No More in the words of those most closely aligned with it, see the Kino-nda-niimi Collective, *The Winter We Danced: Voices from the Past, the Future, and the Idle No More Movement* (Winnipeg: ARP Books, 2014).

30 For more on the context and fallout of this, see Lisa Steacy, "Man Who Allegedly Drove Truck into B.C. Residential School March Charged," *CTV News* November 24, 2022, bc.ctvnews.ca/man-who-allegedly-drove-truck-into-b-c-residential-school-march-charged-1.6166606; and Lisa Steacy, "'He Ran Me Over': Attendees of B.C. Residential School Memorial March Hit by Truck," *CTV News* June,5 2022), bc.ctvnews.ca/he-ran-me-over-attendees-of-b-c-residential-school-memorial-march-hit-by-truck-1.5933849; and The Canadian Press, "Meeting between B.C. RCMP, Indigenous Group Got 'Out of Hand' After Hit-and-Run at Memorial March," *CTV News,* June 9, 2022, https://bc.ctvnews.ca/meeting-between-b-c-rcmp-indigenous-group-got-out-of-hand-after-hit-and-run-at-memorial-march-1.5939667.

31 For example, the Haudenosaunee have a traditional protocol for "adding rafters to the longhouse," that is, making space in their political organization for new national partnerships. The most well-known example is the inclusion of the Tuscarora Nation in the Haudenosaunee Confederacy. These sorts of protocols and processes were historically common among Indigenous Nations as ways to structure the respectful mixing of societies and people and sharing of land. Trade was often conducted under the bounds of ceremony and complex rules of trust and respect.

32 All of this must be understood against the backdrop of Indigenous international trade and diplomacy that was far more globalized and interconnected than is commonly believed. There is increasing evidence suggesting that the idea of the Americas as isolated and static prior to colonization is a Euro-centric fiction that rests on the notion that only Europeans were sufficiently developed and technologically advanced to traverse such great distances. A growing body of evidence suggests that trade and diplomacy across Turtle Island, and around the Pacific Ocean, were relatively common prior to European colonization. While all these trans-oceanic and cross-continental contacts remain controversial, evidence shows sustained contact between often distant Nations, such as the Coast Salish People of the Pacific Northwest and Hawaiians. We first heard both Coast Salish and Hawaiian Peoples asserting that they had a centuries long history of contact during our time living in Lekwungen territory (Victoria, BC) between 2004 and 2009. Paul D'Arcy, in his history of precontact Pacific trade, notes that while traditional scholarship viewed Pacific sea voyages as accidental and haphazard, more recent archaeology has established that Indigenous Peoples of the Pacific have long been skillful long-distance sailors and navigators, and intentional travellers and traders; see Paul D'Arcy, "No Empty Ocean: Trade and Interaction Across the Pacific Ocean in the Middle of the Eighteenth Century," in *Studies in the Economic History of the Pacific Rim*, eds. Sally Miller, A.J.H. Latham, and Dennis Flynn (London: Routledge, 1998). He also notes that the longer distances between land masses in the northern Pacific have been less conducive to tracing archaeological or linguistic contacts but recent genetic testing and cultural comparisons have suggested sustained relationships that extended all the way across the Pacific to Asia. On the technological sophistication and international Indigenous contact and trade more generally, see Charles Mann, *1491: New Revelations of the Americas Before Columbus* (New York: Vintage Books, 2006).

33 Anthony Hall, *American Empire and the Fourth World: The Bowl with One Spoon, Part 1* (Montreal: McGill-Queens University Press, 2003).

34 Alan Taylor, *The Civil War of 1812: American Citizens, British Subjects, Irish Rebels, & Indian Allies* (New York: Vintage Books, 2010).

35 Adam J. Barker and Emma Battell Lowman, "Settler Colonialism and the Criminalization of Indigenous Peoples in Canada," in *Justice, Indigenous Peoples, and Canada: A History of Courage and Resilience*, eds. Kathryn M. Campbell and Stephanie Wellman (New York: Routledge, 2023).

36 See: Ronald Niezen, *The Origins of Indigenism: Human Rights and the Politics of Identity* (Berkeley: University of California Press, 2003).

37 Mamdani has written many articles and books over the years on this topic, most

significant being his 2020 book, *Neither Settler Nor Native: The Making and Unmaking of Permanent Minorities* (Cambridge, MA: Belknap Press, 2020).

38 Alice Broome, "From the Archive: The Indian Diaspora in British Colonial Africa," *British Online Archives,* June 2, 2023, britishonlinearchives.com/posts/category/articles/629/from-the-archive-the-indian-diaspora-in-british-colonial-africa.

39 The debate sparked by Mamdani's work has continued in many fields, most especially in relation to the settler colonization of Palestine by Israel, begun in the twentieth century. This has drawn in questions of citizenship, race, religion, historical land tenure, and many other aspects that would seem to demonstrate that, while settler identity is not simplistic, it remains a necessary point of analysis and debate. See, for example, Raef Zriek, "When Does a Settler Become a Native? (With Apologies to Mamdani)," *Constellations: An International Journal of Critical & Democratic Theory* 23, 3 (2016); "When Does a Native Become a Settler? (With Apologies to Zriek and Mamdani)," *Constellations: An International Journal of Critical and Democratic Theory* 29, 1 (2022); Fazil Moradi, "In Search of Decolonised Political Futures: Engaging Mahmood Mamdani's Neither Settler nor Native," *Anthropological Theory* 23, 4 (2023).

40 The entanglements between identity and power go far beyond the settler colonial focus of this book but are worth grappling with all the same. On the complexity of identity and Canada and the ways that it is entangled with very localized as well as transnational and global cultures, structures of power, and practices of politics and economy, see, Eva Mackey, *The House of Difference: Cultural Politics and National Identity in Canada* (University of Toronto Press, 2002).

41 Anne Waters, "Language Matters: Non-discrete, Non-binary Dualism," in *Native American Thought,* ed. Anne Waters (Malden: Blackwell Press, 2004).

42 Many important works in the development of critical Indigenous studies and settler colonial theory position Indigenous and settler as a binary in part because of the degree to which it often appears to be the case. See for example: Patrick Wolfe, "Recuperating Binarism: A Heretical Introduction," *Settler Colonial Studies* 3, 3–4 (2013); Frantz Fanon, *The Wretched of the Earth* (New York: Grove Press, 1963); Albert Memmi, *The Colonizer and the Colonized* (Boston: Beacon Press, 1965). Our attempt to bring more nuance and flexibility to these constructions is not a critique of the original works cited, all of which are key foundational studies that we rely on throughout this book. Rather, as we specify a contemporary, Canadian, settler colonial framework, we are able to engage with particular historical events or cultural touchstones that add detail within this more constrained scope.

43 Some scholars, such as Jodi Byrd, have expressed discomfort with the stark binaries sometimes employed in discussions of Settler and Indigenous Peoples; see, Jodi Byrd, *The Transit of Empire: Indigenous Critiques of Colonialism* (Minneapolis: University of Minnesota Press, 2011). Other scholars, such as Patrick Wolfe, argue for a strategic essentialism in settler colonial analyses; see Patrick Wolfe, "Recuperating Binarism." Our hope here is to bridge these two concerns.

44 Chris Andersen, *Métis: Race, Recognition and the Struggle for Indigenous Peoplehood* (Vancouver: UBC Press, 2014).

45 Tapii Garba and Sara-Maria Sorentino, "Slavery is a Metaphor: A Critical Commentary on Eve Tuck and K. Wayne Yang's 'Decolonization Is Not a Metaphor,'" *Antipode* 52, 3 (2020).
46 Byrd, *The Transit of Empire*.
47 We thank our dear friends Emanuel and Karen for agreeing to let us recreate this conversation.
48 Alissa Macoun and Elizabeth Strakosch, "The Ethical Demands of Settler Colonial Theory," *Settler Colonial Studies* 3, 3–4 (2013), 435–37.
49 Alex Khasnabish and Max Haiven, *The Radical Imagination: Social Movement Research in the Age of Austerity* (Halifax: Zed Books and Fernwood Publishing, 2014).
50 Margaret Kovach, *Indigenous Methodologies: Characteristics, Conversations and Contexts* (University of Toronto Press, 2009), 20.
51 Sarah Hunt, "Ontologies of Indigeneity: The Politics of Embodying a Concept," *Cultural Geographies* 21, 1 (2013), 4.
52 Vine Deloria, Jr. and Daniel Wildcat, *Power and Place: Indian Education in America* (Golden, CO: Fulcrum Resources, 2001).
53 On issues of colonialism in the academy, see, Devon Miheshua and Angela Cavander-Wilson, *Indigenizing the Academy: Transforming Scholarship and Empowering Communities* (Lincoln: University of Nebraska Press, 2004); Clelia Rodríguez, *Decolonizing Academia: Poverty, Oppression and Pain* (Halifax: Fernwood Publishing, 2018); Billie Allan and VC Rhonda Hackett, *Decolonizing Equity* (Halifax: Fernwood Publishing, 2022); Kathleen Absolon, *Kaandossiwin — How We Come to Know: Indigenous Re-Search Methodologies, 2nd Edition* (Halifax: Fernwood Publishing, 2022); Joyce Green, *Making Space for Indigenous Feminisms, 2nd edition* (Halifax: Fernwood Press, 2017).
54 The Memorial to Laurier is a letter dictated by the chiefs of the "Secwepemc (Shuswap), Nlaka'pamux (Couteau or Thompson) and Okanagan tribes" to anthropologist James Teit in 1910. It "is written in a narrative form from the First Nations' point of view. It tells the Aboriginal side of the first hundred years of contact with non-Native peoples." Details and a full transcript can be found at the webpage of the Shushwap Nation Tribal Council: shuswapnation.org/to-sir-wilfrid-laurier/.
55 There are many excellent accounts from Indigenous People about their own governance structures and how they continue to rely on these in opposition to settler colonialism, environmental destruction, and alienation from territory, and we encourage readers to seek these out in their own areas. As an example and starting point, we highly recommend Leanne Betasamosake Simpson's *As We Have Always Done: Indigenous Freedom Through Radical Resistance* (Minneapolis: University of Minnesota Press, 2017).
56 Jana-Rae Yerxa, "Refuse to Live Quietly!" *Indigenous Nationhood Movement*, March 12, 2014, blog, nationsrising.org/refuse-to-live-quietly.
57 Siku Allooloo, "From Outrage to Radical Love," *Indigenous Nationhood Movement*, March 7, 2014, blog, nationsrising.org/from-outrage-to-radical-love/.
58 For excellent introductory texts, we recommend: Howard Adams, *Prison of Grass: Canada from a Native Point of View* (Saskatoon, SK: Fifth House Publishers,

1989); James Daschuk, *Clearing the Plains: Disease, Politics of Starvation, and the Loss of Aboriginal Life* (Regina, SK: University of Regina Press, 2013); Roxanne Dunbar-Ortiz, *An Indigenous Peoples' History of the United States* (Boston: Beacon Press, 2014); JR Miller, *Skyscrapers Hide the Heavens: A History of Indian–White Relations in Canada* (University of Toronto Press, 1989); Andersen, *Métis*; Asch, *On Being Here to Stay*; the summary of the *Report of the Royal Commission on Aboriginal Peoples*; and the United Nations Declaration on the Rights of Indigenous Peoples, https://www.un.org/development/desa/indigenouspeoples/wp-content/uploads/sites/19/2018/11/UNDRIP_E_web.pdf.

Canada and Settler Colonialism

COLONIALISM IS SUCH AN IMPORTANT PART OF CANADIAN IDENTITY and yet it is so little understood. It is not too bold to claim that colonialism more than any other force drove the creation and shape of Canada and its regions. In this chapter, we will explore settler colonialism in Canada today, its relationship to identity, and how it manifests in the daily lives of Canadians.

Settler colonialism as a concept is a tool for identifying and understanding how complex interactions among power, people, and place produce patterns of violence, dispossession, and destruction across time, and target particular peoples and places. Settler colonialism is a way of thinking about power and migration that allows us to better understand the nature of contemporary Canadian society. As a concept, it was born out of a rejection of the salt water thesis — the twentieth-century international agreement that ensured that once overseas colonies such as Canada, Australia, or South Africa were freed from the control of European imperial powers, they were to be considered "decolonized" even if newly arrived or settler populations remained in control.

In academic contexts, at least two different groups developed the concept to fill a similar role, working across former white British anglophone colonies. First, Indigenous scholars and activists continually demonstrated that colonization was not "over," demanding that both the continuities and differences from "the colonial period" be understood as key to discussing these countries today. Then, non-Indigenous political theorists, anthropologists, and historians began challenging assumptions in their own disciplines and developing tools for more accurately analyzing ongoing and present-day colonization. Over time, as these groups expanded their work, influenced each other, and began working together, settler colonialism became a robust, developed concept within the academy and social discourse.

For this concept to be a useful tool, we need to understand the specific features and functioning of settler colonialism. First, as political theorist Lorenzo Veracini explains, settler colonialism is distinct from other forms of colonialism in that it generates an entirely new people — a Settler society.[1] This is a key point; Canada has neither built and maintained overseas colonies as points of power and wealth extraction, nor has it remained a colony (or collection of colonies) of overseas imperial powers. Canadian colonialism does not look like classic colonialism and the founding of overseas colonies because it is directed *internally*, against an Indigenous population essentially captive within the borders of the state.

We find it useful to explain settler colonialism as having three main pillars. First, "invasion is a structure not an event."[2] Second, settlers come to stay. Third, the end goal of settler colonialism is its own transcendence. Australian anthropologist, Patrick Wolfe, is responsible for the now famous identification of settler colonialism as a structure. Wolfe identifies settler colonization as characterized by specific ways of thinking about heritage, belonging, race and difference, and power. He describes how the justification for the settlement of Australia — and more to the point, the assertion of a myth across history, science, and popular narratives that Australia was empty and open for the taking — has been woven into Australian society at many levels, and continues to drive explicit political and economic decisions and public opinion. This colonialism is directed toward justifying and supporting settlement and its pre-emptive claim to sovereignty on the land itself, which requires enormous buy-in and receives nearly unquestioned public support. Wolfe demonstrates that these things are virtually guaranteed by the structure of settler colonial societies.

Invasion is not the only moment that the foreign army sweeps in; it continues until the occupying force leaves. In Canada, invasion did not happen at the moment that Indigenous lands were first occupied or appropriated by Euro-American people in the past. Rather, it continues to happen because the social, political, and economic structures built by the invading people endure. According to Wolfe, such structures of invasion include cultural norms and practices that develop into institutionalized laws and social taboos. As an example, he identifies the ties in European thought between patriarchy and patrilineal descent, and the intergenerational passing of private property (meaning through a patrilineal line in traditional European societies). In the settler colonial context in Australia, these concepts became the foundation of racist and sexist narratives of Indigenous promiscuity and the assertion that Aboriginal peoples completely lacked a conception of ownership or property. Settlers did not understand Aboriginal concepts of property or family lineage, and so assumed they had none. This lack of "development" was used as justification for dispossessing Aboriginal communities of their lands without purchase or Treaty. Australian property laws and, in fact, the state itself, were then created afterward based on the assumption that these racist precepts were true.

Next we move from the level of structures to people. Lorenzo Veracini developed a nuanced theory of settler colonial political belonging and narrative that differentiates settlers from other colonizers and imperial agents by the "intent to stay" (*animus manendi*).[3] It is contrasted with the "intent to return" (*animus revertendi*) which motivates colonial agents like traders, soldiers, and administrators, and in part defines how colonizers imagine their belonging in a place: is it our home, or a place to be until we *go* home? Settler occupancy is intended to be permanent, and as such, our claims to the land have to be beyond question. One can say that when they move to new places, settlers carry their sovereignty with them and then after selecting a place to live, justify asserting sovereignty — their power of governance over that territory — through narratives of progress and racial or cultural superiority and through coercive and direct force. To exercise the intent to stay, settler colonizers must deny Indigenous presence in (or at least the legitimate claim to) places targeted for settlement and resources targeted for extraction and profit. When groups of settler colonizers then turn to the help of a state government, or form one themselves, in order to expel or incarcerate Indigenous Peoples and open coveted lands for settlement, it helps make these governments seem legitimate. Their justification for being is to manage the "Indian problem," which itself only exists because there is an invasive settler sovereignty.

Finally, we come to settler colonial transcendence. That is, the end of settler colonialism because Indigenous Peoples are eliminated and the presence of this new people — the settler society — becomes so deeply entrenched that it is naturalized, normalized, unquestioned and unchallenged. As Jodi Byrd has shown, settler colonialism is a type of colonialism that "succeeds" not by preserving a given, pre-existing colonial order, but by superseding it.[4] Contrast this, for example, with the British colonial regime in India, which sought to maintain an invasive system of governmental authority and economic exploitation to enrich the empire and select colonial elites at the expense of the colony — the difference between India as a colony and Britain as an empire remained stark. In both cases, resources were extracted to the benefit of a variety of colonizers, but the impact on the colonized place (and peoples) was different in important ways. The French and British colonization of what would become Canada relied heavily on Indigenous producers (of, for example, furs), traders, diplomats, and other interlocutors. Their imperial competitions required that they work hard to attract Indigenous allies. However, once the settlement of Canada became an end unto itself, the importance of Indigenous labour and expertise rapidly diminished and violent displacement of Indigenous People rapidly increased. In order to obscure the violence of persistent invasion and dispossession, histories of the new people are whitewashed. Sanitized emphasis on practices of benevolent or philanthropic colonialism involving peacemaking, treaties, and the giving of "gifts" (technologies, medicines, institutionalized education, etc.) is used to overwrite the realities of how the new nation was formed through warfare, terrorism, subjugation, and theft.[5]

All three of these processes or pillars initiate and rely upon earlier "transfers" of Indigenous lands to settler colonial control. These take many forms, including necrocolonial transfer, in which Indigenous People are literally killed through murder, disease, deprivation, or warfare. They also take the form of narrative transfers, in which stories are told and retold until they are taken as truth and used to undermine Indigenous Peoples. For example, the Bering Strait Theory was first proposed in the late sixteenth century without any scientific evidence, and has since been accepted and promoted by historians, archaeologists, and anthropologists. This theory suggests that during an ice age, the capture of water in massive glaciers caused the water level in the Pacific Ocean to drop, temporarily connecting present-day Siberia and Alaska and allowing nomadic peoples from Asia to cross into North America, and eventually to spread all the way to Tierra del Fuego. This theory was used to position Indigenous Peoples as only slightly earlier arrivals than Europeans, and, despite the lack of evidence for it, the theory has endured as a settler colonial myth — every time more archaeological evidence is uncovered that Indigenous presence on Turtle Island is far older and more complex than the Bering Strait Theory would suggest, the dates are simply pushed back. Indigenous Peoples have long contested this construction. Their own creation stories and oral histories speak of different origins as either emerging in their own homelands or as migrations from different worlds or from across oceans, often borne out in the place-based traditions and practices of Indigenous cultures.[6] These arguments are backed by mounting combinations of linguistic, genetic, and archaeological evidence showing that Indigenous origins on Turtle Island cannot be explained simply. Yet, even in the face of both Indigenous and Western evidence, the myth of the Bering Strait Theory persists, closely aligned with the need to justify settler colonial usurpations of land.[7]

These transfers show how the development of settler societies and their associated cultural, economic, and political practices both require and facilitate the displacement, marginalization, and destruction of Indigenous Peoples. Transfer of the land — claiming it as "ours" and building laws to justify the claim — is exercised as a right by the new settler society. As Indigenous Peoples are physically and conceptually displaced, settler society grows into the (perceived) open space created by their (perceived) absence.

Settlement colonies refer to colonies formed with the intention of importing a permanent newcomer population, and are often discussed in the context of the European age of colonization. Not all colonies were settlement colonies; some colonies were trading posts, and some were the administrative apparatus of territorial governments over lands hardly populated by non-Indigenous Peoples. Even some colonies that were designed for people to be sent there — like penal colonies — can differ significantly from permanent settlement. But in settlement colonies, permanent populations of settlers become, over time, the basis of a new society. A settler society is created when a newcomer people shift from identifying with and being materially reliant upon the distant empires and states that often founded them or from which they emigrated, to identifying primarily with the political constructs, goals, and society in a new homeland that is oriented specifically to sustain and benefit them.

People *may at times* move between imperial and colonial jurisdictions — such as the British imperial core and the Canadian colonies prior to Canadian independence — fairly seamlessly. Historically, there were no borders, visas, or other barriers to crossing between the two, only the economic barrier of passage and settling. However, as settler colonies grow and become rooted in their new places, these new polities often come to see themselves as "different" or "special" and thus deserving of independence from the imperial core. For Canada, the natural environment and hardy culture it produces, the perception of the country as a successful multicultural nation, and its history of internationalism and peacekeeping are contrasted with the European empires that founded it, setting Canada aside as unique. Political rights, responsibility, and allegiance are shifted from one political entity to another, empowering new political and economic structures of settler colonialism that are not dependent on foreign support or control. For settler colonization, this process is called an *isopolitical shift*, and it is an inevitable consequence of people legally and politically detaching from originating political institutions in favour of reinvesting in the new settler society and its associated political structures and authority with which settler communities identify and rely upon. In the United States of America, the radical break of the War of Independence is a dramatic and visible result of this shift. In Canada, the shift from imperial colony to settler colonial society occurred more slowly. However, there are many markers along the path: Confederation in 1867; the seven-day wait to declare war after Great Britain at the onset of the Second World War; and eventually the patriation of the Constitution in 1982. However, beyond and beneath these events there was a constant, increasing tendency for Canadians — no matter how attached to the trappings of empire — to think of themselves as "special," developing national myths and identities different from those of the empire, and expanding and changing their sense of community in ways that defied the boundaries of Britishness. The political acts of claiming an independent Canadian state followed the demand by a settler people to be recognized as a new, distinct society.

Over time, as settler collectives exercise their sovereignty, narratives and stories are developed that construct that particular settlement territory as special — particularly beautiful or productive — and Settler people come to identify themselves through residency and belonging in this special locale. Canada has long been contrasted with England and others in the productivity of its lands and the opportunities available there, and now Canadian identity is often premised on a closeness to nature (socially and culturally) that is both personally positive and largely unique, or so the national myths go. In general, settler colonizers differentiate themselves from their societies of origin by intensely identifying and focusing on the aspects of their new homelands that are special. Frequently, this includes environmental features, but also perceived opportunities for social and economic advancement. But it also involves committing violent or displacing acts against Indigenous Peoples who have competing claims to these unique, special places.[8] Developing nationalisms grow out of this identification, which justifies the Settler community in gatekeeping the special settler homeland.

Beyond Binaries

As a method of identity development, gatekeeping manifests in what Veracini has called a set of "triangular relations,"[9] which we earlier referenced in discussions of terms such as "chattel" versus "arrivants." These triangular relations are premised on the perception of three distinct subjectivities created by settler colonialism. These three groups are settler colonizers, Indigenous Others,[10] and exogenous Others. The final group includes, for example, enslaved peoples, imported and unfree labour, and marginalized migrants. The goals of settler colonialism regarding each of the three perceived groups in this three-way relationship are different. Settler people are the primary beneficiaries of settler colonial structures designed to ensure that the intent to stay is supported by both material structures and by discourses that reflect settler colonial ontological understandings of land and place.

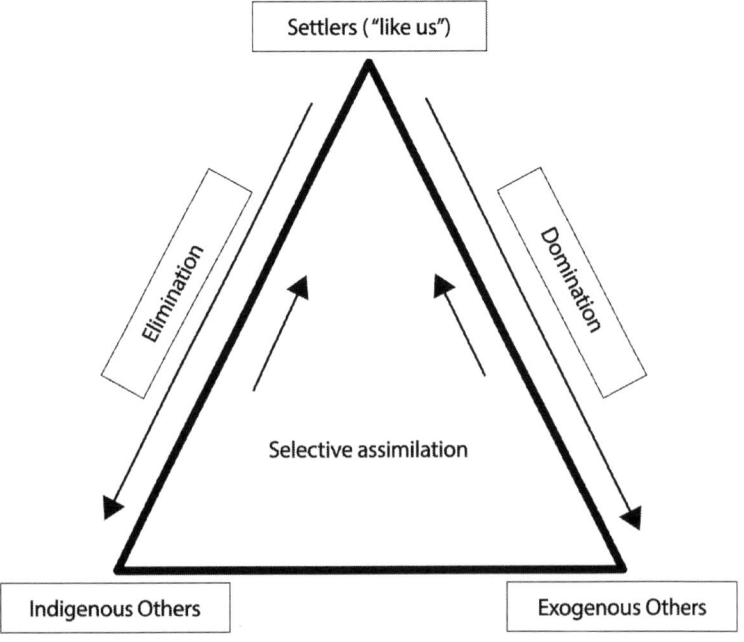

FIGURE 1: Triangular relationship between subjectivities under settler colonialism.

It is important to be clear that these triangular relationships do not refer to an actual relationship between three separate groups or communities. The reality, as expressed in our construction of nondiscrete, nonbinary dualism in Chapter 1, is much more fluid and varied. There are constant tensions around the "belonging" of racialized groups, for example, and not just within Settler or Indigenous communities, as exemplified by the uncertain relationships between Chinese migrant labourers, white Settlers, and Indigenous Peoples all working in salmon canneries on the Pacific coast in the late nineteenth and early twentieth centuries.[11] In the present, undocumented migrant workers — whose intent to stay or return is often uncertain — at times seek to make alliances with Indigenous communities (who are, in turn, often more welcoming than the Canadian state) while also participating in environmentally destructive extractive capital on Indigenous Peoples' lands.[12] Racial and class dynamics in Canada mean that, despite ideals of multiculturalism, there are, in fact, huge variations in how people experience being included or excluded from social structures and systems. As Beenash Jafri has pointed out:

> for people of colour the benefits of being a settler are accrued unevenly. These privileges or social advantages are contingent on things like nationality, class, gender, and migration status. When we account for systemic inequities, underemployment and the racialization of poverty, for most people of colour there are few "benefits" associated with being a settler. Thus, if we follow the logic of a settler/non-settler binary, an argument about people of colour having settler privilege quite easily falls on its face. Many people of colour are settlers without (or with limited) settler privilege.[13]

This is a crucial point: privilege is not evenly distributed through a settler colonial society, and especially as new groups of people move to and across these societies, even these uneven distributions may shift. Given these differences in the ways people experience settler colonial society, we have to remember there is far more dynamism within and between these groups than settler colonial perceptions might suggest. In any particular place and time, the relationships between Indigenous Peoples, Settler peoples, and perceived "Others" who fit somewhere between these categories (or maybe in neither) will constantly shift and change. Framing relationships in this way provides a useful way of thinking about who constitutes *us* and what sort of problematic differences require management to make that perception true. Settler Canadian identity is, in part, typified by the unending renegotiation of what is Canadian, which helps explain why a core of "Canadianness" is so hard to pin down, and why thinkers and writers have spent so much time and energy trying to articulate one. Sociologist Richard Day has shown instead that Canadian identity, from its inception on an Anglo-Protestant/Franco-Catholic axis, has developed as an "endlessly open" method of incorporating and managing difference.[14] That is to say, because the origin point of Canadian identity is the negotiation between two different, and often competing, identities, what defines Canadian identity more than anything else is that it bridges, connects, or aggregates other identities with the notable exception of Indigeneity and racialized populations that are deemed subhuman (in connection to various forms of unfree labour).

Under settler colonialism, all three categories are intended to eventually collapse into one, as illustrated in Figure 1. What that means is, ultimately, all problematic Others will be managed out of existence. Exogenous Others will either be disciplined to fit into the dynamics of the settler collective as a whole (which may include some changes or shifts for the settler collective), or they will be excluded permanently through legal dehumanization or actual removal from the settler state, both of which we can witness in ongoing and increasing deportations of refugees or undocumented migrants.[15] Meanwhile, Indigenous Others and their competing claims to the land are targeted for elimination. This is not always physical in nature: elimination requires that prior Indigenous claims to the land are cut off, subsumed beneath Settler sovereignties, and Indigenous Nations as peoples are extinguished. Elimination, as such, includes limited assimilation of individuals even as societies are dismantled. This can include, then, limited assimilation of Indigenous People as "ethnic minorities" on an individual level as part of the elimination of Indigenous Nations on a collective level.

This last point has received a great deal of attention and has been hotly debated. Does elimination mean genocide? There is a great deal to suggest that the Canadian state, at the least, has engaged in attempted genocide: historian James Daschuk identified John A. Macdonald's policies of starving Indigenous People on the plains so they would accept reservations as genocide and ethnic cleansing; following the final report of the TRC on residential schools in 2015, Chief Justice Beverly McLachlan asserted that Canada had "attempted cultural genocide;"[16] and the 2019 final report of the Inquiry into Missing Indigenous Women Girls concluded this to be an ongoing genocide in Canada[17] — the examples could continue. However, not every instance of settler colonial violence is necessarily genocidal, which is vitally important to remember lest we become distracted into thinking that only the most egregious acts qualify as settler colonialism. Rather, what the Settler society desires is not necessarily the death of Indigenous People per se (though this has been all too common); settler colonialism requires the death of Indigenous Peoples *as peoples*, meaning as nations and communities capable of exerting governance over their own lands and lives.[18] There are many ways that settler colonizers seek to make this happen, including interfering with or preventing traditional forms of governance, removing people from traditional territories so they cannot practice their relationships to the land, and seeking to erase Indigenous histories that contradict nationalist narratives.[19]

This does not stop at the elimination of Indigenous Peoples, nations, and identities in the present. The ultimate goal is to remove Indigenous connections to the land from history as well. It is not enough that Indigenous Peoples no longer exist to challenge Settler sovereignty: Indigenous Peoples have to disappear in the past as well as the present or Settler societies like Canada risk exposure as illegal and unjust. Consider the case of Mistaseni (or Mistusinne) Rock in Saskatchewan, a massive four hundred–ton rock that resembled a sleeping buffalo and was both a sacred site and a historically significant feature of the landscape for Cree peoples. Settlers first dynamited then submerged the rock in an artificial lake created as part of a hydroelectric project in 1966. Soon after, all "official" memory or records of the rock's existence disappeared. The elimination of Cree presence was so great that, despite Cree efforts to pinpoint and memorialize the rock, the site of Mistaseni was not reconfirmed until 2014.[20] This is the logic of elimination in action: first, a physical erasure, then a conceptual forgetting.

A monopoly on the narrative as well as the physical landscape, were it to be achieved, would do several things. It would put to rest any legal doubt about where Settler sovereignty comes from. By erasing competing prior histories and stories, Settler societies seek to possess and maintain the only legitimate claims to their territories. It would also free Settler peoples of the moral and ethical conundrum of membership in a nation founded on genocide, racism, and dispossession. The end of the Settler story is the clearing of the ground to begin a new story, one where colonialism is simply something that happened in the past, possibly regrettable but definitely inevitable, and certainly not worth critiquing given the overwhelming benefits of our "great nation." This is a sort of inward-looking invisibility, where the violent force, racism, and destruction of land and relationships to those lands that accompany colonization are made invisible to the Settler society itself through long-term social processes and generation of powerful myths. Of course, the violence and illegitimacy of settler colonization is never invisible to Indigenous Peoples, and that is why so long as Indigenous Nations remain — and remain in resistance — the settler colonial story cannot be finished.

Settler colonialism can be summarized as a process through three goals: elimination, indigenization, and transcendence. As we have laid out here, Settler societies seek to eliminate competing assertions of sovereignty, and so seek to eliminate Indigenous Peoples and their land-based relationships. Then, Settler societies seek to erase the evidence of those competing sovereignties having existed, both supporting Settler claims to the land and obscuring the violence and criminal nature of colonial dispossession. Settler societies then seek to claim an "Indigenous" status, posing as postcolonial societies. Nations like Canada are portrayed as natural successors to "primitive, past" Indigenous societies, and so Canadians born in the country can consider themselves "native" to the land without contending with Indigenous claims and relationships to the same lands. This is complemented by Settler Canadians as individuals or groups claiming a fictitious "status" as Indigenous People, and often appropriating spaces and resources intended to strengthen Indigenous sovereignty and identity. These include a number of high-profile cases of individuals in academia and the arts,[21] and communities claiming "Aboriginal" rights to hunt and fish, or be exempted from paying taxes, from the government.[22] These are not authentic claims to being Indigenous, but rather attempts to conflate Indigeneity with land tenure, to romantically or cynically use family histories in place of political and relational methods of identification, and sometimes simply to economically benefit from programs put in place specifically to confront economic injustices experienced by Indigenous People and communities. Finally, colonialism is transcended — put into the past — when settler colonial societies absorb or assimilate Indigenous People as minority populations, indistinguishable from any other Canadian, with no recognition of any kind of "status" and no obligations owed by the government. Efforts have been made to abolish the Indian Act, dismantle reserves and "absorb" Indigenous People into Canada many times, and though promoted as inclusion or progress, have rightly been opposed by many Indigenous People and communities unwilling to accept attempted federal extinguishment of the few recognitions accorded Indigenous Peoples.

Spaces, Systems, Stories: Structures of Invasion at Work in Canada

We find it helpful to think of how settler colonialism manifests in three broad groups. This is not the only way of examining settler colonization but it is useful to focus on how power is concentrated and used by colonizers. Canadian structures of invasion come in three types: spaces, systems, and stories. First, settler colonial spaces displace and replace Indigenous spaces. Spaces in this sense are social — they are the animate geographies of our everyday lives. Spaces are not predetermined but empowered by collective agreement that they exist and have meaning. Settler colonial society ignores Indigenous spiritual spaces, for example, and asserts its own "secular" spaces based on dividing up and owning land. They include the broad ideas of "property" and real estate: what are these but spaces premised on ideas of ownership, surveying, and commercial value of land, that contradict Indigenous conceptions of communal, non-exclusive responsibility of, for, and to the land? These spaces are then subdivided into private and public spaces and also formalized in aggregate as towns and cities, regions, territories, and provinces. The city of Toronto or the city of Vancouver is a settler colonial space: a space that is intended to displace and cover the Anishinaabe or Salish spaces, respectively, that preexist settler colonization.[23] We think of these spaces as urban because we contrast their built environment with the rural spaces associated with the prairies or northern Québec, which are, in turn, contrasted with the undeveloped "wilderness" beyond. But all these spaces say nothing of who else might have a claim on the land, or really, even of the land itself.

They instead speak of us, of Settler Canadians, and our history of drawing the boundaries and shaping the landscape of these spaces. Settler Canadian history glorifies acts of homesteading — of taking a piece of property and making it your own, ignoring the violence and dispossession that so often preceded and accompanied these claims. This pattern persists. When we, Settler Canadians, buy a house in the suburbs, we are doing more than engaging in a private financial transaction: we are purchasing the *idea* of that land as *ours* — our own circumscribed space with amenities like a backyard and privacy fences. Our purchase is a benefit of our placement on the inside of the structures of settler colonialism and a denial of Indigenous claims to those same lands. There are often violent reactions from Settler Canadians when Indigenous

People challenge those claims through actions like blockading roads, as happened when Mohawk warriors shut down the Mercier Bridge during the Oka Crisis. When Québécois people in Chateauguay burned effigies of Mohawks, they did so not just because the occupation was "against the law," especially since the Settler riots and clashes with police were equally disruptive and against the law. The Québécois protesters demanded that Canadian law be asserted over the Mohawks even as they broke the law themselves, and examining their words revealed a deep anxiety about how Mohawk claims to the land could undermine Québécois (and Canadian) sovereignty.

We return to the example of the events in Oka in 1990 frequently because they reveal clear patterns in how Settler Canadians think about space, how they will respond to challenges to their perceived spaces from Indigenous People, and because they set the stage for understanding Indigenous resistance to settler colonialism in the twenty-first century. The Mohawk blockade asserted an Indigenous presence in a place where it was assumed to be illegitimate and in a way that questioned how Québec as a province gained authority to assert a political economy exclusive of Mohawk systems.[24] The idea of Montréal as a place of commerce, a metropolis where Canadians may freely enter and exit to enjoy shopping, culture, or entertainment, to conduct business and political discussions and eventually go back to a different space, a private home space, was physically, unmistakably challenged by the Mohawk blockade. The benefit of movement, the structures that claim the right to say how a space is used, by whom, and when, and the insistence that Indigenous Peoples were not part of that space and did not belong, all were shaken by the physical, embodied disruption of settler colonial space. The response by Settler Canadians — rioting, demands for military intervention, assaults on Indigenous People — shows how tightly bound up Canadian identity can be with the spaces of settler colonialism. And these events have been repeated many times since, for example in both 2006 and 2020 when residents of Six Nations of the Grand River occupied lands under development for subdivisions which they still claimed under the Haldimand Grant in 1784. Or, consider the example of the dispute around Indigenous fisheries that spans decades in the Maritimes. In 1993, the Supreme Court decided in favour of Donald Marshall of Membertou First Nation, recognizing his right to earn a living from fishing. The response from commercial Settler Canadian fishers was violent. As journalist Moira Donovan explains:

The violence that followed in Miramichi Bay lasted into the early 2000s. The Lobster Wars, as the conflict became known, were the first sign that implementing the Marshall decision would not go smoothly. In the decades since, tensions have flared again and again, including in late 2020, when lobster fishers from Sipekne'katik First Nation faced similar violence in southwest Nova Scotia. In April 2023, DFO [Fisheries and Oceans Canada] closed the elver fishery early after a series of altercations, including one person allegedly hitting a fisher with a metal pipe. Then, in August, four people allegedly stole a crate of lobster from a wharf in southwest Nova Scotia, dumped the contents, and threw the empty crate at its owner, a fisher from Sipekne'katik ... The conflict started with fish, but it ultimately reaches to the heart of how Canada recognizes First Nations' rights and sovereignty.[25]

Settler Canadians' tendency to react with violence toward even qualified recognitions of Indigenous rights has everything to do with the all-or-nothing imperative of settler colonization. These lands must be "ours" (meaning Settler Canadians, however hazily defined), and at some level Settler Canadians recognize this absolute claim cannot coexist with Indigenous sovereignties.

The second structure of invasion is more fluid: settler colonial systems can be defined as the processes by which Canada runs and through which settler colonization is asserted and changed over time. Some of these systems are obvious — perhaps the most obvious, thanks in part to the much-discussed 2015 TRC Final Report, is the Indian Residential School (IRS) system. As a system of "education," the residential schools attempted to assimilate Indigenous children into Canadian society by severing their connection to family, land, community, and culture, and disciplining them into accepting and preferring Settler languages, religions, and social practices. Comparatively few Settler people participated directly in the schools and benefitted personally — at the very least in the form of wages and personal power. However, *all* Canadians have benefitted and continue to do so to some degree, even if they do not choose to, or even if they actively struggled against the system, because a key function of the schools was to clear the land of Indigenous Peoples, setting the basis for Canadian prosperity. It is nearly impossible to imagine what Canada would look like if residential schooling had not happened, if Indigenous resistance to colonization had not been curtailed by actively abusing Indigenous children for generations — the languages that would be spoken, the oral histories that would be passed on, the ecosystems that would be tended, and so on. But the Residential School System did happen, and it victimized Indigenous People with the intent of ending their cultures and their peoples. In so doing, this system both weakened Indigenous communities and contributed to beliefs that Indigenous Peoples were *inherently* weak, backward, and in need of civilizing. And, of course, this did not end with residential schools — the same paternal attitudes guided social workers and others with the ability to intervene in Indigenous lives for decades, even after the schools began to decline in number. Currently in British Columbia, as one example, Indigenous People make up 10% of the population but 70–80% of all children in care.[26] This number reflects the incredibly invasive and authoritarian techniques of the Canadian social care system that intervenes in the lives of Indigenous parents and parents-to-be (especially women) to an extraordinary degree. In their research, Buchner, Pearson, and Burke interviewed Indigenous mothers who had experienced interventions from the BC Ministry of Children and Family Development (MCFD) during or immediately after pregnancy, which revealed a pervasive sense of authority and surveillance on the part of social workers:

> Janita stated that she saw a social worker when she was pregnant and the social worker said, "'see you again,' and I'm like, what? She's like, 'oh I'll just see you around' …. I'm like ok … I left, and I'm like uh I don't think so." After this encounter, a birth alert was put on the system so that the hospital would notify MCFD when she delivered her baby. Janita stated, "I know they'll [MCFD] never leave me alone … I was still on watch after my oldest was born."[27]

These interventions are justified as protecting children, but the real impact is that of disempowering Indigenous parents, denigrating Indigenous parenting methods, and ignoring the very real generational impacts of residential schools, and the continuation of the work of residential schools through pernicious forms of "care" and "social services."

Public education systems in Canada offer a related example of settler colonial structures in the systemic biases against Indigenous knowledge and learning strategies. A key role of these systems is to socialize children and youth into Canadian society and to instill the values of "good citizenship." As many education researchers have pointed out, "The mainstream education system that is provided to Aboriginal people acts to assimilate them into the mainstream economy,"[28] which puts Indigenous students in public education in the position of having to choose "between assimilating and dropping out of school."[29] Other examples include economic systems, which use the impoverishment of reserve and rural communities to leverage deals for resource extraction that will destroy the land for very few jobs,[30] or, likewise, political and legal systems of Canada in which traditional Indigenous forms of justice are displaced while Indigenous People, making up only a small fraction of the overall population of Canada, count for a full third (33%) of all federal prison inmates, which is actually an increase from 25% ten years earlier. Ivan Zinger, the head Correctional Investigator at the Office of the Correctional Investigator, has stated that the "steady and unabated increase in the disproportionate representation of Indigenous peoples [sic] under federal sentence is nothing short of a national travesty and remains one of Canada's most pressing human rights challenges."[31] This is a result of a complex set of biases in the justice system that assumes Indigenous Peoples are likely to be criminals, and also that social problems rooted in economic marginalization and the legacies of residential schools, among other factors, are best treated with imprisonment.[32] These systems have been created to discipline and coerce all peoples, including Settler and Indigenous Peoples, to meet the needs of expansive capital and nationalist governance, what we have elsewhere discussed as a "society of control."[33] However, what is often ignored is the particular effects these systems have on Indigenous Peoples, and the ways that Settler identity and governance are especially dependent on anti-Indigenous violence and erasure.[34] And these structures reinforce each other, disempowering and displacing Indigenous Peoples, knowledge, and practices.[35]

Narratives are the means through which violent colonization is transformed into the story of heroic struggle and the inevitable establishment of an exceptionally successful, just, and distinct society, and they comprise the third structure of invasion. Narratives underpin the spaces and systems described earlier, and are remarkably powerful and pervasive structures of invasion. Narratives form the basis of the stories Settler Canadians tell ourselves and each other about who we are as a people. These narratives link diverse stories of heroic adventurism that work to cover larger projects:

> the seizure of land and its conversion to private property; the destruction, forced migration, or removal of indigenous communities; the assertion of ideological justifications for dispossession and repossession; the structural antagonism between settler and imperial actors; the development of creole settler cultures; and the construction of a doubled settler identity as both colonizer and colonized.[36]

In the settler colonial context, Canadians are encouraged to tell many different origin stories, and yet those stories must remain consistent in some core ways.

Consider, for example, the story in which people come to a new land, a land full of opportunity, and with little but the sweat of their brow and a dream go on to build a prosperous life that is an example to others. This is an expression of the frontier narrative and it takes many forms: in the nineteenth century, we have stories of pioneering Doukhobor farmers in Saskatchewan or "gentlemanly" English cattle ranchers in British Columbia. In the twentieth century, immigrant success stories proliferate with the post–Second World War immigration boom from the United Kingdom — which includes both of our families — and later the multicultural, liberal narrative of Canada's international peacemaker reputation attracting immigrants from Pakistan, Lebanon, Syria, and many other countries. In the twenty-first century, Canadian media is replete with narratives of immigrant success, including Canadian Broadcast Corporation (CBC) television hits *Little Mosque on the Prairie* (2007–2013) and *Kim's Convenience* (2016–2021). The popularity and persistence of these stories belies the degree to which many immigrant communities continue to struggle against racism and marginalization in Canada — but those stories don't fit the colonial narrative. Further, Canadian immigration policies today, although couched in terms like "high skill" and purporting to be merit-based, effectively create a "two-tiered" immigration system with those immigrants from a wealthy background, with high educational attainment (often connected with class), and with cultural and linguistic fluency being portrayed as "good" (meaning assimilable) immigrants, producing a second tier that does not meet these criteria, which is both economically exploited and displaced in the national narrative.[37]

In today's versions of the frontier narrative, Canada is a container not yet full, a place of opportunity for those who would work hard and boldly venture forth to seek their fortune — or to be parceled off to those whose fortune is already made. It is a narrative that centralizes the individualism and heroic efforts of small groups of people, isolated either by geography or by cultural difference, who make their way in the world through determination and drive and in so doing earn a place in the national fabric, ultimately enhancing the quality and character of the nation for everyone. The frontier narrative excludes Indigenous People by omission or by marginalizing them as tragic obstacles, and fudges the question of the legitimacy of the new people on the lands by focusing on settler hard work, struggle, and effort, and their eventual conquest of the land, as if it made conquest of people inevitable and immaterial. It is tied to tropes of civilization and progress, and the eventual but assumed success of the newcomer, which, in circular fashion, justifies their presence on the land.

It is important to understand the common ways that Settler people interact with these stories, forging a national identity that is welded to settler colonialism at its core. Such stories are key to defining Settler belonging in Canada, and the narratives that normalize Settler people on the land and exclude or eliminate Indigenous Peoples and Indigenous presence on the land further the end goals of settler colonization. Personally, parts of both of our families arrived in Canada from Britain following the Second World War. Our family stories told of perseverance and sacrifice, of the bravery it took to move away from family and homelands to try and rebuild a life in Canada. Our parents and grandparents told us how those who first arrived were often lonely, knowing they might never go home and missing friends and loved ones back in the United Kingdom. These stories emphasized not just that our ancestors did difficult things, but also that they did heroic things — that their motivations were correct, which is borne out by the successes they (and later, we) achieved. These stories also clearly position us as Canadians who had nothing to do with colonization, leaving unexamined any complicity or benefit to ourselves. These and other stories we tell are often attempts to justify Settler Canadians' own histories and actions by retroactively rewriting the history of how we came to be on the land, and under what authority Canada makes this claim. Settler Canadians tell these stories because we want to feel good about ourselves and our pasts, which is understandable. However, these stories, and the exclusions or untruths they rest upon, refuse to acknowledge the many violences required to create colonial spaces of opportunity.

Colonialism in Canada is not just a legacy of earlier times, but an ongoing ideology and practice that is critical to defining the sense of both nation and self in Canada. Settler colonial structures combine to influence and involve nearly everything about life in Canada: from large-scale politics and economics to banal aspects of everyday life, from official histories to family stories, from the sovereign state to the family home. Police officers and lawyers, steel workers and farmers, homeowners and those moving to new places in search of work or education: all are complicit in, and live lives informed by, settler colonialism. However powerful spaces, systems, and stories may be, they only exist because of the actions and decisions of people — from elites to everyday people. This should not be read as a blanket and inevitable condemnation of Settler Canadians. Rather, understanding that we all bear some responsibility for ongoing settler colonization means that we are all capable of making a positive difference as well.[38]

Whiteness and Capitalism

When we talk about oppression and injustice in Canada, we need to understand that there is no one single cause or source of oppression. Transphobia and homophobia, racism and racial discrimination, ageism, ableism, misogyny, classism, and so on: there is no simple explanation for how or why any of these attitudes and structures come about. We do not propose that an understanding of the Settler identity and settler colonialism in Canadian society can explain all of these injustices. But these concepts are necessary to making sense of how Canada remains an oppressive place, and why so few Settler Canadians are able to see and understand the ongoing nature of this oppression.

Activists and scholars, especially those Indigenous women and women of colour who have exposed and articulated these connections through many years of struggle, have created work foundational to understanding these challenging and complex concepts. Harsha Walia's work has had a particularly strong impact on us. Walia is an anti-colonial and migrant justice activist who worked with No One Is Illegal (NOII) for many years and has become a powerful advocate for both Indigenous People and undocumented people in Canada. Her work, along with that of Indigenous scholars such as Leanne Simpson, Sarah Hunt, Michelle Daigle, Vanessa Watts, Gina Starblanket, and Glen Coulthard, has helped to expose the ways that multiple forms of oppression intersect, and also revealed the ways that even scholarly or activist understandings of oppression remain incomplete.[39] The intersections of patriarchy and gendered violence, dispossession and class warfare, and white supremacy and racism are complex, and combine to underpin all manner of imperial and colonial conquests, both in Canada and around the world. As a result of these complex forces, Settler people (despite their many differences) are coerced, forced, or lured with comfortable ignorance into complicity in the oppression of other people — and, in fact, their own oppression. We will return to this complicity later in the book, drawing out how discourses of Canadian multiculturalism and popular movements against poverty, austerity, and neoliberalism can and do contribute to maintaining genocide and colonialism. For now, we hope that it is clear that our focus on settler colonialism and the Settler identity are not meant to erase or diminish the importance of capitalist dispossession, or militarized and racialized state violence, but rather to further demonstrate how we — across racial, class, and other lines of difference — are complicit in Indigenous dispossession, and also what can be done about it.

What we learn from Walia's discussions of the struggles of contemporary migrant and refugee populations is the way these forms of oppression continue to evolve and change. Her work draws our attention to the increasingly complex ways that borders are used to regulate mobile populations, uprooted by capitalism, and to incorporate them into the Canadian economy, while preventing them from ever truly becoming a part of Canadian society.[40] Walia demonstrates that neoliberal capitalist agreements that force people to leave their homelands and come to Canada as often-undocumented labourers — agricultural workers from Mexico, domestic workers from the Philippines, service industry workers from India, and so on — are supported by state policies that legalize the denial of rights for these displaced populations. In this, we see the state, corporate capital, and social racism and apathy continuing to work in concert, while employing increasingly powerful technologies and evolving narratives such as post-9/11 anti-Muslim rhetoric, to achieve their goals. But as Walia warns, attention to migrant justice, anti-racism, and economic equality cannot be sought at the expense of Indigenous Peoples' struggles for survival. If alienation of newcomers is confronted through a universal humanism, the result can be "immigrant and migrant workers ... facilitating the removal and theft of Indigenous land and resources."[41] Meanwhile, organizing around shared victimhood by state and corporate powers can, as Walia explains, collapse "Indigenous Peoples in the category of immigrants ... effectively erasing their relationship to this land."[42] This is the flip side of our earlier discussion of how settler colonialism as a framework can reveal crucial similarities and differences between the experiences of Black and white "newcomer" people, and why terms such as "arrivant" are key: there are also key similarities and differences between the struggles of Indigenous Peoples and racialized newcomers, collectively subjected to white supremacy and patriarchy as part of the colonial project, that need to be understood. Otherwise, there is a clear risk of Indigenous struggles being collapsed into struggles for racial equality, for newcomers and immigrants with little power and agency to be treated as if they were colonial elites in Canada, and for antagonisms between Indigenous and non-white newcomer communities to be normalized with the effect of obscuring the role of colonialism in pitting these groups against each other.

So we must proceed from the understanding that it is impossible to discuss capitalist exploitation, racial oppression, or settler colonialism separately from each other. Why then do we choose to focus to such a great extent on Canadians as Settlers, rather than whiteness and class? We argue here, as do other scholars of settler colonial studies in Canada,[43] that we need to pay sustained attention to Settler people — broadly constituted — to understand how they embody settler colonialism in the present, and how settler colonial structures of oppression continue to both inform and limit legal, political, and economic oppressions. This should not be to the exclusion of other dynamics of oppression and dispossession, but rather to help make sense of them. We cannot focus exclusively on "racism" as such. As sociologist Jeff Denis has demonstrated in his studies of anti-Indigenous racism in northern Ontario, racist attitudes find public expression not just when "difference" is encountered, but when certain kinds of privilege are threatened. As Denis explains:

> prejudice does not stem from a lack of intergroup friendships, but from a historically developed sense of (group) superiority; it is a "defensive reaction" triggered when the dominant group's sense of entitlement to resources and privileges appears threatened by subordinate group gains or aspirations.[44]

That is to say, Settler Canadians often have benign reactions to Indigenous People in the abstract, but if an Indigenous community attempts to buy back land, to lobby for or against a particular development, or to become involved in established politics, then the Othering of Indigenous People as oppositional — an obstacle, a "problem" — suddenly appears to Settlers. If we accept that privilege can be derived from a variety of means and sources, whether through oppression and exploitation of people as labour, or genocide and destruction of people to possess land and resources, then we also need to accept that white Canadians can express different kinds of racism in response to the resistance of different racialized groups of people, and also that various peoples of colour can also participate in racist reactions to Indigenous resurgence and anti-colonialism.

Likewise, even though globalization and neoliberalism portray capitalist oppression as universal and diffuse, occurring "up there" in the boardrooms of multinational conglomerates and at high-level meetings between governments and corporations, these systems still "touch down" somewhere.[45] In Canada, these systems touch down on the lands stolen from Indigenous Peoples that provide both the resources that fuel extractive economies (such as oil, timber, or even fish and agricultural crops), as well as the urban spaces like Bay Street in Toronto, where financial decisions are made. In Canada, capitalism needs settler colonialism to operate. This has often been overlooked in traditional Marxist or socialist critiques of capital.[46] And while reams of paper and years of scholarship and activism have been spent analyzing, critiquing, and confronting capitalism and racism, settler colonialism and the role of Settler people in perpetuating oppression that is specific and particular to places like Canada remains under-analyzed. If we do not attend to settler colonialism alongside capitalist dispossession and white supremacy, we risk constructing a "race blind" socialist society in which the possibility of distinct Indigenous nationhood is again denied.[47]

We are all — even those of us privileged by whiteness, formal education, and class — limited to the lifestyles that are chosen for us with only some latitude, lives that fit within the settler colonial systems of Canada, something we turn to in more detail in Chapters 4 and 5. It makes sense to draw from and make connections to communities that are already engaged in struggles against similar imposed limitations. What is required, however, is a strong grounding in the critiques of settler colonialism that demand we think differently about the land, about scales of struggle, about Indigenous Peoples' aspirations for decolonization, and about how these raise a very different set of critiques than other anti-oppressive frameworks. To understand this better, we need to understand the relationship between Settler identity and settler colonization.

Settler Colonization and the Settler Identity

Settler people are tied together by common — if highly varied — narrative histories of movement and new beginnings, and by participation and membership in various structures of invasion that we have described; they also share similar possibilities for relating to the land differently. As we show in Chapter 3, there are avenues through which Settler people *could* try to relate to land and place in ways that do not depend on settler colonialism and the displacement of Indigenous Peoples. By contrast, settler colonizer is not an identity. It is someone who pursues a relatively narrow range of actions and social participation following the dictates of colonial institutions. A settler colonizer is always, by definition, part of a group that seeks to transfer land from Indigenous Peoples to their own control, exerting sovereignty over territory and wrapping particular narrative forms around this transfer.

Saying settler colonizer in relation to Settler Canadians is like saying European in relation to people from "the West": it might imply many of the things that we associate with being a part of "Western civilization" (as problematic as the term is), but the two are not synonymous. Equally, Canada is a multicultural nation — and specifically with reference to Québécois nationhood — yet these differences in national identity do not undermine our common grounding in settler colonialism. This is an important distinction to make because, as we work to expose the structures of invasion that are built, maintained, and expanded by Canadian settler colonialism, we need to recognize how Settler Canadians, whether newcomers or from long-tenured families, are recruited into supporting these structures. This recruitment works through narratives of national mosaics and other stories of difference and belonging that recognize the many origin points for Settler Canadians, but then conflates and flattens these to arrive at a common patriotic endpoint. We also need to explore the ways that Settler people in Canada can begin to work against these structures, challenging the disavowal and colonial processes that have come to define individual and collective identities.

But, in any practical sense in Canada today, almost all non-Indigenous people, with the notable exception of those excluded for being perceived as "exogenous," are Settler *people* and are also settler *colonizers*. Those who are considered exogenous — such as refugees and migrant workers, but possibly also Black and other racialized communities — are forced into complicity with a settler colonial system that does not benefit them, often based on a vague promise that, someday, it might. In Canada, the structures of invasion that have been built through five hundred years of colonial settlement are pervasive, and almost impossible to avoid. Almost everything most Settler people think about as being Canadian or associated with Canadian identity is caught up in the process of building, expanding, or maintaining the invasive structures of Canada. And that means that the vast majority of people who live within that structure participate in it, benefit from it, or are complicit in colonial dispossession and elimination through it.

We need some attention here to what "race" actually is, and how it works in settler colonial contexts. Race is created through the assertion of power to group perceived "Others" — meaning those seen as "not Settlers" in the triangular relations of settler colonialism — based on assumptions about innate qualities or fundamental differences in human societies usually seen as linked to particular racial characteristics like skin colour. All people may be "racialized" but, of course, there are enormous differences between experiences based on context and privilege or positioning within systems of oppression. Writing in the Australian context in *The White Possessive*, Aileen Moreton-Robinson describes how a key aspect of colonial whiteness is built on the experience of and attendant justification of taking the property and livelihoods of others. So what we think of as a "white settler" is partially tied up with the history of these people exercising dominance, and also usually brings up tropes of masculine frontier violence. This creates a situation where those who wish to perform whiteness more conspicuously can do so in part by embodying a similar kind of dominating persona, often rooted in similar tropes. Performances of conspicuous nationalism, the ownership of property, and adopting vernacular settler colonial aesthetics can all shift how someone is racialized and thus to what degree they are accepted into settler group formations and experience privilege. Meanwhile, the experience of being racialized as non-white usually involves a history of being excluded from positions of power, dehumanized for labour, or treated as expendable in other ways. Conditions of poverty, for example, are part of how settler colonizers have racialized Indigenous People, implying an innate inability to care for themselves that is in actuality an imposed and deliberate material condition. This leads to many debates about group identity and subject group formation given that identities are multiple — even across racial difference — and people can experience greatly varying levels of privilege or access to power from others seen as "like us." The debate around whether Black individuals or communities can ever be considered settlers/Settlers centres on the degree to which people racialized as Black by white settler colonial societies will ever be permitted inalienable humanity in those societies, or whether they will forever remain "abject." This is in part a question about the degree to which the identity of white is dependent on "not Black" as an essential boundary. The debate is also tied up historically with the colonial enslavement and the forced migration of people from Africa to the Americas, and with the ongoing power of whiteness to shape migration, belonging and economic access or dispossession.[48]

Being Settler Canadian

This brings us to a point often overlooked in research and debate on the subject: settler colonialism is produced and upheld not just by governments and corporations — the usual targets of anti-colonial critique — but by people, by Canadians. Settler colonialism is everywhere, and it can be enacted between a small group of people, but those actions coalesce and resonate so that soon systems develop. These systems include our governance and economic systems, but they also include our faith communities, our educational and health systems, our media and recreation — everything. So while it can be tempting to think of settler colonialism as flowing downward from powerful structures such as the Crown, the state, or wealthy multinational corporations, the reality is that the power flows both ways: those structures are empowered to colonize because of Settler Canadians. In Chapter 4, we look at the reasons why people participate in and perpetuate these systems of dispossession and oppression, but here we seek to clarify how, through everyday actions, from seemingly innocuous to explicitly violent, Settler people perpetuate settler colonialism in Canada today.

Appropriation and Extraction

During the height of Idle No More, in the winter of 2012–13, Anishinaabe scholar, poet, and community leader, Leanne Betasamosake Simpson, was interviewed by well-known activist and writer, Naomi Klein. In this high-profile piece, Simpson made the important point that government of Canada legislation that was designed to loosen protections of bodies of water was intended to make it easier for resource extraction companies to gain access, disrupt for construction, or dispose of pollutants in those waters. She articulated the Idle No More protests as a movement against colonialism in Canada because "colonialism is always about extraction."[49] Certainly, the colonization of Canada was and is driven by resource extraction, from furs to timber, and from gold to oil. But beyond the well-documented drive to extract resources from Indigenous lands, one of the most common ways that Settler Canadians perpetuate colonialism is through appropriation.

Appropriation can be understood as the removal of an element of culture, a concept or idea, or a symbol or practice out of its original context, and its redeployment in a new cultural or social context for the gratification or profit of the appropriating person or group. We say appropriation rather than simply "theft" in recognition of the fact that there is often no Canadian law or regulation preventing this extraction, and therefore little recourse for the targeted group to prevent the loss or seek redress. Appropriation in colonial contexts is the assertion that one has the right to take something, regardless of what the group being taken from may say, think, or feel.

In Canada, the Settler identity is closely bound up with symbols, objects, and practices appropriated from Indigenous Nations. The inukshuk originating with the Inuit, Yupik, and other Arctic Peoples was used as the symbol of the Vancouver 2010 Olympics without consultation with either those Peoples or those on whose lands the Games were being held. Transportation technologies like the canoe — which originated with many nations, including the Anishinaabe and Haudenosaunee — or dogsled — again, developed by many Arctic Peoples — are proudly held up as distinctly Canadian. Maple syrup, a staple of the Algonquian-speaking people of eastern North America, is sold around the world stamped with the red maple leaf. The list could go on: igloos, pemmican, mukluks, dream catchers, feathered headdresses or war bonnets, snowshoes, and so forth, are all Indigenous inventions and technologies, all shared by multiple nations with different meanings and uses in many traditions, and yet they are all taken out of context and claimed by Canadians as part of a simplistic and unified national culture. Appropriation of Indigenous art styles has become big business and non-Indigenous producers are unironically and cynically labelling their art as "Indigenous" to increase their sales. A 2022 investigation in Vancouver found that 75 percent of "Indigenous arts and crafts" shops were selling "inauthentic art."[50] This speaks to the perceived right to control — and extract value and profit from — these technologies and cultural symbols. These claims to a right of control are accompanied by deep resistance to addressing the power imbalances that have allowed us to take these objects and techniques as our own while at the same time denying and contesting Indigenous claims of ownership on the grounds that no one can "own" symbols of our heritage.

Appropriation also applies to ideas and concepts; Indigenous ways of knowing are myriad and complex, and have the potential to reveal a great deal about human–environmental relationships, social practices, and time and space. Some Settler Canadians perceive a value in Indigenous thought and, often without intending to "offend" or cause harm, exert their power as part of a dominating society to take these concepts for themselves. Across Canada, there are New Age and mystical movements which rely on Indigenous symbols such as the medicine wheel, knowledge of medicinal plants and herbs, and rituals and spiritual practices like the sweat lodge. Often, the practitioners of these kinds of appropriation will claim to be honouring Indigenous People, but this form of "postmodern quotation"[51] repackages Indigenous knowledge outside of its original context, warping the meaning, and benefitting Settler peoples.

Further, appropriation has to be seen against the historical backdrop of efforts by Settler peoples to wipe out Indigenous ways of knowing and spiritual practices through residential schooling, bans on religious and ceremonial practices, and forced social reorganization. Appropriation relies on the belief that Indigenous Peoples, as colonized and subjugated, do not have the power to refuse, or simply should be "flattered" that "civilized" people have taken interest. As Sarah Hunt has written in response to appropriations of Indigenous symbols and images by "hipsters" in Vancouver:

> This is an old tactic, part of broader political efforts to forget the history of colonialism upon which this country is founded ... So a tomahawk is not just a tomahawk. It is a symbol of my silence. It is a history of resistance turned into a symbol of cool, devoid of any meaning or political significance.[52]

Of course, pop culture appropriations, like New Age appropriations,[53] are often expressed as attempts to "honour" or be inspired by profound Indigenous traditions. These excuses ignore the massive power imbalances and the lack of knowledge of and connection to the sacred significance of many aspects of Indigenous culture. At worst, the incorporation of Indigenous images and symbols into Canadian society is an informal enactment of the "politics of recognition" that undermine Indigenous nationhood.[54] Hunt develops effective suggestions for ethical ways of engaging with Indigenous cultural symbols and objects — such as supporting local Indigenous artists who control their own expression and distribution, rather than buying mass-produced dreamcatchers — but all too few engage respectfully. In the context of ongoing colonial power imbalances, appropriation intended as "honouring" is clearly ridiculous.

There are many reasons why Settler Canadians appropriate from Indigenous Peoples and cultures, some of which are obvious. Financial gain is a key motivator, as it so often is in settler colonial extraction: something taken from Indigenous cultures need not be paid for but can then be sold for significant profit. There is also the "cool" factor: Indigenous symbols and aesthetics — disconnected from the reality of Indigenous lives and bodies — are claimed for their exoticism and beauty. Academics, scholars, and researchers appropriate because, as "experts" on a field related to Indigenous Peoples or cultures, they feel they have a right to "collect" elements of those cultures; this is an enduring concern with respect to bioscience, but also for museums, which often display Indigenous artifacts, artwork, and images without any acknowledgement of the problematic ways in which these things were acquired, and the implications for contemporary communities separated from sacred or ceremonial objects.[55]

But more than anything else, Canadians appropriate Indigenous symbols, objects, and knowledge because we feel that these things are always already a part of our national identity. The settler colonial claim to the land comes along with a claim to all the parts of it. Indigenous cultures are seen not as the lived expressions of people but as things on the land, and therefore available to Settler Canadians to claim. In this way, appropriation is a method of building and differentiating a national identity. As such, it is a part of the process through which Canadian society is created, set apart, and rooted in the landscape. Appropriated symbols and objects become a taking-on rather than a putting-down of roots.

In a related sense, Settler people attempt to claim authority on Indigenous identities and cultures or the right to use Indigenous symbols and objects by referencing Indigenous ancestry. This happens so frequently that it has become expected that appropriations will be accompanied by a claim of having a "Cherokee grandmother."[56] As scholars like Daryl Leroux, Adam Gaudry, and Chelsea Vowel have argued, this claiming of ancestry has been systematized through the spread of "eastern Métis" and other dubious claimants to Métis Status and identity based on a long ago ancestor.[57] Some of these individuals do so to gain an advantage, such as claiming an Indigenous-specific grant or scholarship, while others work collectively to create fake "First Nations" in order to try and claim rights from the government. Most recently, in 2023, it was revealed that two women — the

Gill sisters — with no Indigenous ancestry and born in Mississauga, had been fraudulently enrolled in the Nunavut Tunngavik, which would make them legally Inuit. Their birth mother claimed she had adopted them from an Inuit woman and provided false information on their enrolment applications. The goal was to benefit from government programs designed to support Inuit education:

> both daughters received sponsorship funding from the Kakivak Association, an organization that provides funding to Baffin Inuit for education-related expenses. Nadya and Amira Gill received $158,254 from September 2020 to March 2023, says the document. Another $64,000 was on hold for Amira Gill in the spring of 2023 but was not paid out.[58]

In the words of Choctaw researchers Erin Spiceland and Rachel Byington, "Claiming Native ancestry where none exists leads to the dilution of our culture and visibility, and using any connection to Native people to justify such unacceptable use of Native culture is an affront to all Indigenous Peoples."[59] It also causes material harm, taking supports from already underfunded communities. And each time we Settler Canadians choose to do these things, or choose not to challenge the appropriations by and of others around us, it reinforces the mutual contract of settler colonialism.

Racism and Violence

One of the ways in which Settlers participate in settler colonialism in Canada is through racism and race-based violence. Colonialism and racism are not coterminous, though one is often deployed in the service and context of the other. In Canada, settler colonialism involves the taking of land, power, and symbols, and the building of a new society in place of Indigenous Nations. Race-based prejudice and discrimination are used to justify these colonial actions. When newcomers took over lands that were clearly owned and occupied by Indigenous Nations, Settlers justified their acts — morally, religiously, and in legal frameworks — by claiming that as a race, "Indians" could not own the land because they were not sufficiently "civilized."

Racism is not a singular, unified way of thinking, but rather, it is the deployment of particular strategies to justify particular treatments of different groups of peoples. Different kinds of race-based judgements and systems are used to justify different kinds of colonialism. For example, the enslavement of Africans and Black Americans was justified by similar but subtly different kinds of racism than anti-Indigenous racism. The neocolonialism inflicted on Mexican and other Latinos resulting in forced migration, poverty, and extreme precarity is justified through yet another different (but related) set of racist practices and ideas. Excellent work has been done especially by Black and Indigenous scholars to untangle how these different forms of racism overlap and intersect; the notes of this book contain references that we would encourage readers to peruse. Among the key points raised are that Black and Indigenous alliances and hybridity are completely ignored, erasing the powerful and fruitful histories of cooperative resistance movements. While we cannot go fully into these discourses here, it is important to note their links to different colonial regimes, and their interlocking but unique characteristics.

A great deal of anti-Indigenous racism is structural racism. Various institutions and processes that we take for granted in everyday Canadian life are designed in a way that inherently marginalizes or disserves Indigenous People. Educational systems, as discussed above, have received harsh criticism for excluding Indigenous educational practices. Combine the multiple ways that public schools have racially profiled and discriminated against Indigenous students, and the legacy of residential schools specifically designed to destroy Indigenous identity, and it is unsurprising that there are generational layers of distrust from Indigenous communities toward mainstream formal education. Likewise, social services have been frequently criticized for failing to understand — or intentionally ignoring — Indigenous parenting methods when apprehending children and putting them in custody. The "Sixties Scoop," in which children were taken out of Indigenous communities almost by default whenever social workers visited, was predicated on the assumption that Indigenous children would automatically be better off with white families. To justify seizing children in huge numbers, social workers applied a middle-class, suburban, white Canadian standard to communities with very different cultural norms and values. These communities were also often dealing with extreme economic marginalization. Today, despite the good intentions of many social workers and attempts to reform the child welfare system, the situation is not much improved. "Birth alerts," a process in which an "at-risk" mother-to-be is identified and the baby taken into custody of the state immediately after being born (and therefore before the mother has even had a chance to be a mother), continue to be used against Indigenous People at much higher rates than other groups. As staunch and successful Indigenous child welfare advocate and scholar, Cindy Blackstock, has discussed, there are currently more Indigenous children in care than were incarcerated in residential schools at the height of that shameful project.[60]

Police at all levels have also been the subject of much public and media discussion about their treatment of Indigenous People in Canada. Prominent scandals and stories of police include the murder of Dudley George, an Anishinaabe protester at the Ipperwash standoff in Ontario in 1995.[61] "Starlight Tours" became infamous practices in several provinces: officers picked up solitary Indigenous individuals — often those they perceived as vulnerable due to homelessness or intoxication — drove them outside of the city limits, and dumped them in remote areas of the countryside, often in lethally cold conditions. Outside Saskatoon, several Indigenous individuals, including Neil Stonechild, have died as a result of this type of police brutality.[62] Police violence also includes specifically gendered abuses, such as widespread allegations of RCMP officers sexually and physically assaulting Indigenous women and girls,[63] or refusing to investigate the disappearances or murders of Indigenous women who are assumed to be sex workers and therefore disposable.[64]

Twenty-first century police violence against Indigenous People continues a long historical trajectory. As an institution, police have often been used as a tool to suppress Indigenous sovereignty, from the Northwest Mounted Police invasions of Métis territory (present-day Manitoba and Saskatchewan) between 1869 and 1885, to the provincial police interventions in Oka and Ipperwash in the 1990s, to the use of the RCMP to break up Indigenous protests in Elsipogtog and Burnaby Mountain in 2013 and 2014.[65] In 2020, the use of the RCMP and threat of lethal force to clear Wet'suwet'en occupiers and their allies off disputed land to facilitate the construction of a gas pipeline raised shock and consternation across Canada, but have not slowed the use of police force to further business and government interests in the face of Indigenous efforts to protect lands and water and assert Treaty Rights and self-determination. These are, of course, just a few high-profile examples. The pattern of surveillance, arrest, and incarceration of Indigenous People for political activism – or everyday activities that the Canadian state perceives as political and threatening – extends across centuries at this point.[66]

Anti-Indigenous prejudice is not limited to systems of policing and education, but extends to everyday Canadians. Specific individual acts include the emergency room doctors and nurses who ignored Brian

Sinclair, an Indigenous man in distress in Winnipeg in 2008, assuming he was drunk when in reality he was dying. The same occurred in September 2021 in Joliette, Québec, to Joyce Echaquan, an Atikamekw woman who livestreamed nurses calling her stupid, and assuming that her pain was the result of opioid withdrawal. It was not; she died from "pulmonary oedema linked to a rare heart condition." The Québec coroner called this systemic racism, and noted that if Echaquan had not recorded herself, no one would ever have known.[67] Then there are more direct physical attacks. In 2017, Brayden Bushby, a Thunder Bay man, threw a trailer hitch out of a moving car, striking Indigenous woman Barbara Kentner who had been walking with her sister; as the car carrying him and his friends sped off, he was heard to declare he "got one." Kentner died several months later. A court found Bushby guilty of manslaughter.[68] That is a far cry from the case of Gerald Stanley, who shot and killed a young Cree man, Colton Boushie, in 2016. Despite overwhelming evidence of murder, Gerald Stanley was acquitted in 2018, a decision only made possible because, as political scientist David MacDonald argues, it relied on tropes that young Indigenous men are inherently threatening and that it is reasonable and common sense for white men like Gerald Stanley to attack them, articulated as pre-emptive self-defence.[69]

Violence, of course, does not occur in a vacuum. Racist tropes that condone or encourage violence spread in subtler forms. For many Canadians, it is a common thing to make jokes about "Indians" or create parodies using Indigenous images, especially if they play on tropes of drunkenness, laziness, violence, or sexualization. Dressing in "red-face" for *any* reason also falls under this category of racism. Assumptions that any missing or murdered Indigenous women were sex workers (and that Indigenous sex workers deserve the violence they experience), or that Indigenous men are inherently violent and thus responsible for the Missing and Murdered Indigenous Women (MMIW) epidemic, have been common responses even to the Inquiry into Murdered and Missing Indigenous Women. The defensive prejudice apparent in demands that "angry Indians" should "get over it," and perhaps the simplest, easiest act of privilege — saying nothing when others do these things — all happen in the day-to-day lives of many Canadians.

What ties all these acts together, from the institutional to the individual, is the dehumanization and oppression of Indigenous individuals and Peoples. These acts all rely on the belief that Indigenous Peoples do not have the same right to life or to defend their cultures and homelands that we would expect for ourselves. As such, their assertions of sovereignty or even just attempts to survive in a hostile society are met with contempt, violence, and degradation. For each action and attack that goes unchallenged, and each dehumanizing story or statement that is uncritically repeated, settler colonial society becomes more secure in its judgement of Indigenous People as powerless and inferior.

National Myths

Colonial behaviours of many sorts are bound up with the ways Canadians understand themselves as peoples — that is, how our histories explain how we came to be and justify our claims to belonging on the land. Particularly important to Canadian collective identities are narratives of multiculturalism, peacekeeping, socially progressive politics, and hard-earned prosperity. These attract newcomers and assure Canadians of our moral righteousness on the world stage and at home. They are expressed and reinforced through the way Canadian history is made, marketed, and reflected back to us. Through what is included and what is excluded, these narratives are the basis for political action and talk, as well as general, day-to-day discourses of being a good Canadian citizen. Our national myths structure our values and our sense of belonging with those who share our values, and those values are often directed toward owning property and prosperity, or obeying the law and getting along — peace, order, and good government. In fact, these positive ways of seeing ourselves are not truly traits that Canadians possess but shared myths that bind us together as a people. One of these myths warrants particular attention here.

The peacemaker myth, a term coined by historian Paulette Regan,[70] is the story of Canada as founded in Treaty-making and honourable dealing, where Indians welcomed French, British, and Canadian people as mutually beneficial partners. This is a story often told in direct contrast to the violence of American colonization. The peacemaker myth is tightly entangled with the perception of Canada as a multicultural mosaic, compared to the United States' melting pot. It is a story of a Canada that, while once troubled by racial and cultural strife, has achieved enlightenment and now welcomes all people as equals with the same rights and responsibilities, the same respect and dignity, regardless of where they may come from or how and why they have come to the lands everyone now shares. And it underpins the idea of Canada as an international leader. Canada is the snowy little nation that could, that fought on the "right" side of both World Wars, that helped found the United Nations, that is a peacekeeping nation in international conflicts, that is a paragon of justice, free of corruption, ranked among the best places to live and the envy of many other nations, and with absolutely "no history of colonialism."

In the narrative form of the peacemaker myth, European (particularly British) and later Canadian colonization was enacted through peaceable and benevolent efforts — marked by the proffering of the gifts of civilization (education, medicine, agriculture, access to materials and markets), not under threat of violence as in the US Indian Wars and removals of Indigenous Peoples, which were marked by forced marches, mass executions, bounties for kills, and soldier and settler removal of Indigenous People from the American West. It's a comforting story for Canadians, but it is not true.

Canada also relied on violent tactics and displacements to dispossess Indigenous Peoples. The Northwest Mounted Police, forerunner to the RCMP, were originally deployed as an invasion force against the Métis of the Red River to suppress their declaration of sovereignty — even though their territory fell outside of the official boundaries of the Dominion of Canada.[71] Plains nations, including the Cree and Blackfoot, were intentionally starved to make them more pliable in Treaty negotiations.[72] All this is, as are many similar stories, historical fact that should put paid to the notion of Canada as a peacemaker nation. Moreover, while much scholarship in recent decades has gone into exposing these violent acts, they were known and discussed among Settler Canadians when they were happening. Consider the efforts by Dr. P.H. Bryce, Chief Medical Inspector for Indian Affairs, to expose an epidemic of student deaths in the IRS system in 1907. Many of these deaths were due to tuberculosis and other common, treatable illnesses. His report found that, including students sent home sick, an average of 42 percent of Indigenous children died in the schools, with some individual schools reporting much higher rates. His report was ignored, he was dismissed, and Bryce spent the rest of his life campaigning publicly to expose this truth, but with little interest or engagement from others.[73]

Regan, writing in 2010, explains that Settler Canadians often react with surprise and disbelief to revelations about systemic physical and sexual abuse in residential schools and to the fact that the intent of the Residential School System was to eliminate Indigenous Peoples through the deliberate interruption of cultural transmission, family life, and removal of Indigenous

People from their lands. Many claim to have "not known" about residential schools at all. Yet thousands pass by the huge physical structures of the schools every day in urban environments like Brantford, Ontario, or walk through the halls of the school building now converted into a hotel and casino in Cranbrook, British Columbia. Now, following so much publicity around the schools, the privilege to "not know" has been greatly reduced. Instead, politicians like Lynn Beyak and media outlets from the *New York Times* to the far-right *True North News* engage in rampant denialism of the harms of residential schools and in refusals to admit that the schools were not only complicit in genocide, but explicitly designed to achieve it.[74] This kind of denialism is no different from the preceding denial of the schools' existence: both, fundamentally, are a disavowal of all of the harms that we know occurred to preserve the comfort of Settler Canadians.

It is possible to imagine that the schools were so closed off to Settler Canadians that they were truly ignorant of the role and function of these institutions, the physical structures appearing to be just another part of the urban or rural landscape. But in reality, thousands of Canadians over many years worked in and with the Residential School System, from truant officers and Indian Agents, to teachers and principals, to janitors and nurses. Some spoke out about the insufficiencies and violences of the schools, and newspapers openly discussed the role of schools in "civilizing" (meaning deculturing or assimilating) Indigenous children. There was social knowledge — and approval — of what went on in those physical structures up until there wasn't. Canadian ignorance of residential schools is not so much rooted in a lack of education, but a broad social "forgetting." Acknowledging residential schools, and the violence of settler colonialism that they were designed to administer, would violate the peacemaker myth that underpins Settler Canadian identity. As a result, Canadians en masse refuse to really see the schools, the systems, and their own culpability and responsibility, whether that entails denying the existence of the schools wholesale, or denying the most egregious crimes of the schools as part of sanitizing their intent and impact:

> At the core of denialism is deception. People who engage in residential school denialism seek to call irrefutable historical facts into question. They either ignore or soften the actions of both churches and governments in Canadian history. Worst of all, denialism seeks to silence survivors and discredit their

experiences ... To disregard or undermine survivors' experiences and knowledge is one example of how denialism persists in contemporary times. It is underpinned by racist beliefs that Indigenous Peoples are inferior, inept, incapable, and backwards when compared to white settlers or European societies. This ideology was the main driver of settler colonialism in Canada and was used to justify the creation of the residential schooling system and other harmful policies.[75]

Denying the impact of the schools is no different from denying knowledge that the schools existed.

It is more than the peacemaker narrative itself that underscores Canadian national identity — it is the individual choice to participate in a collective "dysconsciousness," an "uncritical habit of mind ... that justifies inequity and exploitation by accepting the existing order of things as given."[76] The willful ignorance that buttresses settler colonial narratives and myths must also be understood as an act and a choice: an intentional forgetting of histories that are known, an intentional blindness to facts placed right in front of us. These myths, as powerful as they are, exist in no small part because, generation after generation, day after day, Settler Canadians choose the comfort and glory of believing in the national culture and the national story of Canada, "the true north, strong and free," over understanding our history and present-day actions as participating in a protracted project of dispossession, elimination, and one of the largest land grabs in the history of humankind.

Looking to the Land

What does it mean to say that Canada is a colonial nation or, as has become common in academic research, a "settler state"? Let us start with the historical recognition that Canada was forged by settler colonialism, and as a contemporary settler state maintains legal, political, and economic systems rooted in the settler colonial usurpation of Indigenous lands and the dispossession and elimination of Indigenous Peoples.[77] More simply, Canada's present laws, politics, economic systems, cultures, and social practices are all to some extent rooted in the ideologies, practices, and histories of settler colonization.

Settler Canadians and settler colonialism are two sides of the same coin: a process-based identity and the process that currently produces the identity. The identity comes to shape the process too, and so all Settler identities have their own specificities: Settler Canadians and Settler Australians have differences, even if, in the broad strokes, the settler colonial premises of our societies are similar. In Settler Canada, no matter how comforting our national myths, we remain a society based on violent dispossession of Indigenous Nations that is both unable — yet — to complete the settler colonial trajectory, and that remains bent on appropriating, assimilating, or disappearing any aspects of Indigenous identity that threaten our claims to the land.

Notes

1   Lorenzo Veracini, *Settler Colonialism: A Theoretical Overview* (London: Palgrave Macmillan, 2010).
2   Patrick Wolfe, "Settler Colonialism and the Elimination of the Native," *Journal of Genocide Research* 8, 4 (2006), 388.
3   Veracini, *Settler Colonialism*, 149-150.
4   Jodi Byrd, *The Transit of Empire: Indigenous Critiques of Colonialism* (Minneapolis: University of Minnesota Press, 2011).
5   Regan, Paulette. 2010. *Unsettling the Settler Within: Indian Residential Schools, Truth Telling, and Reconciliation in Canada*. Vancouver: UBC Press.
6   This charge has been led by the Lakota scholar, Vine Deloria, Jr., in scathing writings such as the chapter "Low Bridge, Everybody Cross"; see, Vine Deloria, Jr., *Red Earth, White Lies: Native Americans and the Myth of Scientific Fact* (Golden, CO: Fulcrum Publishing, 1997), 67–92.
7   A good summary of these debates and the ways that science and research are being used both by and against Indigenous communities can be found in a series of articles in the electronic newspaper, *Indian Country Today*; see, Alex Ewen, "Bering Strait Theory, Pt. 1: How Dogma Trumped Science," *Indian Country Today* June 13, 2014, https://ictnews.org/archive/bering-strait-theory-pt-1-how-dogma-trumped-science.
8   Scott Lauria Morgensen, "Queer Settler Colonialism in Canada and Israel: Articulating Two-Spirit and Palestinian Queer Critiques," Settler Colonial Studies 2, 2 (2012); Veracini, *Settler Colonialism*.
9   Veracini, *Settler Colonialism*.
10 To be clear: people identified as "Indigenous" by a settler colonial state are often identified according to some imposed standard, like Status (via the Indian Act) or "blood quantum" (via government band rolls), regardless of how Indigenous communities might identify themselves.
11 Renisa Mawani, *Colonial Proximities: Crossracial Encounters and Juridical Truths in British Columbia, 1871–1921* (Vancouver: UBC Press, 2010).
12 Harsha Walia, "Transient Servitude: Migrant Labour in Canada and the Apartheid of Citizenship," *Race & Class* 52, 1 (2010)
13 Beenash Jafri, "Privilege vs. Complicity: People of Colour and Settler

Colonialism," *Equity Matters*, March 21, 2012, blog), ideas-idees.ca/blog/privilege-vs-complicity-people-colour-and-settler-colonialism.

14 Richard Day, *Multiculturalism and the History of Canadian Diversity* (University of Toronto Press, 2000).

15 Harsha Walia, *Undoing Border Imperialism* (Oakland: AK Press, 2013).

16 Sean Fine, "Chief Justice says Canada Attempted 'Cultural Genocide' on Aboriginals," *The Globe and Mail*, May 28, 2015, theglobeandmail.com/news/national/chief-justice-says-canada-attempted-cultural-genocide-on-aboriginals/article24688854/.

17 Jorge Barrera, "National Inquiry Calls Murders and Disappearances of Indigenous Women a 'Canadian Genocide'," *CBC News*, May 31, 2019, cbc.ca/news/indigenous/genocide-murdered-missing-indigenous-women-inquiry-report-1.5157580.

18 Wolfe, "Settler Colonialism."

19 Patrick Wolfe, "After the Frontier Separation and Absorption in U.S. Indian Policy," *Settler Colonial Studies* 1, 1 (2011). While we ourselves have no problem describing many instances of settler colonial elimination as genocide, we want to avoid relying too heavily on the use of the term because of its highly particular usage in international and legal studies, which creates unnecessary debate about whether settler colonial elimination of Indigenous Peoples "counts" as genocide or not.

20 Indigenous Saskatchewan Encyclopedia, "Mistusinne," University of Saskatchewan (ND). teaching.usask.ca/indigenoussk/import/mistusinne.php; Post Media, "In 1966, a Sacred Aboriginal Rock Was Blown Up to Make Way for a Man-Made Lake. Now Divers Search for Remnants," *The National Post* August 27, 2014, nationalpost.com/news/canada/in-1966-a-sacred-aboriginal-rock-was-blown-up-to-make-way-for-a-man-made-lake-now-divers-search-for-reminants.

21 Jean Teillet, "Indigenous Identity Fraud: A Report for the University of Saskatchewan," University of Saskatchewan (2022); Melanie Brice et al., "Wena ka tapaymish ekwa kakway ka dipayhtamun? (Who Claims You and What Do You Claim?)," in *Unsettling Education: Decolonizing and Indigenizing the Land*, eds. Anna-Leah King, Kathleen O'Reilly, and Patrick J. Lewis (Ottawa: CSP Books, 2024: 282–298).

22 Darryl Leroux, *Distorted Descent: White Claims to Indigenous Identity* (Winnipeg: University of Manitoba Press, 2019).

23 Victoria Freeman, "'Toronto Has No History!': Indigeneity, Settler Colonialism, and Historical Memory in Canada's Largest City," *Urban History Review* 38, 2 (2010); Natalie Baloy, "Spectacles and Spectres: Settler Colonial Spaces in Vancouver," *Settler Colonial Studies* 6, 3 (2016).

24 This was not the first time — in fact, Québec has a history of clashing with Indigenous Peoples over issues that might appear economic or legal, but were framed heavily in land-based terms by many commentators. Alanis Obomsawin's documentary *Incident at Restigouche* (1984), which detailed a series of raids on Mi'kmaq communities for out-of-season fishing, demonstrated this in stark detail. In conversations, then Minister of Fisheries, Lucien Lessard, fundamentally asserted that the lands and waters belonged to Québec, and that Mi'kmaq challenges to Québécois sovereignty would be met with violent force as a matter of principle.

25　Moira Donovan, "Why Are Indigenous Fisheries Still Drawing Anger and Violence?" *The Tyee*, October 27, 2023, thetyee.ca/News/2023/10/27/. Canada-Ignoring-Supreme-Court-Indigenous-Fisheries-Violence/. For more on these violent incidents and the "logic of possession" see, Ardath Whynacht, *Insurgent Love: Abolition and Domestic Homicide* (Halifax: Fernwood Publishing, 2021).

26　Katelynn Buchner, Tammy Pearson, and Susan Burke, "Indigenous Women's Experiences with Child Protection at their Child's Birth," *Practice* 34, 4 (2022), 255.

27　Buchner, Pearson, and Burke, "Indigenous Women's Experiences with Child Protection at their Child's Birth", 262.

29　Yatta Kanu, *Integrating Aboriginal Perspectives into the Curriculum: Purposes, Possibilities, and Challenges* (University of Toronto Press, 2011), 21.

30　Glen Coulthard, *Red Skin, White Masks: Rejecting the Colonial Politics of Recognition* (Minneapolis: University of Minnesota Press, 2014).

31　Ivan Zinger, "Office of the Correctional Investigator Annual Report 2022–2023," Office of the Correctional Investigator (2023), 54.

32　AC Hamilton, *A Feather Not a Gavel: Working Towards Aboriginal Justice* (Winnipeg: Great Plains Publications, 2001).

33　Adam J. Barker, "The Contemporary Reality of Canadian Imperialism: Settler Colonialism and the Hybrid Imperial State" *American Indian Quarterly* 33, 3 (2009).

34　Morgensen, "The Biopolitics of Settler Colonialism."

35　Adam J. Barker and Emma Battell Lowman, "Settler Colonialism and the Criminalization of Indigenous Peoples in Canada," in *Justice, Indigenous Peoples, and Canada: A History of Courage and Resilience*, eds. Kathryn M. Campbell and Stephanie Wellman (New York: Routledge, 2023).

36　John Mack Faragher, "Commentary: Settler Colonial Studies and the North American Frontier," *Settler Colonial Studies* 4, 2 (2014), 185.

37　Stuart Tannock, "Points of Prejudice: Education-Based Discrimination in Canada's Immigration System," *Antipode* 43, 4 (2011).

38　We make this point in the spirit of Paulette Regan's work, which we have relied on throughout this book, and which discusses her own coming to grips with settler colonial complicity and responsibility in her work and life. We also make this point remaining conscious of the critiques raised by postcolonial theorists that "taking responsibility" must be deeply considered and worked out collectively lest it be used as a means to appropriate the agency of Indigenous Peoples in deciding how to address settler colonialism; see, Pat Noxolo, Pavarti Raghuram, and Clare Madge, "Unsettling Responsibility," *Transactions of the Institute of British Geographers* 37, 3 (2012). We return to discussions of how Settler Canadians can think through responsible ways of relating to Indigenous communities in Chapter 6.

39　Harsha Walia, *Border and Rule* (Haymarket Books, 2021), and *Undoing Border Imperialism* (Oakland: AK Press, 2013).

40　Walia, "Transient Servitude: Migrant Labour in Canada and the Apartheid of Citizenship," *Race & Class* 52, 1 (2010), 81; see also, *Undoing Border Imperialism*.

41　Walia, "Transient Servitude."

42　Walia, "Transient Servitude," 69–70, 73.

43 Ravi Da Costa and Tom Clark, "Testimonial Textures: Examining the Poetics of Non-Indigenous Stories about Reconciliation," in *Storytelling: Critical and Creative Approaches*, eds. Jan Shaw, Philippa Kelly and L.E. Semler (London: Palgrave Macmillan, 2013); Ravi Da Costa and Tom Clark, "On the Responsibility to Engage: Non-Indigenous Peoples in Settler States," *Settler Colonial Studies*, 6, 3 (2016); Eva Mackey, *Unsettled Expectations: Uncertainty, Land and Settler Decolonization* (Halifax: Fernwood Press, 2016); Mollie McGuire and Jeff Denis, "Unsettling Pathways: How Some Settlers Come to Seek Reconciliation with Indigenous Peoples," *Settler Colonial Studies* 9, 4 (2019); Paulette Regan, *Unsettling the Settler Within* (UBC Press 2010); Adam J. Barker, "The Contemporary Reality of Canadian Imperialism," *American Indian Quarterly* 33, 3 (2009).

44 Jeff Denis, "Transforming Meanings and Group Positions: Tactics and Framing in Anishinaabe–White Relations in Northwestern Ontario, Canada," *Ethnic and Racial Studies* 35, 3 (2012).

45 Richard Day, *Gramsci Is Dead: Anarchist Currents in the Newest Social Movements* (London: Pluto Press, 2005).

46 Coulthard, *Red Skin, White Masks*

47 Adam J. Barker, *Making and Breaking Settler Space: Five Centuries of Colonization in North America* (Vancouver: UBC Press, 2023), specifically Chapter 4; Daniel Salée, "Indigenous Peoples and Settler Angst in Canada: A Review Essay," *Journal of Canadian Studies* 41 (2010).

48 We recommend Iyko Day's "Being or Nothingness" and Justin Leroy's "Black History in Occupied Territory" as articles that provide much more nuanced discussions of these concepts. See, Iyko Day, "Being or Nothingness: Indigeneity, Antiblackness, And Settler Colonial Critique," *Critical Ethnic Studies* 1, 2 (2015), 102–121; Justin Leroy, "Black History in Occupied Territory: On the Entanglements of Slavery and Settler Colonialism," *Theory & Event* 19, 4 (2016).

49 Naomi Klein, "Dancing the World into Being: A Conversation with Idle No More's Leanne Simpson," *Yes! Magazine,* March 5, 2013), yesmagazine.org/peace-justice/dancing-the-world-into-being-a-conversation-with-idle-no-more-leanne-simpson.

50 Riley Yesno, "Fake Indigenous Art is the Tip of the Iceberg of Cultural Appropriation," *CBC News*, October 5, 2002), cbc.ca/documentaries/the-passionate-eye/fake-indigenous-art-is-the-tip-of-the-iceberg-of-cultural-appropriation-1.6606937.

51 Celia Haig-Brown, "Indigenous Thought, Appropriation, and Non-Aboriginal People," *Canadian Journal of Education* 33, 4 (2010).

52 Sarah Hunt, "An Open Letter to My Local Hipsters," *Media Indigena*, September 20, 2011, mediaindigena.com/sarah-hunt/issues-and-politics/ an-open-letter-to-my-local-hipsters.

53 Lisa Aldred, "Plastic Shamans and Astroturf Sundances: New Age Commercialization of Native American Spirituality," *American Indian Quarterly* 24, 3 (2000).

54 Glen Coulthard, "Subjects of Empire: Indigenous Peoples and the 'Politics of Recognition' in Canada," *Contemporary Political Theory* 6, 4 (2007).

55 For more on museums and collection, see: Gloria Jean Frank, "'That's My Dinner on Display': A First Nations Reflection on Museum Culture," *BC Studies* 125/126

(Spring/Summer 2000); Ruth Phillips, "Re-Placing Objects: Historical Practices for the Second Museum Age," *Canadian Historical Review* 86, 1 (March 2005); and Naohrio Nakamura, "The Representation of First Nations Art at the Art Gallery of Ontario," *International Journal of Canadian Studies* 45–46 (2012).

56 See for example the controversy over the racist Adam Sandler film *Ridiculous Six* in early 2015. Many Indigenous actors walked off the set in response to dehumanizing and grotesque portrayals of Indigenous Peoples. One actor, Robert Van Winkle — better known as the hip hop artist Vanilla Ice — defended the racist script by claiming that he was not offended despite his "Chactaw [sic] Indian" heritage. This claim was quickly fact-checked by an article in *Indian Country Today*, and not only was there no evidence of Indigenous ancestry, but Van Winkle also eventually retracted his claim and apologized. See, Erin Spiceland and Rachel Byington, "'Fact Check: Is Vanilla Ice Really Native?' Choctaw Researchers Investigate," *Indian Country Today*, April 28, 2015, indiancountrytodaymedianetwork.com.

57 Adam Gaudry and Darryl Leroux, "White Settler Revisionism and Making Métis Everywhere: The Evocation of Métissage in Quebec and Nova Scotia," *Critical Ethnic Studies* 3, 1 (2017); Adam Gaudry, "Communing With the Dead: The 'New Métis,' Métis Identity Appropriation, and the Displacement of Living Métis Culture," *American Indian Quarterly* 42, 2 (2018); Chelsea Vowel and Darryl Leroux, "White Settler Antipathy and the Daniels Decision," *TOPIA: Canadian Journal of Cultural Studies*, 36, (2016).

58 Colette Derworiz, "Woman Pleads Guilty in Inuit Identity Fraud Case, Charges Dropped Against Daughters," *CTV News,* February 10, 2024), ottawa.ctvnews.ca/woman-pleads-guilty-in-inuit-identity-fraud-case-charges-dropped-against-daughters-1.6763947.

59 Spiceland and Byington, "Fact Check: Is Vanilla Ice Really Native?"

60 Cindy Blackstock, *National Children's Alliance Policy Paper on Aboriginal Children* (Ottawa: First Nations Child and Family Caring Society of Canada, 2004).

61 Peter Edwards, *One Dead Indian: The Premier, the Police, and the Ipperwash Crisis* (Vancouver: Stoddart Publishing, 2011).

62 Rob Renaud and Susanne Reber, *Starlight Tour: The Last, Lonely Night of Neil Stonechild* (Toronto: Random House Canada, 2005).

63 Human Rights Watch. "Those Who Take Us Away: Abusive Policing and Failures in Protection of Indigenous Women and Girls in Northern British Columbia, Canada," Research Report (2013), hrw.org/reports/2013/02/13/those-who-take-us-away-0.

64 Warren Goulding, *Just Another Indian: A Serial Killer and Canada's Indifference* (Calgary: Fifth House Publishers, 2001).

65 On October 17, 2013, Mi'Kmaq protesters from the community of Elsipogtog (New Brunswick) attempted to prevent surveying for future fracking operations on their traditional territories. They were met with a violent and overwhelming RCMP response, in which forty protestors were arrested en masse (few were charged and even fewer convicted of any crimes) and dozens more pepper sprayed or shot with rubber bullets at close range. See, Miles Howe, *Debriefing Elsipogtog* (Halifax: Fernwood Publishing, 2015). In November of 2014, a loose coalition of Indigenous

and Settler protestors led by local First Nations occupied surveying and drilling sites for a Kinder Morgan pipeline proposed for Burnaby Mountain in BC. Video taken at the protest showed multiple random arrests by local police and RCMP, with police at times simply grabbing protestors out of the crowd, and in some cases, dragging elders down a steep road in handcuffs. Grand Chief Stewart Philip of the Union of BC Indian Chiefs was among those arrested.

66 Andrew Crosby and Jeffery Monaghan, *Policing Indigenous Movements: Dissent and the Security State* (Fernwood Publishing, 2018); Kevin Smith, *Liberalism, Surveillance, and Resistance: Indigenous Communities in Western Canada, 1877–1927* (AU Press, 2009).

67 Leyland Cecco, "'Dead Because She Was Indigenous': Québec Coroner Says Atikemekw Woman a Victim of Systemic Racism," *The Guardian*, October 12, 2021), theguardian.com/world/2021/oct/06/joyce-echaquan-coroner-indigenous-systemic-racism-death.

68 CBC News, "Man Who Threw Trailer Hitch at Indigenous Woman Found Guilty of Manslaughter," *CBC News*, December 14, 2020, cbc.ca/news/canada/thunder-bay/bushby-thunder-bay-trailer-hitch-ruling-1.5840583.

69 David MacDonald, "Settler Silencing and the Killing of Colten Boushie: Naturalizing Colonialism in the Trial of Gerald Stanley," *Settler Colonial Studies*, 11, 1 (2021); Gina Starblanket and Dallas Hunt, *Storying Violence: Unravelling Colonial Narratives in the Stanley Trial* (Winnipeg: ARP Books, 2020).

70 Regan, *Unsettling the Settler Within*.

71 Howard Adams, *Prison of Grass: Canada from a Native Point of View* (Saskatoon, SK: Fifth House Publishers, 1989).

72 Daschuk, *Clearing the Plains*.

73 Adam Green, "Telling 1922s Story of National Crime: Canada's First Chief Medical Officer and the Aborted Fight for Aboriginal Health Care," *Canadian Journal of Native Studies* XXVI, 2 (2006).

74 Sean Carleton, "'I Don't Need Any More Education': Senator Lynn Beyak, Residential School Denialism, and Attacks on Truth and Reconciliation in Canada," *Settler Colonial Studies* 11, 4 (2021); Emelia Fournier, "Federal Government Needs to Counter Rise in Residential School Denialism Says Kimberly Murray," *APTN News*, September 28, 2023, aptnnews.ca/national-news/federal-government-needs-counter-rise-in-residential-school-denialism-says-kimberly-murray/.

75 Crystal Fraser, "Residential School Denialism Is an Attack on the Truth," *The Conversation*, July 3, 2024, theconversation.com/residential-school-denialism-is-an-attack-on-the-truth-233318 [paragraph breaks removed].

76 Daniel Johnson, "From the Tomahawk Chop to the Road Block: Discourses of Savagism in Whitestream Media," *American Indian Quarterly* 35, 1 (2011).

77 For more on the conceptual "disappearance" of Indigenous People through the creation of spatial and temporal boundaries around notions of "Indianness," see, Kevin Bruyneel, *The Third Space of Sovereignty: The Postcolonial Politics of U.S.–Indigenous Relations* (Minneapolis: University of Minnesota Press, 2007), and *Settler Memory: The Disavowal of Indigeneity and the Politics of Race in the United States* (Chapel Hill, NC: UNC Press Books, 2021). For more on the biopolitics of "elimination" in Canada,

see: Morgensen, "The Biopolitics of Settler Colonialism." For Settler conceptual blindness to residential schools, see, Regan, *Unsettling the Settler Within*. For more on Wolfe's theories of elimination, see, Wolfe, "Settler Colonialism and the Elimination of the Native."

It's Always All About the Land

IN THE NEWS — and indeed in this book — Indigenous Peoples' "issues" appear in many forms. Racism in the health care system, provision deficits in education, dangerous and inadequate housing and infrastructure in reserve communities, over-incarceration of Indigenous People, and on and on. But, and with no exaggeration, at the heart of all these issues is *the land*. The land is what sustains Indigenous communities and identities. The land is what Settler people need to have a home and economic stability. The land is what is contested, what is shared, what is danced upon, and what is discussed without words. In Chapter 2, we made clear the way that settler colonialism functions in Canada, both in the past and in the present, and the way that it impacts the Settler identity and Settler Canadians. In this chapter, we move to examine the ways Settler people *settle* — that is, the way Settler identities become rooted in particular places. In Canada, who we are as Settler Canadians and who Indigenous Peoples are trying to be through resurgent nationhood are tied together by an inescapable truth: it's always all about the land.

Societies rely on a sense of place to make sense of themselves and the world around them.[1] Settler Canadians are no different in this regard, and as a people, they often become deeply attached to land, forming strong emotional relationships with particular places and features of the landscape and cultures there. Both Indigenous and Settler people have attachments to land but they must be understood as having particular kinds of relationships with the places that they call home. We must understand what makes these relationships distinctly settler colonial to discover what land means to the Settler identity, and how particular relationships to land contribute to producing and reproducing settler colonialism in Canada.

Identity and the Land

This returns us to the tensions introduced in the first chapter around the different ways we come to know ourselves through the places we live. We must think carefully and deeply about a settler colonial worldview, contrasted with Indigenous place-thought in order to emphasize that the ontological understanding of land and belonging — the basic ways that concepts like "home" and "place" are articulated and positioned in Indigenous and settler colonial philosophies and cultures — prevents simple political or economic solutions to settler colonial dispossession and displacement. We must recognize that the incommensurability of Settler political economies and Indigenous nationhood is not a result of simple mismatch or intentional, Machiavellian domination. Neither should we read Indigenous–Settler conflicts through the lens of a "clash of cultures" — culture, like governance, is after the fact of how we relate to the land, something that is practiced and acted upon as a reflection and reinforcement of our place-based relationships. Indigenous relationships to land and place are often articulated in overly simplistic ways — like Indigenous People being at one with nature and similar tropes that reduce Indigenous People to a natural phenomenon rather than peoples, nations, and societies. The opposite is true: Indigenous place-relationships are exceptionally detailed, complex, and dynamic. Crucially, these relationships have been developed through long, experiential histories with particular lands and places not just as a geography, a topology, or a resource, but as living beings.

As Vanessa Watts discusses, a problem with non-Indigenous ways of thinking about land and place is the separation of ontology and epistemology — the way of thinking about the land and the experience of being on the land (Figure 2). In this diagram, "the left is a depiction of how an Anishinaabe and/or Haudenosaunee cosmology might be represented … the right, the process by which a Euro-Western meta-understanding can contribute to colonization of these Indigenous cosmologies":[2]

> In Indigenous traditions, ontology and epistemology are inseparable: the way of thinking about the land and the experience of relating to it are essentially the same.[3]

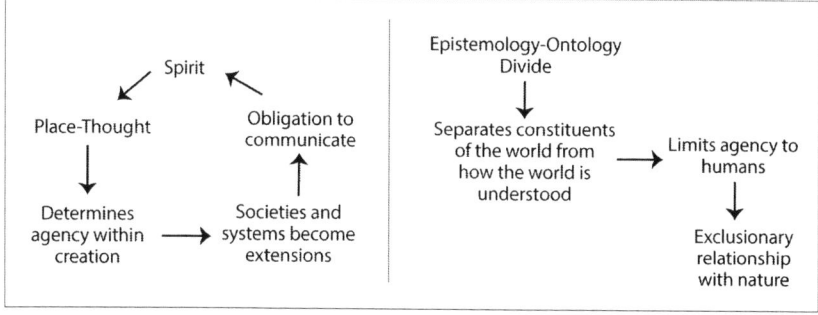

FIGURE 2: Indigenous versus European knowledge relationships to the natural world. From Watts, "Indigenous Place-Thought & Agency Amongst Humans and Non-Humans." (reproduced with permission from the author)

We engage here with Indigenous knowledge and place-thought but not in an attempt to define some fixed core or foundation of what it means to be Indigenous. As Sarah Hunt has noted, Indigenous knowledges:

> are rarely clear, neat, linear or straight-forward, but are instead productively confusing. This might entail embracing the shifting relationality, complexity and circularity of Indigenous knowledge as productive and necessary. The situatedness and place-specific nature of Indigenous knowledge calls for the validation of new kinds of theorizing and new epistemologies that can account for situated, relational Indigenous knowledge and yet remain engaged with broader theoretical debates.[4]

Our challenge as Settler Canadians is to accept this "productively confusing complexity" not as some sort of problem to be rationalized, but as complex, fully constituted ways of knowing.

Now and in the past, Settler people have constructed Indigenous Peoples as simplistically tied to "the land," in ways that engage or approach dehumanization and racism that positions Indigenous Peoples as simply features *of* the landscape rather than autonomous nations *on* the land. Consider the construction of the "noble savage" — an admirable animal but not a complex or modern human being. Simultaneously, it is no exaggeration to say that Indigenous societies are rooted in particular and powerful relationships to land and place that inform and produce collective identities. As expressed in creation stories and oral histories, economic practices and systems, that Indigenous Nations are rooted in land and place is not a myth or a metaphor.[5] Rather, it is an established fact and an important and powerful way for Settlers to work toward understanding how Indigenous

People understand themselves and their societies. It is essential that we appreciate just how complex these place-based relationships are, particularly if we do not understand the specific details. Settler Canadians are likely to live on or move through the territories of many Indigenous Nations and cultures over our lives; we need to understand these concepts so we can engage effectively with local particulars, and simultaneously hold space for understandings we may not have yet.

Indigenous relationships with the land are the source of intricate systems of thought and vast stores of knowledge, dynamic and durable structures of governance, ecological and resource management systems, and cultural and spiritual traditions of incredible power and profound meaning.[6] Working from Indigenous scholars and experts who have engaged and communicated these understandings in powerful ways, the first and most essential point is that Indigenous identities are based, historically and in the present, on living, dynamic relationships with land. The powerful and extensive writings of the late Lakota philosopher, Vine Deloria, Jr., centralize spiritual relationships between a tribe and sacred places, with each informing the identity of the other.[7] The place can be a particular feature of the landscape such as a mountain, ridge, or butte where particular ceremonies or rituals are conducted. It can be rivers or streams where purification rituals and rituals around fishing or aquaculture intersect. Blackfoot writer and scholar, Leroy Little Bear, has expressed this relationship as centred on the need to maintain balance by consistently visiting and interacting with sacred sites in a ceremonial way, which ensures that both the land and people can continue in a sustainable fashion; these "rituals of renewal" come to define the circular movements of Indigenous Peoples on the land, and as societies.[8] In the work of Watts, Indigenous identities and histories are shaped by "place-thought," which is the inseparable relationship between how Indigenous Peoples understand and interact with the world as a living entity with will and agency of its own, and the ways in which living, intelligent elements of the world shape Indigenous thinking, culture, and social practice.[9] As Cree and Saulteaux researcher, Margaret Kovach, has argued, land relationships link Indigenous People with the past, with collective Indigenous identities, and with kinship groups and communities.[10] The land becomes the source of stories that children learn about values and cultural precepts; by the time they become adults, they transmit those same stories of the land to the next generation, linking generations of family across time through the same practice, in the same place. Further, Kovach shows that it is particular relationships with land and specific places that differentiates Indigenous Peoples from one another and also differentiates them from other groups in settler societies.

No two Indigenous Peoples have the same relationship to a specific place. In general, places in Indigenous traditions are understood to have their own "personality,"[11] so the relationship one group has with a specific place may be different from that developed by another. What a sacred forest space is to one group might be a good place to hunt for another. It is the concept of a place-based identity, forged in long-standing and intimate relationships with particular lands and sacred sites that is common to Indigenous Peoples across the continent (and the world). In the abstract, this may sound straightforward. In practice, it can be difficult for those of us not experienced or trained in Indigenous worldviews and traditions to understand how these place-relationships inform the lives of Indigenous individuals and communities.

As Settler Canadians, we ourselves found it challenging to understand what is meant by a place-based identity. During our time as researchers and students of Indigenous politics, geography, and history, we developed an intellectual understanding of the central role of land in Indigenous identity. But to understand the lived reality of having a place-based identity constantly under assault, to be continuously striving against colonial dispossession to enact and reassert relationships to the land — as is the case for Indigenous Peoples all across Canada today — was a different and more difficult process. We were challenged over many years to understand Indigenous struggles as being about more than holding private property title to land in Canada and fair payment for land appropriated by the state, and more than equal rights under the law. They are about more than eliminating racism and other social barriers that have prevented Indigenous People from participating fully in Canadian society. It took time and experience and a great deal of help from our Indigenous friends to understand that owning private property could never take the place of relationships to the land, nor could any amount of money compensate for losing those relationships. Likewise, we had to learn that the purpose of anti-Indigenous racism is to facilitate the removal or erasure of Indigenous People from the land. We also struggled to understand relationships to land as being more than something that happened only during cultural ceremonies, to see these relationships as something that informed, at a very deep level, worldview and everyday choices. When we talked about issues of colonialism, we approached these discussions as questions of policy and politics, education, power, and the harm perpetuated by systems of racism and poverty. We were passionate, educated, and wrong.

It was Nuu-Chah-Nulth scholar, storyteller, and leader, Chaw-win-is, who, over the course of many conversations, arguments, and shared experiences, taught us to know better. Each time we got carried away, Chaw-win-is told us firmly, "No, it's not about that — it's always all about the land." Through storytelling and conversation, involvement in events and action, and nuanced analysis of colonialism at work on Turtle Island, Chaw-win-is slowly helped us learn. Land in the context of Indigenous cultures and colonial appropriation is far more than *property* or *territory*. It is the water, the air, the living things like plants and animals, the rocks and earth that have thoughts of their own, and the spirits that bind all of it — including people — together. When Chaw-win-is talked about *the land*, she was talking about everything that surrounded her people, made them who they are; it was at risk if colonialism turned that land into property or territory. We also learned how deep, complex, and profound her relationship to the land is through hearing her share stories with her grandfather, as he told her where their people came from on the land, and then we heard her tell those same stories to her children so they, too, could visit those places and know them. The land sustains her physically, culturally, and spiritually and connects her to family and nation across generations.

Indigenous Peoples have powerful, long-standing relationships to particular places, relationships which cannot be easily or simply articulated but have time and again proven profound, staggeringly complex, and critical to identity, nationhood, and survival. It is these relationships that settler colonization seeks to sever so colonizers can achieve undisputed claim to the land. Based on this, we seek here to put Indigenous knowledges in conversation with what Mark Rifkin has called "settler common sense."[12] This refers to the way the logics of settler colonial domination are woven through almost every aspect of contemporary settler societies no matter how diverse different communities or political economies may appear. Our goal here — in focusing on the ways that Settler people "think place" in particularly settler colonial ways by contrasting them with Indigenous place-thought — is to expose and de-normalize that common sense. Before understanding the role of settler colonialism on the land, we need to understand the ways in which the Settler identity relates to land and place.

Homeland: Settlement, Diaspora, and Difference

A key component of the Settler identity is the intent to find a homeland and settle there, to stay long term, and to build a sense of belonging through social and political structures such as citizenship in a state, or stories of achieving success through a "pioneering spirit" and "up by the bootstraps" struggle. Settler identities are also forged in relationship to land: it is the location and basis for security, opportunity, and identity as a new people. Settlers, be they recent arrivals or long-standing residents, have actual or remembered roots of some sort in other countries. However, they do not have another homeland to which they expect to return and identify primarily with the settler colonial society to which they belong. The Settler identity is invested in social relationships between people and places, and the stories and histories, structures and systems of economics and politics, and cultural and social practices on both local and much broader scales that these produce. But this investment in and connection to the land is based on a very different idea of "the land" from the Indigenous concept described earlier. Settler sovereignty is essentially "portable" anywhere inside the Settler's perceived domain.

This is a simple but important difference in the ways that Indigenous and Settler identities operate with respect to place: one is integrated into the land and one is imposed upon it. There is a difference between a relationship *with* the land, in the case of Indigenous Peoples, and a relationship *to* the land, in the case of settler societies. Indigenous societies include all elements of land and place as part of the community, from rocks, water, and air to plants and animals. This means that Indigenous Peoples relate to land as part of an integrated network of personalities and powers, all of which gives rise to a dynamic social identity. Settler people, by contrast, relate to the land as the site on which their society is built. Settlers create potent stories about the land — as sites of conquest, as hard-won property, or even as "natural" places that inform our national identities[13] — and can form strong emotional and historical attachments to these places that become our home. We build monuments to remind ourselves and others of where our formative struggles occurred, like Brock's Monument near Niagara Falls or the Battlefield Monument in Hamilton that mark key sites from the War of 1812. Settlers spend time, energy, materials, and wealth in the pursuit of marking the places where our own identities connect to the territories we claim. But these investments still treat places as territories or objects that have meaning not in and of themselves, but because of what Settler people (or the empire builders from who we arise) did in these places. It is our history in a place that makes a place matter, not the place itself.

In some senses, the conflicts between Indigenous Peoples and Settlers with respect to the land are grounded in very different experiences of having or losing a homeland. Indigenous Peoples have always been mobile, and many societies moved around their homelands in complex patterns. Jon Parmenter's history of Iroquoia in the sixteenth century begins with a vignette of Iroquoian chiefs drawing an extensive, complex map of transportation routes, river and lake systems, and associated villages and trading sites. Throughout the rest of Parmenter's research, the ability of Iroquoian traders, diplomats, warriors, and ordinary people to cover vast distances with few troubles is incredibly apparent.[14] None of these movements interfered with the place-based relationships that underpin Indigenous nationhood and culture, and even after colonial imposition has forced Indigenous communities to relocate, Indigenous identities are often maintained through stories and spiritual connections to "lost" or denied sacred lands. Settler people, by contrast, often relate to the lands through the lens of peoples whose originary connections to land have been severed, either by some self-motivated break in the case of religious communities such as Mennonites who relocated to places like Pennsylvania in the United States and Waterloo, Ontario, or through enslavement and forced, permanent relocation and disassociation like the economic migrant populations discussed previously.

Daniel Coleman has drawn a stark contrast between the way that poets and writers — coming from the perspectives of Indigenous communities, fighting for land, and diasporic communities, articulating their relationships to new homelands — express their views on land and place in Canada.[15] He notes that there is an evident disconnect between "Indigenous commitments to literal places as compared to diasporic distrust of nativism and its reputed essentialism." Coleman's description of diasporic suspicions of place-relationships that hint at "nativism" and "essentialism" are based largely in the experiences of the African diaspora. This is truly important to understand because, for many, their presence in Canada is a result of being forced to move by capitalist and white supremacist violence, either through enslavement and transportation, or through destruction visited on their homelands that has forced them to relocate. Once in Canada, these same people are often viewed with suspicion and treated with hostility by white Canadians who do not accept them as "legitimate" Canadians. The racist nativism of Settler Canadians can be easily mistaken for Indigenous claims to land, and it is easy to see how Black folks and other people of colour would feel very uneasy about narratives that seem to speak to an essentialized belonging that can be misread as exclusive and exclusionary. However, there is a larger point that can be drawn out here.

Nativism is a reactionary trend in many societies in support of an essentialist nationalism, and opposing multiculturalims and immigration. It is not exclusive to settler societies. It often invokes racist tropes or mythistories of prior occupation that present the perceived "Other" as a threat. Nativism has been repeatedly a driving force in the antisemitic persecution and expulsion of Jewish populations across Europe, for one well-known example. In this way, there is a close link between nativism and several historical diasporas, not just in settler colonial contexts. However, nativism takes on particular connotations when deployed in settler colonial societies. For example, in the United States during the 1800s, white people born in America were often violently opposed to mass immigration of Irish, Italian, and other nationalities, and styled themselves "Native Americans" — with nativism here referring to birth in the American state rather than Indigenous connections to land. These Native Americans were not claiming to be "Native American" as we might use the term today, but rather claiming particular rights by being born in this place versus more recent arrivals. Similar claims have been exercised in Canada, with Richard Day pointing out that that Catholic, non-English speaking Europeans were not accepted as "white" in early Canada, which was built on Anglo-Protestant dominance of, especially, Québécois.[16] Crucially, these claims can blur the lines of claims to Indigeneity, as they can be seen to mirror Indigenous territorial claims to particular homelands based on, in part, long-term occupation and relationship. Nationalist and exclusionary place-relationships are frequently weaponized by states, empires, and racist societies to force a variety of populations into mobility and to bolster nationalist support for the existing order.[17]

In that vein, many Settler Canadians come from diasporic peoples — Irish, Jewish, Doukhobor, Tamil, the many descendants of enslaved West Africans, and so on — who, while all related differently to whiteness, histories of slavery, and experiences of political, economic, or social marginalization, do share the experience of being displaced and struggling to "re-place." Their experiences of (coerced or forced) mobility are frequently expressed through common anxieties and desires with respect to finding a "homeland" in Canada. Among other commonalities is a preoccupation with how permanent that homeland might be. Recalling that settler colonizers come to stay, the anxieties and suspicions of diasporic peoples toward Indigenous claims to land can be read as anxieties that a particularly tenuous settler status — not rooted in long-term land tenure, Anglo- or Francophone versions of whiteness and Christianity or other core aspects of Canadian culture, or sufficient power and wealth — could be undermined by a "competing" Indigenous claim.

Settler societies, of course, are not free of these forced mobilities and displacements. But places like Canada and the United States have often proclaimed themselves to be bastions of freedom and liberty, cosmopolitan nations where anyone can come and succeed. While whiteness, especially manifested as anti-Black racism, continues to hold powerful sway over the ways that many Settler people perceive difference and engage in "Othering," many Canadians of diverse backgrounds are proud of the multicultural heritage of their composite nations. The same suspicions that Coleman discusses in the context of diasporic populations toward deep Indigenous connections to land run through much of Canadian society because they are positioned as inherently opposed to a multicultural, pluralist society. As Coleman argues,

> The scandal of the relation between Indigeneity and diaspora is that, despite their shared challenge to the settler state's claims to liberal equity and justice, their different histories of displacement by colonialism and by the racial nation state have tended to set very different, even opposed, political and social objectives for Indigenous and diasporic peoples.[18]

The flip side of the diasporic anxiety is the humanist insistence that "there is only one race: the human race," a liberalist argument that is often used to simultaneously argue for racial equality under the settler colonial system, and to deny Indigenous critiques of the system itself.

The fact that many people from marginalized or racialized communities might identify more strongly with Settler Canadian society and ways of being on the land than with the struggles of Indigenous Peoples for the land underscores the need to pay attention to how settler colonialism has shaped various identities. Returning to our discussions of the work of Harsha Walia in the previous chapter, we cannot rest on an assumption of shared experiences of oppression or dispossession to unite Indigenous Peoples and people of colour, because the experience of being on the land itself is likely different between these groups. Further, even white Settler Canadians can often reference a historical oppression or forced relocation as a reason why they should be exempted from responsibility for settler colonialism. While this claim obscures the power of whiteness and class privilege, it also obscures the differences between Indigenous Peoples displaced on their own lands and diasporic or migrant peoples seeking to construct their new homes on those same lands. Even as we must continue to deconstruct racial and economic inequality within Canada, we must be careful not to allow "diversity" to become a cover for settler colonization.

Settler Colonialism, Identity, and the Land

Indigenous and Settler conflicts over land have been discussed in some senses as a clash of sovereignties. However, we have shown that these sovereignties are not at all alike. Indigenous sovereignties are bounded by sacred responsibilities to interact with particular places while Settler sovereignties are "carried with us" until we decide to root them somewhere.[19] Sovereignty in this case does not refer to a particular political philosophy, but rather to the ability to govern and define the basic patterns of living in a territory. Settler society relates to land indirectly, the relationships mediated through structures such as regimes of property or the peacemaker myth. We described these in Chapter 2 as spaces, systems, and stories in the settler colonial context.

Indigenous Peoples cooperate with the land as an extensive community of diverse beings to increase their collective capacity for sustainable and balanced coexistence:

> for [Indigenous Peoples], the foundation of values arises from and is invested in land; being born in a landed context creates birthright responsibilities to uphold the collective community agenda of land tenure and retention of that land base. Thus American Indian communities carry an identity of being intimately tied to sustainable territories, where an individual's identity of time, space, and place create a land-based worldview, complete with sustainable values.[20]

Indigenous relationships to land are balanced by what the people give to, and do for, the land, and how the land cares for and provides for the people. The rituals of renewal that we discussed previously are a key example of this, but so are practices like seasonal burns through which human society and the land itself both benefit.

By contrast, Settler Canadian identities require the creation of social and cultural structures which need to be constantly rebuilt in a material sense as the land is adapted to the uses that Settler societies desire, and in a conceptual sense as Settler people generate histories and stories and political and legal systems that anchor them in place. Vine Deloria, Jr. once contrasted the difference between Indigenous societies whose sacred places are fixed upon the landscape, and European societies that built churches and other places of worship wherever was most convenient for themselves. These places, then, become seen as inviolable, permanently altering the landscape and how people can relate to it. These are human-centric relationships: they are about what the land can be made to give and how it can be made to give it. As such, it is directly at odds with the relationship between Indigenous Peoples and their sacred places and home environments. Canadian political theorist, James Tully, describes this opposition as fundamental to Canadian society:

> the ground of the [settler colonial] relationship is the appropriation of the land, resources and jurisdiction of the Indigenous Peoples, not only for the sake of resettlement and exploitation ... but for the territorial foundation of the dominant society itself.[21]

For concrete examples demonstrating the importance of land in Canada and to Canadians, consider moments of Indigenous reclamation or reoccupation. In iconic examples such as the standoffs at Oka in 1990 and Ipperwash in 1995, Mohawk and Anishinaabe protesters (respectively) claimed the right and responsibility to determine how land was used. These communities rejected the assertions by settler society that their views — of land as undeveloped and better off as a golf course, of land as intentionally undeveloped and kept for all as a public park — should be the only ones that matter. They rejected these views forcefully. After years of frustration and disappointment in legal, political, and diplomatic proceedings, they took over roads and access ways, disrupting Settler Canadians' perceived rights of access to and through Mohawk and Anishinaabe territories. For this, they were met with heavily armed police and the military. Dudley George was murdered by an Ontario Provincial Police sniper at Ipperwash, and entire communities like the Mohawk reserve of Kanesatake were besieged by armoured vehicles and helicopters, violently searched, and repeatedly fired upon.

The Caledonia standoff of 2006, also known as the Grand River Land Dispute, is somewhat less well-known, in part because it did not involve the explosive violence and loss of life associated with the earlier two events. Here, residents of Six Nations Reserve reclaimed a partially constructed subdivision that, according to Canadian law, was being built on lands within the municipality of Caledonia, Ontario, adjacent to the reserve. Six Nations protesters claimed the land had been illegally sold; it belonged to them under the Haldimand Land Grant of 1784. The governments of Ontario and Canada have countered that the grant holds no legally binding status, that all land transactions that have shrunk the reserve are valid, even when individuals sold off lands not belonging to them and other such irregularities. Settler Canadians in Caledonia led by several notable racists who campaign under "free speech" and "equal rights" banners rallied against the Six Nations reclamations. Despite this opposition, the reclamation site — renamed "Kanonhstaton" which translates as "the protected place" still stands free of development. Moreover, in 2020, another developer attempted to build a similar housing development adjacent to the reserve lands and on territories still disputed by the Haudenosaunee. This site too was quickly occupied and renamed "1492 Land Back Lane." Reporter Jorge Barrera has called these sites "the front line of a land battle older than Canada — one that has been waged by Six Nations of the Grand River through parliamentary committees, federal land claim processes, the courts and now, again, on the streets of Caledonia."[22]

Another key example was introduced in Chapter 1: far to the west, the Unist'ot'en Camp is an ongoing assertion of sovereignty in Wetsuwet'en territory, in the Interior of British Columbia. The Unist'ot'en clan of the Wetsuwet'en constructed an action camp, including a permanent cabin and pithouse, directly in the pathway of several proposed oil and gas pipelines. Construction companies have responded by trying to sneak in survey crews or by changing their construction routes to circumvent the Unist'ot'en Camp. Meanwhile, unknown individuals have left explosive packages and tried to burn down the main bridge leading in to the action camp. More recently, this site and others in the area have been raided by the RCMP who have used violence and the threat of imprisonment to try and disperse Indigenous "protesters." Regardless, the Wetsuwet'en and their allies remain committed to putting their lives on the line to protect their lands. Efforts like these are important and powerful, but pushback makes the situation precarious and dangerous.[23]

Land reclamation efforts like these are often met with violence while they are simultaneously constructed as fundamentally *not* about the land in public and political arenas. Many of these conflicts are popularly articulated by Canadian pundits and news commentators as battles over rights, financial obligations, self-government, or a clash of cultural practices, in ways that leave land to one side. When Indigenous People assert that the land itself is important, beyond value as property or the source of resources for extraction, they are derided for being "mystical" or "nostalgic" or "essentialist," all of which are deflections to avoid actually taking seriously the challenging relationships with the land asserted in Indigenous identities.

Land is important to everyone, and the priority that Indigenous and Settler people put on the land is, in fact, the source of most conflicts. Settler colonialism in Canada is not a clash between a people who are connected to the land and a people who are not, but rather between a people who have always been connected to the land and a people whose connection to the land is premised on the displacement and destruction of Indigenous Peoples' pre-existing relationships to place.

Mediating Structures

As we have demonstrated, Settler identities flow from particular attempts to relate to new lands as "home." Of course, newcomers and settlers are not bound to relate to the land only through the practice of colonization, and in fact, can and have developed strong personal relationships to place that complement rather than displace Indigenous relationships. Historical examples of moments like this are few and far between, and certainly anomalous amid the wider history of colonial invasion. We will consider some of those examples and what they tell us about the possibility of Settlers co-existing with Indigenous Nations absent colonial domination. But first we must consider how Settler Canadians' relationships to place are circumscribed by settler colonial structures of invasion in the present. For Settler Canadians, these structures, in the form of spaces, systems, and stories, currently mediate the relationship between Settler and land in Canada, thereby providing the basis for Settler belonging in Canada.

Recall the "intent to stay" that characterizes settler colonialism.[24] Settler people, unlike visitors, sojourners, or others passing through, seek to establish and maintain a new homeland. This intent to stay is a powerful motivation, accompanied by the creation of equally powerful discourses that assert that not only can Settler people live "here," but in fact should do so. The legal and political structures that attach us to places, and the regional identities such as Québécois that are situated in specific places are taken as evidence of our justifiable claims, rather than seen as techniques of dispossession and colonial replacement. In settler colonial contexts, these structures of invasion serve to mediate that relationship between Settler people and the land. They define how the land should be and can be understood, who can own it, and how that ownership is justified in both moral or ethical and legal or political contexts.

Stories of Belonging

Settler colonizers encounter the land through lenses created by inherent biases that are passed down generationally through our stories of settlement and belonging. These biases are reflected in the structures we build socially and politically, including traditions of property and ownership, and human-centric understandings of sovereignty and relational responsibility. These complexes of tradition, expectation, perception, and interaction form what are called "imagined geographies," which necessarily differ from the spatial perceptions and relationships of Indigenous Peoples.[25] Before settler colonial collectives construct obvious legal and political relationships that bind them to the land, they construct narratives that justify their being on the land at all and that begin the process of shifting their identity from rootedness in original homelands to the new settlement.

As we discussed earlier with respect to diasporic peoples, one of the most common and historically important Settler Canadian narratives is that of being forced out of a prior homeland. This narrative has a long history. Many settlers coming from Europe in the eighteenth and nineteenth centuries pointed to decadent and corrupt regimes as the reason for their displacement. This was not pure perception, but did, in fact, have a basis in reality. Class hierarchies in European societies, the enclosure of common lands that destroyed traditional livelihoods and forced people to become urban poor, and the criminalization of the poor in multiple ways could very much be understood as a sort of disaster for anyone without inherited wealth. Economic refugees, such as the Irish, were common, as were religious communities escaping persecution, from Puritans to Quakers, Mennonites, and Amish, to Anabaptists and Lutherans. As a now common narrative, these stories are a shorthand explaining why a people would become Settlers

— that is, adopt the intent to stay in a new land, forsaking a connection to the place of their origin — and also what sort of opportunities they have come looking for in settler society. However, the story often leaves out the agency of Indigenous Peoples in letting early settlers stay and in helping them survive, or that the present bounty and opportunity of Canada are rooted in profits from lands unjustly taken from Indigenous Nations. This limited understanding of history strongly influences how many people around the world see Canada: as a bountiful, welcoming place, regardless of the realities of increasing poverty, a widening wealth gap, and racism and prejudicial treatment of foreign workers. Canada is portrayed as a vast country of natural beauty and resources, even as its industrial economy contributes more to climate change than most others — and the benefits that would-be Settlers often hope to find in Canada are very much linked to these destructive practices.[26]

Of course, the reality is much more complex than what these powerful but simplistic narratives depict. For example, many Scottish merchants in the 1800s emigrated to the settlement colonies not escaping persecution or marginalization so much as seeking individual fortune. Parts of Canada were subjected to a well-heeled form of settlement at the hands of British middle- and upper-class colonists seeking to increase their already considerable wealth and social standing through land purchases and business ventures such as ranching or plantations built on enslaved or unfree labour. These groups of settler colonizers also often monopolized large tracts of land and took advantage of less-powerful settler communities — such as the abuse heaped on Chinese immigrants who worked on the construction of the railroads or the dangerous, uncertain, underpaid, and often lethal back-breaking labour of the Italian and Irish immigrants who dug the Welland Canal.[27] To be sure, many migrant people came to settle in Canada because the conditions in their homelands and places of origin were hostile, threatening or limited — warfare and class exploitation, natural disasters and famine, and fascism and ethnic cleansing all forced people to move and relocate — but the point here is how Canada, through stories of opportunity and harmony, attracted those dispossessed populations. The narratives of victimization and escape from a prior homeland, and opportunity and redemption in the settlement colony, become a powerful narrative that displaces Indigenous Peoples' narratives, and even stories of interaction between Settlers and Indigenous communities.[28]

Another common and important narrative in justifying settler colonial belonging on the land is terra nullius: that settlement happened on "empty land." According to this story, the lands claimed by settler colonizers were uninhabited or occupied in a fashion not worthy of respect or legal recognition. Colonizers were therefore both morally justified and legally protected in taking and altering the lands as their own. In fact, "unimproved land" — meaning land not worked according to European concepts of agriculture, labour, and production — was considered wasteful, while the toil of farming was considered good and just. This same logic is applied in the present. For example, the exploitation of oil and gas resources in northern Alberta and British Columbia is lauded for making otherwise empty and unused land productive and profitable. However, as anthropologist and geographer Hugh Brody noted all the way back in 1981, the lands can only be considered "empty" because of the generations of efforts to enclose Indigenous People on reserve lands and disconnect them from their wider territories. This is a pattern, repeating what happened on the plains following John A. Macdonald's starvation policies that, to paraphrase James Daschuk, "cleared" the land. However, in the face of overwhelming evidence to the contrary, it has always taken remarkable intellectual contortions for settler colonizers to ignore or avoid the existence and visible presence of Indigenous Peoples. Even when legally and politically constrained to reserve lands, Indigenous People have not only fought for rights and access to traditional territories, but also maintained active and vital relationships to the lands through hunting and trapping, ceremonial practices, and other activities. No matter how much settler colonial narratives portray these lands as "empty," they were never even "emptied" despite the colonizers' best efforts.

Historically, Indigenous Peoples' relationships to place were marked on the land just as surely as European and Settler fences marked out property. Many Indigenous Nations had advanced farming societies, and lived in large villages and towns, whether permanent, semi-permanent, or seasonally occupied. In early trade relationships, Indigenous traders often got the better end of deals with settler and other colonial agents,[29] and had complex and nuanced understandings of governance, economics, and cross-cultural interactions. This means that, both in the past and present, settler colonizers have to work hard to erase or deny Indigenous presence and authority on the land.

Terra nullius (as a popular concept and through active efforts required to sustain it) is a narrative and practice of erasure, but it is also a way of rooting and justifying settler colonial societies on the land. The excuse that the land was empty and waiting to be occupied is often the basis of Settler claims to legitimate belonging on the land. But there are a host of claims that go together to set the basis of Canadian legal and political institutions, combining as shorthand for the argument that "we were here first" even in the face of indisputable Indigenous counterclaims. In the present, social media, especially in the context of far-right conspiracy theories, repeatedly posits Indigenous People as trying to take "something" — land, funding, legal protections — that does not "belong" to them, and this too is an example of terra nullius. Even to the extent that Indigenous People are seen to exist, they are seen also as being after the fact of Canada's creation and claims to land. Though clearly a well-worn fiction, terra nullius has proven a surprisingly durable and powerful narrative, rising from the grave when least expected.

The zombie-version of terra nullius argues that, yes, the land was not empty; yes, Indigenous People existed on the land and had some recognizable claim to it, but earlier or ancestral settler collectives, in their ignorance and inability to perceive Indigenous "civilization," simply took space that they thought was free. This narrative tends to reframe the discourse to focus on the "good intentions" of early settlers, who struggled against great odds to help build a democratic land of opportunity out of the perceived wilderness — all of which continues to echo racist tropes of civilization and development that cast Indigenous Peoples and lands in need of saving from their own savagery.

Of course, histories — both academic and Indigenous oral histories — put paid to this line of argumentation. Indigenous People and Settlers interacted for decades and centuries. Colonists may have viewed Indigenous Peoples through their own lenses, but there are many references to early settlers describing political leaders or "chiefs" as being akin to monarchs and "kings," underscoring their recognition of the authority wielded by them as something like authority in their own societies.[30] Some settler groups negotiated complex agreements with Indigenous Peoples to occupy certain parts of the land, and developed long-term trade and even mutual-protection relationships, the marks of advanced diplomacy that could not have occurred in an empty space. Today, terra nullius continues to hold a powerful sway over how Settler Canadians think about concepts like "development," with Indigenous Peoples being understood as present on the land but without the markers that would indicate sovereign polities, able to challenge our own preemption of those lands. This modern version of the empty land myth posits the land as empty of civilization if not of people. But of course, terra nullius, both as an enduring myth and as a historical excuse, does not and never has reflected reality.

Of Settler States and Canadian Citizens

Beyond these narrative mediations of Settler Canadian relationships to the land, Canada, as a state, maintains a variety of important political, legal, and economic structures designed to affirm the legitimacy of Settler society. Westphalian sovereignty, the political doctrine that, since the mid-1600s, has defined the nation state as the highest order of political territorial authority, should not be read in isolation from settler colonialism. The development of the modern state and the development of Settler Canadian society have been connected for centuries. The Canadian Constitution is, in many ways, not unique among those of other nation states. The definition of internal territorial jurisdictions, the designation of the rights of citizenship, the creation of checks and balances such as a separate legislature and judiciary, and the enshrinement of procedures for voting and elections of a representative government are all common. But it is significant, especially in the context of a settler colonial nation state like Canada, to remind people that citizenship — the official recognition of an individual's membership in a state — is not value-neutral, nor is it universally positive.

Being a Canadian citizen means, in theory, having one's rights defined in the Constitution and protected by the machinery of the state, and being able to claim entrance to and belonging in any of the territory within the state. That means that for Settler Canadians, citizenship conveys a right to reside on, own, and exert control over lands taken from Indigenous Nations, while Indigenous Peoples are assigned fractions of their traditional territories, if any. So if citizenship, which derives from the Constitution, is the fundamental "proof" that Settler Canadians have a valid connection to the land claimed by the Canadian state, what does the Constitution itself say about Indigenous claims to the land?

Section 35 of the Canadian Constitution (1982) states: "The existing aboriginal and treaty rights of the aboriginal peoples of Canada are hereby recognized and affirmed." This might seem like a clear recognition of the legitimacy and importance of Indigenous Peoples' claims to land. However, this section of the Constitution exists not as a stand-alone but as part of a much larger colonial legal tradition, which includes both Treaty relationships and important decisions by the Supreme Court of Canada on "Aboriginal title." Consider, first, that many treaties between Indigenous Nations and the Crown do not exist in a form easily integrated with Canadian law. How do treaties written in wampum fit into common or statutory law? How do treaties signed between Indigenous Nations but not directly with the Crown or Settler Canadian governments — such as the Bowl With One Spoon Treaty between the Haudenosaunee Confederacy and Anishinaabe Nations — become recognized under section 35? (Simple answer to both questions: they don't.)

Second, consider that when the Constitution was drafted, a series of Supreme Court cases had already begun to set decisions that circumscribed how and to what extent "Aboriginal and Treaty Rights" could be exercised within the boundaries of Canadian sovereignty.[31] Among other caveats, Aboriginal rights to land can only be claimed if it can be proved to the satisfaction of Settler Canadian officials that the land in question is part of a traditional territory, shows evidence of being used by Indigenous Peoples, and has been continually occupied by Indigenous Peoples since before the assertion of Canadian sovereignty. Given that Settler Canadians have done their best to push Indigenous Peoples off their traditional lands, undermine their economies and methods of survival, and erase the evidence of Indigenous communities' tenure on the land, as well as actively and tacitly support the striking depopulation of Indigenous Nations, these criteria are nearly impossible to fulfil.

Should an Indigenous Nation overcome all these legal barriers and win recognition of Aboriginal title to a territory in the courts, the relationship between Aboriginal title and the Crown's claim to "underlying title" remains muddy. Legal decisions have been premised on the condition that Aboriginal title cannot be said to interfere with Canadian sovereign claims to territory. The Canadian government has repeatedly reserved the right (supported by Supreme Court decisions) to simply ignore Indigenous claims if it is in the national interest (broadly defined) to do so. All of which demands that we ask the question: What does Aboriginal title actually do if it only exists subordinate to and subject to the will of the Crown? It is clear both in wording and in practice that Settler Canadian governments consider Indigenous belonging on the land at best a minor concern and at most a major nuisance. The Constitution of Canada exists not to balance Indigenous and Settler relationships, but to ensure Settler Canadian sovereignty over the land, and subsume Indigenous belonging within that sovereignty.

Belonging Through Treaty?

Myths like terra nullius and political systems of constitution and citizenship serve to justify Settler Canadian belonging on the land, and to actively displace Indigenous place-relationships. But if we continue to work from the assumption that Settler identity and settler colonialism are not by strict definition the same, what other ways could a Settler identity be mediated with respect to the land? More simply, are there ways for Settler people to "belong" on Indigenous lands that are not reliant on settler colonialism?

In thinking through this question, it is helpful to start with the core features of settler colonial place-relationships so that we can see the picture in negative. These are things that we already know must change. First, Canadian sovereignty — constructed as absolute, invested in a state territory, and codified in the Constitution, legislation, common law, and regimes of property — cannot stand, and needs to be reformulated. Second, Settler Canadians must exist in a system that does not perpetuate marginalization of Indigenous presence or generate contemporary excuses echoing the fiction of "empty land," and instead must find ways to reconcile their own presence on the land with the preceding and continuous presence of Indigenous Peoples and Nations. Third, the spaces that Settler people occupy cannot be based on the imagined geographies of settler colonialism, but instead should correspond to spaces of Indigenous political and social life on the land. That is the barest set of conditions that must be met for Settler people to find ways to belong on the land that do not rely on the structures of settler colonialism. Helpfully, we have some historical examples of these kinds of relationships in action (not many, but some).

Religious communities like the Quakers, diaspora communities such as the Irish expelled from the American colonies, and even some communities of pastoral homesteaders who lived far closer to the political jurisdiction of nearby Indigenous Nations and confederacies than distant European empires, all had to negotiate some sort of relationship with Indigenous Nations, whether based on respectful sharing or violent imposition. In the most equal and respectful cases, the cross-cultural protocols developed through these encounters are embodied in "peace and friendship" treaties. This makes more sense when we remember that there is a crucial difference between Settler Canadian legal interpretations of treaties and Indigenous understandings of Treaty agreements: in Indigenous political and legal traditions, treaties are living documents describing an ongoing relationship rather than one time political agreements that cede land. Political scientist Dale Turner articulates the Indigenous Treaty position as "the political stance that the treaties represent not only binding political agreements but also sacred agreements, and that to violate them is morally reprehensible."[32] This was often symbolized through gift-giving, which the Crown and Settler Canadian governments often regarded as a payment or transaction, but which Indigenous communities regarded as a necessary part of ceremonially renewing a relational covenant. Other treaties, such as the Haudenosaunee "Two Row" or Guswenta Treaty — which is the core of January Rogers' poem that opens this book — were intended to expand political relationships to include newcomers, but not any kind of land surrender or sale. They codified a relationship of mutual respect and negotiated coexistence.

Rather than a written, legal document, the Guswenta consists of two parts: an oral history that explains the meaning of the Treaty and a beaded belt that serves as the visual metaphor and physical embodiment of the agreement. The belt consists of long strings of wampum — beads made of shaped, polished shells. The pattern is two thick, parallel bands of purple running the length of the belt on a field of white. The purple bands represent the Haudenosaunee canoe and the European ship, travelling together on the river of life, present but never intersecting. The Two Row Treaty is a metaphor for coexistence based on mutual noninterference, but it would be wrong to suggest that these treaties call for segregation or noninteraction. Between the two bands of purple are three strands of white beads, a number chosen to represent the values of peace, friendship, and respect that maintain the "middle row" between the canoe and the ship.[33] The two peoples — Haudenosaunee and Settler — are always in contact, connected by a respectful relationship and sharing of place, but also responsible for maintaining a respectful distance, neither seeking to control the affairs of the other. The Guswenta is more than a legal document: it is one possible way in which Settlers can (and have, even if only briefly) mediate their belonging on the lands of the Haudenosaunee Confederacy without doing so through settler colonialism. The Guswenta explicitly defines the principles, protocols, and practices that Settler people must adhere to in order to legitimately live in Haudenosaunee territories, and the responsibilities that come with that privilege. This provides a glimpse of what a relational, non-dominating, non-colonial arrangement for belonging on the land could look like. It also retains direct application in the present, as demonstrated through public, participatory reenactments of the Treaty in

2013 through a joint Indigenous and Settler canoe journey across upper New York State, part of the traditional Haudenosaunee homeland. Geographer Penelope Edmonds relates that "The Two Row Wampum campaigners aimed to use community-based initiatives to draw attention to Native sovereignty rights, land rights and environmental concerns, brokered and publicly performed through an agreement made four centuries ago."[34] Similar acts are certainly possible on the Canadian side of the border as well.

However, for the majority of Settler history, these sorts of nuanced Treaty relationships have not informed Settler belonging. Instead, Treaty has been used as a strategy to extinguish Indigenous Peoples' claims to land to extend the sovereign control of the settler state. Consider the clash over the meaning of the Douglas Treaties (1850–1854), which "acquired" parts of Vancouver Island for the British Crown at the expense of Coast Salish Nations and communities. These agreements were and are understood very differently by the Lekwungen, WSÁNEĆ, and other Coast Salish signatories to these treaties. For the Coast Salish, the ability to "fish as formerly" — a keystone clause of the treaties — implied an entire system of governance and unique relationship to the land. The centrality of this clause in the Douglas Treaties reveals that the Coast Salish expected newcomers and Settlers to uphold Indigenous place-relationships as part of the founding of their colony.[35] To do otherwise would, by definition, breach the Treaty that had been signed, delegitimizing any Settler claim to belonging in that place and voiding the privilege of staying. That is, of course, exactly what happened: the British Crown and the Canadian state used the Douglas Treaties as a foothold to gain purchase on Vancouver Island, and once the colony and developing settler society was secure, the Salishan way of life was physically and politically attacked.

The history of Treaty-making in Canada has been one of imposing sovereign Settler Canadian belonging through a process designed to appeal and appear to Indigenous perspectives as if it were in accordance with Indigenous Treaty concepts. The Royal Commission on Aboriginal Peoples (RCAP; 1996) as well as the work of scholars, from Anishinaabe legal scholar John Borrows to Settler political theorists James Tully and Michael Asch, have pointed out that if the treaties that were signed in Canada were respected and honoured according to the spirit and intent ascribed to them by Indigenous Nations, many colonial conflicts in Canada could be resolved.[36] What this means is that Settler belonging on the land needs to be moderated through Indigenous nationhood rather than against it.

In Indigenous perspectives, treaties are long-term frameworks for equitable relationships rather than documents detailing land surrender or short-term political alliance-making.[37] Further, when treaties are not understood and embodied in this way, the result can be more than the violation of domestic or international law: breakdowns in respectful relationship can subvert Indigenous nationhood in a profound way.[38] Indigenous Nations, in extending the offer of relationship through Treaty to Settler peoples, accepted newcomers onto their lands and into their spiritual and intellectual traditions in a way that could either empower both communities of people, or leave them vulnerable to abuse. Indigenous Peoples historically entered into Treaty-making processes with Settler peoples by relying on declarations of trust and mutual respect as guarantees that their new partners would not take advantage of them. However, Settler Canadian political authorities never intended to act on treaties in that way.

The Numbered Treaties (negotiated between 1871 and 1921), which were used to bring much of what is now Canada north and west of the Great Lakes into the legal possession of the Canadian state, constitute a case study in the extent to which government officials and Treaty negotiators twisted treaties from their inception. There are multiple accounts of Treaty negotiators relying on interpreters who did not even speak the language of the Peoples they were negotiating with, of arbitrarily altering Treaty provisions after the treaties were signed, and of obtaining consent from individuals with no authority to speak on behalf of a given Nation, or taking the consent of one Nation to a treaty over a given territory as the consent of all Nations of that territory.[39] This is to say nothing of the Nations coerced into signing treaties after a campaign of starvation — through the slaughter of buffalo and driving Indigenous communities away from traditional hunting and farming grounds — that forced people into a position of dependency.[40] Little has changed, conceptually, between the time of the Numbered Treaties and the contemporary process of land claims and modern Treaty negotiations in Canada. By forcing First Nations to rack up huge legal costs in order to stay at the negotiating table, and face endless appeals in a long and uncertain process, the Canadian government ensures that the finite resources of Indigenous communities are consumed by legal process, and the communities involved are slowly "starved" until any deal seems like a good deal.

Earlier in this chapter, we asked whether it could be possible for a foreign people to settle on Indigenous lands in a way that is non-colonial. In theory, the answer is yes. Indigenous Peoples since long before

European colonization have had protocols for permitting movement and settlement across and in their lands. According to some oral histories, the place where the city of Toronto is located was once Mississauga land, but the Mississauga claim itself is based on their leasing the area from the Haudenosaunee Confederacy. On the West Coast, where Salish Nations and communities overlapped and intermingled through complex clan lineages and marriage relationships, there are many stories of various Peoples and Nations requesting (or in some cases purchasing) the right to live on certain lands. The forging of these international agreements on land sharing continues today. You can see an example of this if you've visited Victoria, British Columbia. Wawaditła (Mungo Martin House) is a Kwakwaka'wakw big house built adjacent to the Royal British Columbia Museum in downtown Victoria, BC. This is traditionally Songhees territory, but the construction of Wawaditła was negotiated through complex relational agreements and protocols that continue today. These sorts of arrangements became the basis of why Indigenous Peoples let Europeans stay at all: sharing space was a normal thing to do.

"We Are All Treaty People" or Are We?

"We are all Treaty people" is a rallying call popularized in progressive political circles and among social justice advocates. It is a positive step to see Settler Canadians developing awareness of treaties with Indigenous Peoples, and understanding that the treaties signed by the state imply responsibilities for both Indigenous Peoples and Settlers. For far too long, treaties were considered by many Canadians to be at most a legal construct under which Indigenous People could make limited claims on the government. There is now some popular recognition that treaties also form the basis for Settler people to belong on the land in a more ethical and legitimate fashion. However, caution is necessary: the full meaning and import of "being a Treaty person" is still too often ignored or misunderstood.

As described above, treaties in Indigenous contexts are living covenants. Claiming belonging as a Treaty person means accepting and practicing a dynamic set of responsibilities that will be specific to a given Treaty, on the territory of a given Nation, determined in an open-ended fashion through dialogue with that host Nation (or Nations in the case of territories where more than one Indigenous Nation overlap). We previously described the complex and reciprocal relationships between Indigenous Peoples and their lands, and while Settler people should not try to copy these relationships, they must figure out ways to relate to the lands they occupy that enhance rather than hinder Indigenous place-relationships. This is not the same as developing a set of codified laws and procedures that give certainty or finality. Many treaties between Indigenous Peoples and Settlers must be understood as having been signed under duress and having been intentionally misinterpreted or disregarded. A respectful Treaty person has to throw out what they think they know about any given Treaty and engage with the many potential other meanings beyond the "official" version. This includes the imperative to understand how the language of Treaty — which can be encompassed in written documents that (imperfectly) represent Indigenous languages or concepts, in symbols like wampum belts, and in the oral histories and political traditions of Indigenous communities themselves — cannot simply be translated into English or French, and incorporated into common terminology without misrepresenting or oversimplifying the meaning of the Treaty. Understanding must be relational. Treaties understood according to Indigenous perspectives and respectful relationships raise fundamental questions about Canadian sovereignty, the authority of the state, and the meaning of citizenship, as well as official and popular narratives of Canadian history. Claiming an identity as a Treaty person cannot be done without a deep critique of one's own relationship with Settler Canadian society and present-day settler colonialism.

Finally, and perhaps most importantly, we are quite simply *not* all Treaty people. Huge areas of British Columbia are not covered by treaties between any Indigenous Nation and Settlers. There are many areas of eastern Canada whose only agreements are peace and friendship treaties that are inadequate to the task of informing a resident Settler society how to respectfully share land with Indigenous Nations. There are places all across Canada where treaties were signed with one Nation that do not reflect the will or desires of other Nations that share those places. Again, let us consider the Douglas Treaties, which were often negotiated with only one Nation or community in places usually defined by overlapping Indigenous jurisdictions. That has continued to create confusion in the present, as some modern land agreements, such as the Tsawwassen First Nation Final Agreement (2007), have finalized the exclusive jurisdiction of the Tsawwassen over islands and seaspaces despite concurrent and competing claims by other Indigenous communities, including the Saanich communities of Vancouver Island. Similarly, the creation of the Territory of Nunavut (1999) — though a government statute rather than a treaty — resulted from years of negotiations between the Crown and Inuit Peoples, leaving out the Dene, whose homelands are now obscured beneath the federally recognized "Inuit homeland."

Claiming Status as a Treaty person cannot be a bandaid for Settler Canadian uncertainty, discomfort, or guilt. The critical difference between treaties as respectful bases for coexistence, or colonial frameworks that justify Settler Canadian claims to land resides in which comes first: either Indigenous relationships to land are centralized and Settler social structures developed that are respective of these place-relationships, or settler colonial structures of invasion such as constitutions and state boundaries are prioritized and Indigenous place-relationships are treated as a problem to be managed. This is, of course, the basis of Indigenous and Settler Canadian conflicts, and the root of Indigenous struggles for sovereignty.

Notes

1   For a general introduction to this topic, see, Tim Cresswell, *Place: A Short Introduction* (Oxford: Blackwell Publishing, 2004).
2   Vanessa Watts, "Indigenous Place-Thought & Agency Amongst Humans and Non-Humans (First Woman and Sky Woman go on a European World Tour!)," *Decolonization: Indigeneity, Education & Society* 2, 1 (2013), 22.
3   Shawn Wilson, *Research Is Ceremony: Indigenous Research Methods* (Winnipeg: Fernwood Publishing, 2008).
4   Hunt, Sarah Hunt, "Ontologies of Indigeneity: The Politics of Embodying a Concept," *Cultural Geographies* 21, 1 (2013), 5.
5   Watts, "Indigenous Place-Thought."
6   For more on these subjects see, Vine Deloria, Jr., *The World We Used to live In: Remembering the Powers of the Medicine Men* (Golden, CO: Fulcrum Publishing, 2006); Nancy Turner, Marianne Ignace, and Ronald Ignace, "Traditional Ecological Knowledge and Wisdom of Aboriginal Peoples in British Columbia," *Ecological Applications* 10, 5 (2000).
7   Vine Deloria, Jr.'s writings are extensive and cover a wide range of topics, from legal philosophy and theology to Jungian psychology and the scientific method, all with a great deal of wit and challenging intellect. On this particular topic, see, *God Is Red: A Native View of Religion, 30th Anniversary Edition* (Golden, CO: Fulcrum Publishing, 2003/1973); "Philosophy and the Tribal Peoples," in *American Indian Thought*, ed. Anne Waters (Malden, MA: Blackwell Publishing, 2004); and *The World We Used to Live In*.
8   Leroy Little Bear, "Land: The Blackfoot Source of Identity," Presented at Beyond Race and Citizenship: Indigeneity in the 21st Century Conference, Berkeley, CA: University of California (2004).
9   Watts, "Indigenous Place-Thought."
10 Margaret Kovach, *Indigenous Methodologies — Characteristics, Conversations, and Contexts* (University of Toronto Press, 2009).

11 Vine Deloria, Jr. and Daniel Wildcat, *Power and Place: Indian Education in America* (Golden, CO: Fulcrum Resources, 2001).
12 Mark Rifkin, "Settler Common Sense," *Settler Colonial Studies* 3, 3–4 (2013).
13 Tracey Banivanua Mar, "Carving Wilderness: Queensland's National Parks and the Unsettling of Emptied Lands, 1890–1910," in *Making Settler Colonial Space: Perspectives on Race, Place and Identity*, eds. Tracey Banivanua Mar and Penelope Edmonds (New York: Palgrave Macmillan, 2010).
14 Jon Parmenter, *The Edge of the Woods: Iroquoia, 1534–1701* (Michigan State University Press, 2014).
15 Daniel Coleman, "Indigenous Place and Diaspora Space: Of Literalism and Abstraction," *Settler Colonial Studies* 6, 1 (2016).
16 Richard Day, *Multiculturalism and the History of Canadian Diversity* (University of Toronto Press, 2000)
17 For an overview of this practice, see, Harsha Walia, *Undoing Border Imperialism* (Oakland: AK Press, 2013).
18 Coleman, "Indigenous Place and Diaspora Space," 2.
19 Sovereignty is a contested and inaccurate term with respect to Indigenous governance. We use it here as an approximation, knowing that Indigenous People and Settlers often speak past each other when discussing sovereignty across the settler colonial divide. For more on Indigenous uses of and problems with the term, see Taiaiake Alfred, "Sovereignty — An Inappropriate Concept" in *The Indigenous Experience: Global Perspectives*, eds. Roger Maaka and Chris Anderson (Canadian Scholars Press, 2006). On settler colonialism and sovereignty see, Lorenzo Veracini, "Isopolitics, Deep Colonizing, Settler Colonialism," *Interventions* 13, 2 (2011); and *Settler Colonialism: A Theoretical Overview* (London: Palgrave Macmillan, 2010).
20 Anne Waters, "Introduction," in *Native American Thought*, ed. Anne Waters (Malden: Blackwell Press, 2004), xxiv.
21 James Tully, "The Struggles of Indigenous Peoples for and of Freedom," in *Political Theory and the Rights of Indigenous Peoples*, eds. Duncan Ivison, Paul Patton, and Will Sanders (Cambridge University Press, 2005), 39.
22 Jorge Barrera, "Beyond the Barricades," *CBC News* (25 November 2020), newsinteractives.cbc.ca/longform/1492-land-back-lane-caledonia-six-nations-protest/.
23 On Oka, see, Geoffrey York and Loreen Pindera, *People of the Pines: The Warriors and the Legacy of Oka* (Toronto: Little Brown, 1991). On Ipperwash, see, Edwards, *One Dead Indian*. On the Caledonia reclamation, see, Laura DeVries, *Conflict in Caledonia: Aboriginal Land Rights and the Rule of Law* (Vancouver: UBC Press, 2011); Theresa McCarthy, *In Divided Unity: Haudenosaunee Reclamation at Grand River* (Phoenix: University of Arizona Press, 2017). On the Unist'ot'en Camp, see their website unistotencamp.com. On Indigenous land occupations and protest camps more generally, see, Anna Willow, *Strong Hearts, Native Lands: The Cultural and Political Landscape of Anishinaabe Anti-Clearcutting Activism* (Albany: State University of New York Press, 2012); Warren Magnusson and Karena Shaw, eds., *A Political Space: Reading the Global Through Clayoquot Sound* (Minneapolis: University of Minnesota Press, 2002); Nicholas Blomley, "'Shut the Province Down': First Nations Blockades

in British Columbia, 1984–1995," *BC Studies* 111 (Autumn 1996); Linda Pertusati, "The 1990 Mohawk-Oka Conflict: The Importance of Culture In Social Movement Mobilization," *Race, Gender & Class* 3, 3 (1996).

24 Veracini, *Settler Colonialism*.

25 Lorenzo Veracini, "The Imagined Geographies of Settler Colonialism," in *Making Settler Colonial Space: Perspectives on Race, Place and Identity*, eds. Tracy Banivanua Mar and Penelope Edmonds (Hampsire, UK: Palgrave Macmillan, 2010).

26 Jaela Bernstein, "Canadians Are among the World's Worst Carbon Emitters. Here's What We Can Do About It," *CBC News*, October 8, 2021, cbc.ca/news/science/how-canadians-can-cut-carbon-footprints-1.6202194.

27 We are grateful to historian Melanie Battell for sharing her work on the under discussed poor treatment of immigrant workers, particularly Italian and Irish, in the construction of the Welland Canal between Lake Ontario and Lake Erie.

28 For an example of the power of this narrative in the American context, see the introduction in Ilan Stavans, *Becoming Americans: Immigrants Tell Their Stories from Jamestown to Today* (Washington: Library of Congress, 2014).

29 For example see the stories about Nuu-chah-nulth communities trading with British explorers and traders in the eighteenth century in Daniel Clayton, *Islands of Truth: The Imperial Fashioning of Vancouver Island* (Vancouver: UBC Press, 1999).

30 Karen Kupperman, *Indians and English: Facing Off in Early America* (London: Cornell University Press, 2000).

31 We recommend *Unstable Properties: Aboriginal Title and the Claim of British Columbia* (Vancouver: UBC Press, 2022) by David Rossiter and Patricia Burke Wood, for a thorough treatment of these cases, why the law unfolded through court decisions as it has, and how provincial and federal governments have responded. Many of the most significant cases were raised in British Columbia because of its clear lack of treaties across most of the territory claimed by the province, but they have massive implications across Canada.

32 Dale Turner, *This Is Not a Peace Pipe: Towards a Critical Indigenous Philosophy* (University of Toronto Press, 2006), 26.

33 Turner, *This Is Not a Peace Pipe*, 48.

34 Penelope Edmonds, "'Polishing the Chain of Friendship': Two Row Wampum Renewal Celebrations and Matters of History," in *Settler Colonialism and (Re)conciliation* (London: Palgrave Macmillan, 2016).

35 Nicholas Claxton, "ISTÁ SĆIÁNEW, ISTÁ SXOLE 'To Fish as Formerly': The Douglas Treaties and the WSÁNEĆ Reef-Net Fisheries," in *Lighting the Eighth Fire: The Liberation, Resurgence, and Protection of Indigenous Nations*, ed. Leanne Simpson (Winnipeg: Arbeiter Ring Publishing, 2008).

36 John Borrows, *Canada's Indigenous Constitution* (University of Toronto Press, 2010); Tully, *Strange Multiplicity*; Michael Asch, On Being Here to Stay: Treaties and Aboriginal Rights in Canada (University of Toronto Press, 2014).

37 Turner, *This Is Not a Peace Pipe*.

38 Harold Cardinal and Walter Hildebrandt, *Treaty Elders of Saskatchewan: Our Dream Is That Our Peoples Will One Day Be Clearly Recognized as Nations* (Calgary: University of Calgary Press, 2000).

39 For more on this, see, John Borrows, *Recovering Canada: The Resurgence of Indigenous Law* (University of Toronto Press, 2002); JR Miller, "'I Will Accept the Queen's Hand': First Nations Leaders and the Image of the Crown in the Prairie Treaties," in *Reflections on Native-Newcomer Relations: Selected Essays*, ed. James Miller (University of Toronto Press, 2004).

40 James Daschuk, *Clearing the Plains: Disease, Politics of Starvation, and the Loss of Aboriginal Life* (Regina, SK: University of Regina Press, 2013).

"Settling" Our Differences

SO FAR, WE HAVE DISCUSSED THE HISTORICAL ROOTS of the Settler identity, the political relationship between the Settler identity and settler colonialism in Canada, and the ways Settler Canadians relate to the land. We have constructed Settler identities as situated, process-based, disavowed, and relating in complex, nondiscrete, nonbinary relationships with Indigenous identities. Settler identity, then, is not based on having experienced any particular type or level of privilege. Some have used "settler" as equivalent to "white," even conflating the two — "white settler" — to describe all colonizing peoples in Canada. Others have used settler as a synonym for "non-Indigenous," a catchall for anyone on the continent that does not claim an Indigenous identity and connection to an Indigenous community. These constructions, in the ways that they blur lines and impose or imply particular traits to large, diverse groups of people, raise important questions about intersections of colonialism, race, and patriarchy, and the history and legacy of Canada as a deeply hierarchical society, both through economic exploitation and racial stratification. However, constructions of Settler-as-white or Settler-as-non-Indigenous ultimately shut down opportunities for change.

Settler Canadians are a multi-ethnic people, encompassing disparities of wealth and economic opportunity, huge ranges of education and experience, and a massive variety of ways of identifying with respect to gender, sexuality, and other overlapping markers of identity. However, this diversity does not prevent most of us from being complicit (or being made complicit) in settler colonialism, and identifying strongly with settler colonial national myths, understandings of public and private space, and systems of government and economy. In this chapter, we draw out some of these complexities and diversities and consider how settler colonialism, as a flexible and durable ideology of relationship to the land, has adapted and continues to adapt to challenges and shifts in the social make up of Canadian society. We show how people are recruited into the Settler Canadian identity and discuss what sorts of purported (if not actual) benefits come with participation in Settler Canada.

Settler Colonial Complicity

When we discuss the Settler identity separately from racialized or class-based identities, it does not mean that the Settler Canadian identity is postracial, or postcapitalist, or post any other hierarchy in Canadian society. Rather, as we have discussed previously, in Canada as elsewhere, settler colonialism has a long history of deploying racism and class antagonism and playing on other structural inequalities as tools to both motivate expansionist settlement and justify colonial dispossession and violence.[1] We argue that, while strongly shaped by whiteness, the Settler Canadian identity is racially, politically, and economically flexible. Because settler colonialism is concerned with asserting control over land rather than a particular historical event or a specific social structure, it can "shapeshift" into many different forms, accommodating different social practices and informing a variety of, at times contradictory, subsets of Settler identity. As such, settler colonialism exerts a great deal of influence over how racism and capitalism are embodied and practiced in Canada.

The Settler Canadian identity is defined by broad-based ways of relating to the land, but there is also a great diversity within it. How we experience the world as Settler people is also shaped by our experiences of race and racism, wealth and social mobility, gender and sexuality, and many other very real differences. Understanding the diverse manifestations of the Settler identity as *intersectional* helps make sense of the varied and at times conflicting manifestations of Settler identity.[2] Being white, presenting as middle class, speaking English — these all still bring relatively high levels of privilege *within* Settler society. But this does not mean that only white, middle-class English speakers should be understood as being Settler. As we discussed in Chapter 2, the "we" of Settler Canadians is a constantly changing one, and people experience a wide range of privileges and prejudices simply by being part of Canadian society. However, complicity is not based on privilege but on power and relationships. Privilege in any political economic system may come or go, but the conflict over belonging on the land remains.

Other powerful socioeconomic structures intersect with settler colonialism in Canada. White supremacy has been a feature of Canada since its inception. John A. Macdonald, in addition to starving Indigenous Peoples on the plains, aimed to create a white, Christian nation despite the presence of significant and well-established populations of people of colour. Racialized groups have historically been marginalized and oppressed in Canadian society and continue to be. Despite the oft-repeated stories of Canada as a haven for those escaping enslavement in the United States in the nineteenth century, segregation and violence were and continue to be imposed on Black communities in Canada.[3] Historically this included events like the hanging of Marie-Joseph Angélique, a 29-year-old Black enslaved woman in Montréal in 1734. As Afua Cooper describes in her book, *The Hanging of Angélique,* Marie-Joseph was accused, tried, and found guilty of setting a fire that burned forty-six buildings. She was publicly tortured before being executed. Cooper's research demonstrates just how harsh and brutal life was for an enslaved person in early Canada, and we need to be aware that the racist attitudes and structures of those times do not just disappear, but instead persist in different forms. Much like in the United States, though this is often uncomfortable for Canadians to admit, Black individuals and communities are subject to assumed criminality and presumption of violent behaviour by police as justification for the use of excess force and intervention, and also by white Canadians justifying police intervention in the everyday lives of people simply for being Black. People of colour are often also conceptually separated from "real" — meaning white — Canadian society. For example, nationalism in Québec often constructs Black people as "immigrants" or "newcomers" despite many having roots that extend back before the founding of Canada itself.

Further, white supremacist ideology and practice in Canadian society has been directed against many different groups and communities. For example, the infamous head tax imposed through the Chinese Immigration Act of 1885 demanded that would-be Chinese immigrants pay a steep fee to enter the country, in an effort to discourage immigration from China following the completion of the Trans-Canada railway and its use of imported Chinese labourers. This was despite the fact that many of these would-be newcomers were coming to join family already living and working in

Canada, including those who had laboured under brutal conditions building the railway itself and gone on to set up lives and livelihoods.[4] Or consider the exclusion of immigrants from India, epitomized in the events in Vancouver in 1914 when the Komagata Maru sailed from Hong Kong — a British protectorate at the time — carrying British subjects from India. When it arrived in Vancouver, Canadian officials used an order-in-council that demanded that immigrants must have made a "continuous journey" from their country of origin to prevent the passengers from disembarking, forcing them to remain on board ship in rapidly deteriorating conditions. The Komagata Maru was eventually sent back to India with most of the passengers still aboard, and when it arrived, British soldiers arrested and killed several passengers.[5] During the 1930s, many Jewish refugees fleeing the spread of antisemitic fascism in Europe were denied entry to Canada. Though other countries also worked to close their borders to Jewish refugees, Canada made a particular effort and admitted the fewest number of Jewish people of all Western states during this time.[6] Or as another example, consider the internment of Japanese people during the Second World War, in which many people of Japanese heritage, including those who were Canadian citizens, were imprisoned, forcibly relocated, and had their property seized because of their ethnicity.[7] The list goes on.

And lest anyone believe these forms of discrimination are in the past, consider the attacks on mosques and Hindu temples in places such as Surrey, British Columbia, and Hamilton, Ontario, in the early twenty-first century, or the work of a sociologist at the University of New Brunswick attempting to resuscitate fear of an influx of Asian immigrants threatening Canada's "European character" — that is, its whiteness.[8] Robyn Maynard, in her book *Policing Black Lives*, documents many more cases of anti-Black racism and violence perpetrated by agents of the state:

> Bony Jean-Pierre, an unarmed Haitian man in his forties, was killed in Montréal North, shot multiple times with rubber bullets at close range ... Later that same year, the police in Ottawa beat to death Abdirahman Abdi, an unarmed Black Somali man living with mental health issues ... witnesses saw the police subject him to repeated blows to the face and neck, kneel on his head and then leave him unconscious in a pool of his own blood, handcuffed, without medical attention ... He died a few days later in the hospital.[9]

These extreme examples are the tip of the iceberg that is the much larger system of exclusion and oppression in "whitestream" Canada — Canadian society, dominated by a culture of white supremacy.[10]

In this context, it would be easy to assume that racially oppressed and marginalized communities would seek out alliances with Indigenous People, but this is not commonly the case. It is entirely possible for communities of marginalized peoples to buy into the structures of invasion, to identify strongly with Settler Canadian myths and narratives, and to participate in systemic dispossession of Indigenous Peoples, all the while struggling against their own marginalization or oppression. Under conditions of settler colonialism and white supremacy, racially oppressed communities are encouraged to identify with and support whiteness under the belief that this is necessary for them to be treated as "equal," and that includes anti-Indigenous racism. Muscogee sociologist Dwanna McKay (née Robertson) has argued that, in the United States, while many racialized people experience forms of racial violence and discrimination, anti-Indigenous racism remains both acceptable and encouraged in ways that reflect the foundational racialization of Indigenous People as part of the colonial claiming of land,[11] and we would argue that the same very much applies in Canada. Likewise, Jodi Byrd has identified how Black American struggles for life and liberty have at times come at the expense of obscuring Indigenous sovereignties, and how some Hawaiian independence discourses have relied on rhetorically trying to separate themselves from being treated like "American Indians."[12] A somewhat parallel situation in Canada can be found in the mutual dispossession of both Black Nova Scotians and Mi'Kmaw Peoples in the nineteenth century. Despite there being what would seem obvious resonances between the struggles of these groups, many "African Nova Scotians failed to appreciate the meaning of [Mi'Kmaw] relationship with the Crown."[13] Rather than building solidarity between different communities engaged in mutual struggles, these two communities became estranged through resentments born out of perceptions of competition for limited rights and recognition, and an inability to appreciate the particularity of differently racialized struggles. The struggles of groups such as these are significant and have produced important social change, but they have at times done so at the cost of perpetuating settler colonialism and all its attendant harm and implications.

We should point out here that similar dynamics can occur among communities whose oppression is based in subjectivities other than race or ethnicity. For example, political theorist Scott Morgensen has shown that many queer social movements, in fighting for equality and against violence and oppression, prop up powerful settler colonial narratives of peacefulness, equality, and opportunity.[14] As such, everyone — of all backgrounds — needs to understand that they can be made complicit in settler colonialism. Otherwise, even well-intentioned activists and discourses of fairness and equality can actively further settler colonialism's end goals. The efforts of many social justice activists, even those aware of some history of colonialism and who act out of sympathy with Indigenous dispossession, have repeatedly fallen into patterns of behaviour that buttress settler colonial structures of invasion or replace existing structures with new ones that are just as powerful and even more pernicious in form. On one hand, Canadian hallmarks such as multiculturalism, anti-racism, and equality have repeatedly been co-opted to serve the settler colonial agenda. On the other, even radical anti-capitalist actions relying on direct action and raising fundamental questions about the political economy of Canada have not escaped settler colonialism. The risk of equating the struggles of Indigenous Peoples against settler colonialism to struggles against racism or capitalist exploitation is pressing, and we turn now to a brief examination of both.

Multiculturalism and Anti-Racism

Canadian multiculturalism is held up internationally as an example of a successful and progressive strategy for creating a nation state where people of any cultural or racial group can come together and live side by side, peacefully and respectfully. It has also been critiqued for not actually producing equal opportunity or equal treatment for Canadian citizens, as governments and communities have struggled over the best ways to pursue the creation of a multicultural, respectful society in practice. For example, the controversial 2013 Charter of Québec Values, which banned religious symbols and clothing, was heavily criticized for being racially and religiously discriminatory, yet received widespread support among many people on the grounds that it promoted universal, secular human rights. Similar examples could be picked from many other provinces — multiculturalism in this country has not been a smooth or simple path.[15]

However, the fact remains that, since 1971, Canada has maintained an official policy of multiculturalism, with the Canadian Multiculturalism Act signed into law in 1988. More importantly, Canadians continue to strongly identify multiculturalism as a distinctly Canadian value: Canada is made up of people whose identities originate in many different cultures and religions and individuals should have the right to practice those cultures and religions. While we are aware that in fact many groups are discriminated against at various times — for example, in 2016, police in Toronto beat and gassed peaceful Black Lives Matter protesters — the ideal of the multicultural mosaic remains a powerful part of Canadian identity. So, when sizable (in scale, violence, impact, etc.) incidents of racism and violence against Indigenous Peoples occur, some Canadians react with outrage. Various groups, from the Council of Canadians to the New Democratic Party and the Green Party, and any number of ethnic and religious community associations, have made public statements in support of equality for Indigenous Peoples, often pointing to the Charter of Rights and Freedoms and the guarantees of equality for all Canadians. Moreover, with Canada finally ratifying the United Nations Declaration on the Rights of Indigenous People (UNDRIP), and with British Columbia passing harmonizing legislation — the imaginatively titled Declaration on the Rights of Indigenous People Act (2022) — there would seem to indicate a broad consensus on this.

Yet there is a paradox, exemplified by the presence of an openly racist and race-based piece of legislation. The Indian Act, which has evolved from an amalgam of bits and pieces of colonial-era legislation designed to "gradually civilize" Indigenous People, literally sets the terms for a separate, racialized legal Status for "Indians" in Canada. The Indian Act denies Indigenous Peoples and communities the power to determine their own membership, continues to link Status to restrictive lineage rules, denies the right to self-determination by enforcing band council governments on designated and federally regulated "First Nations" as the only legitimate system of governance, and otherwise gives the federal government enormous authority to micromanage the lives of Indigenous People. There have been repeated attempts to remove or replace the Indian Act, the two most famous instances being the 1969 White Paper and the proposed First Nations Governance Act in 2002. These attempts occurred more than thirty years apart, but both were explicitly designed to end government responsibility to Indigenous Peoples — to get Canada out of "the Indian business" — and to assimilate Indigenous Peoples into Canadian civil society. The 1969 White Paper approached this by proposing that Canada do away with all government recognition of Indian Status, and absorb Indigenous Peoples as multicultural, rights-bearing citizens, with no differential relationship to land, Treaty, or the Crown. The First Nations Governance Act took a more subtle approach, attempting to restructure First Nations governments and reserve lands as municipalities, using terms like "self-governance" to elide the same dissolution of financial obligation and Treaty responsibility and turning reserve lands into private property. Both would have the practical effect of allowing the state to legally disregard Indigenous nationhood, and finalizing the primacy of the settler state as the sole, sovereign authority over the land. Despite the deeply problematic construction and negative effects of the Indian Act, Indigenous communities and political leaders actively opposed both attempts to abolish it.

Recall that the goal of settler colonization is to eliminate Indigenous nationhood and sovereignty and competing claims to land. The Indian Act, for all its considerable problems, forces the government of Canada to recognize the existence of Indigenous Peoples and to treat them differently from others in Canada. As such, it is at times a thorn in the side of settler colonialism because it makes it more difficult for the government to disregard Indigenous Nations. Even as a holdover from the pre-Confederation era, The Indian Act stands in some respects as a marker that Indigenous Peoples cannot simply be incorporated or disappeared into Canadian society — even though it is racist legislation that causes harm, it is better than the alternative.[16]

Multiculturalism in Canada, as a concept and a practice, has little to say about relationships to land and place. Culture is constructed as a set of practices, something that one does wherever one is, and rights as the freedoms and privileges of individuals, guaranteed by the state and protected by law. However, Indigenous Peoples have very different notions of how rights function: collectively rather than individually, and with a far greater focus on responsibilities to one's community, to the land, to ancestors, and future generations. When Indigenous Peoples were constructed simply as another ethnic or cultural group meriting the same rights as all other Canadians under the Charter and Multiculturalism Act, then Indigenous Peoples' only means of redress was through Canada's institutions of elected governments and courts. As such, Indigenous Peoples' own systems of governance are treated as invalid, and Indigenous sovereignty is subsumed under the state. Multiculturalism that does not recognize the difference between racism deployed against Indigenous People in order to dispossess them of the land, eliminate Indigenous identity, and disappear them as autonomous nations, and racism deployed against immigrants and minority populations in order to "discipline" them and uphold white supremacy, risks reinforcing settler colonialism through a flattened, colonialism-blind notion of equality. As Eva Mackey has presciently argued:

> [The] Canadian nation-building project has lived "with difference" from the outset, and has done so through flexible strategies of managing, appropriating, controlling, subsuming, and often highlighting it. This process has shown that the recognition of difference, in and of itself, is not necessarily the solution.[17]

Anti-racist, multicultural responses to "racist ideologies that insist on the dichotomy between white and non-whites" often ignore the important and compelling difference between Indigenous and Settler, taking the settler colonial society for granted, and allowing settler colonialism to advance behind the veil of racial tolerance and inclusion.[18]

Occupy and Anti-Capitalism

Among leftist activists and social commentators, from the social democrat base of New Democratic Party voters to more radical campaigners for anti-capitalist or socialist economics, capitalism is often given pride of place as the source of most social ills. This includes centralizing capitalism as the primary driver of exploitation of Indigenous Peoples, with evidence of extreme poverty among many reserve communities in Canada, and the destruction of sites and regions through development and resource extraction driven by capitalist expansion. There is, obviously, some truth to this. Capitalism has had, historically and in the present, an enormous impact on Indigenous Peoples. By driving the appropriation of land for profit, the transformation of complex webs of environmental relationships into extractable resources, and the migration of large groups of Settlers and temporary workers to work on resource extraction and development projects, capitalist endeavours often go hand in hand with settler colonialism. It was the potential for developing gold deposits in the Northwest Territories that drove the forced relocation of the Sayisi Dene to Churchill, Manitoba, in 1956, a move that had catastrophic effects on the lives and culture of the community. It is the same potential for massive profits that drives the mass exploitation of the Athabasca Tar Sands, one that attracts large numbers of immigrants to Alberta to work in the oil industry but destroys the lands of Cree, Blackfoot, Métis, and other Indigenous Nations, depleting and polluting water and entire ecosystems and Indigenous ways of life along with them. And it was the capitalist development logic that drove the conflicts at Oka in 1990 and Caledonia in 2006 and 2020, as golf courses and subdivisions encroached on Haudenosaunee lands in Québec and Ontario, threatening the few protected areas that these communities could still actively claim through state processes. Further, neoliberal capitalism and austerity policies stand as a threat to the well-being of Indigenous People and Settler Canadians alike. As poverty spirals out of control in Canada, as the wealth gap widens; as cutbacks to health care, education, and social services continue to harm the most vulnerable; as capitalist elites further hijack the democratic process; and as industry and development continue to devastate the basic ecosystems that all humans need to survive, we all need to seriously question the Canadian — and global — economic system.

However, settler colonialism also functions in the absence of capitalism. Consider Soviet socialist settler colonization in Siberia during the twentieth century that shows many of the same patterns as settler colonialism in capitalist Canada, perhaps best summed up by the observation that "though the active phase of settler colonization may be over, the actual phenomenon is not. The assimilation and Russification of Indigenous Peoples continues, and their ethnic territories are gradually losing special status."[19] While there are ongoing debates over "how socialist" the Soviet project was, leftist political philosophies including socialism and anarchism have been broadly critiqued by Indigenous and anti-colonial scholars for submerging concerns about settler colonialism beneath triumphant anti-capitalist rhetoric.[20] Indeed, critiques of capitalism *and* socialism have identified that both systems require the elimination of Indigenous connections to land. Be it to achieve profit or rational efficiency, capitalism and socialism are concerned with achieving control over territory. Indigenous People cannot be considered simply individualized consumers or undifferentiated parts of the proletariat.

These arguments are not new, but it is important to highlight the fact that settler colonialism and capitalism are not one and the same. As such, anti-capitalist efforts may overlap with Indigenous Peoples' struggles, but settler colonialism does not depend on capitalism alone to function. Anti-capitalism is not the same as anti-colonialism. Eve Tuck and Wayne Yang clarify the relationship between settler colonialism and capitalism in North America: "colonialism is not just a symptom of capitalism … Capitalism and the state are technologies of colonialism, developed over time to further colonial projects."[21] Even when well-intentioned, it is misguided to reduce *all* social ills — Settler and Indigenous — to a single, exploitative, exterior force such as capitalism. We have to ask: if a capitalist economy is defeated or dismantled in Canada, what does this actually do to address the illegitimacy of Settler people on the land? The answer is, potentially, very little.

A useful example can be found in the Occupy movements, which flourished during the autumn and winter of 2011 and 2012. Although originating in the United States as Occupy Wall Street, Occupy movements spread around the globe, including major encampments in Montréal, Toronto, and Vancouver. The Occupy movements had no central or defining ethos, but were inspired by anti-austerity measures and opposition to neoliberal capitalism in the wake of the global financial crisis of 2007–8, which saw a huge transfer of wealth to a few capitalist elites. This spawned the slogan "We are the 99 percent," an effort to unite people in struggle against capitalist exploitation by this small, powerful, mega-wealthy group. The Occupy movements created positive shifts in the politico-economic discourse of Canada, but they also demonstrated that it is possible to be a politically radical Settler person, and still a settler colonizer.

In Canada, the concerns of Indigenous communities are not necessarily those of the "99 percent," and "occupation" as term and tactic needs to be understood in the context of Indigenous lands that are and have been occupied by settler colonizers for centuries. As Sandy Grande has noted, the anti-austerity goals of Occupy do not, by definition, contradict settler colonialism:

> the discursive trope and strategy of "occupation" reconstitutes (territorial) appropriation as the democratic manifest and, in so doing, fails to propose something distinct from or counter to the settler state. Indeed, activists are adamant in their assertions that OWS [Occupy Wall Street] is not a protest (one time event) but rather a form of "place-based activism" contingent on local (re)possession. As such, "occupiers" take over public spaces, constructing virtual homesteads complete with kitchens, outdoor classrooms, libraries, sleeping areas, etc.; a strategy that presupposes a colonialist logic that not only proffers its citizens the right to assemble but also the freedom to settle.[22]

In many ways, the Occupy movements returned to powerful settler colonial stories: the exceptional nation, individual equality, and a liberal economy that generates fundamental freedoms if only properly tended and regulated.

The other settler colonial narrative on which the Occupy movements seemed to rely was that of "empty land" — in this case articulated as "public space" — as equally available to all:

> The Occupy movements seek to claim the spaces created by state power and corporate wealth — specific sites such as Zuccotti Park or Wall Street, and more general spaces of urban poverty and suburban collapse. Indigenous occupations, by contrast, have sought to reclaim and reassert relationships to land and place submerged beneath the settler colonial world. Their occupations do not question simply the divisions of wealth and power in [Canada and the United States]; they question the very existence of settler colonial nation states.[23]

Despite the history of Canadian wealth being generated from the exploitation of Indigenous lands, Occupy largely chose to focus on the abuse of power and position by individuals and corporations. Rather than addressing the roots of inequality, the "99 percent" sought to level the playing field *within* the imposed settler colonial system and state, completing the settler colonial end game: Settler and Indigenous disappear, along with the history of colonization, leaving only homogenized (in this case, liberal and progressive) rights-bearing individuals.

From early on in Occupy encampments, Indigenous People expressed concern and frustration with the movements' philosophy and tactics. However, participants only partially engaged with Indigenous concerns. Despite a variety of dialogues in which Indigenous speakers and community leaders exhorted Occupy Toronto members to rethink their approach, asking them to commit to "decolonizing Toronto" instead of re-occupying already contested lands, they were met with resistance.[24] Eventually, Indigenous activists moved to tend a sacred fire at the Occupy Toronto site, continuing to support some of the goals of Occupy Toronto but separating themselves from the mass meetings and other actions of the group. Similar patterns occurred in Montréal, with Indigenous concerns portrayed as an "add on." In Vancouver, despite an initial acknowledgement of Indigenous territory and a strong analysis of settler colonialism in many public forums, this marginalization of Indigenous Peoples and concerns persisted.[25]

The settler colonization of Canada created and creates a vast amount of wealth for colonizers, while forcing Indigenous Peoples to the extreme margins.[26] It is impossible not to feel for the "average Canadians" whose lives have been devastated by job loss, increasing cost of living, decreasing government spending and support, and seemingly no avenue for aid as the wealth gap continues to widen. At the same time, it cannot be ignored that Canadian wealth (especially that of the esteemed home-owning middle class) was and is generated from the exploitation of stolen land. It is hard to seriously claim that "we" are all in this together, when no level of redistribution of wealth that benefits average folks would in any way address Indigenous Peoples' dispossession of their lands. In order to enter that kind of mass movement, Indigenous People must ignore generations of difference-making and dispossession by governments and Settler communities, and assume the role of a politicized minority in solidarity with other minority groups making equivalent claims. Participation is contingent on abandoning fundamental aspects of Indigenous identity and nationhood.

Becoming Settler People

At this point, we have painted a rather unflattering picture: Canada is a state founded on stolen land, predicated on the elimination of Indigenous Peoples, and a nation steeped in racism, violence, and denial. Even social justice movements, from widely accepted multiculturalism to radical anti-capitalist campaigns may fall into the trap of reinforcing this immoral, unethical society of domination and dispossession. Settler colonialism requires that Settler people, in exchange for many purported but often immaterial benefits, participate in systems that commit genocide and seek erasure of Indigenous identities, while also profoundly limiting the possible ways that Settler people can pursue their own economic and political interests. Settler colonialism monopolizes the potential ways that Settler people can *be Settler*. If the cost of belonging is so high, it is awfully hard to see why anyone would want to be a member of Settler Canadian society. And yet, settler society continues to grow and continues to be seen as natural and normal. It continues to evolve, changing to admit new peoples and accommodate various differences that it would or could not in times past. The question, then, is how are people continually recruited to the settler colonial project? How are people convinced to assume and even fight for membership in Settler Canadian society?

Let us recall the triangular relationships described in Chapter 2. In the settler colonial perception, there are three kinds of people: Settler "selves," exogenous "Others," and Indigenous "Others." In this construction, the endgame of settler colonialism will be realized when all exogenous Others are absorbed into or accounted for by the Settler identity, and Indigenous Others are eliminated as a functional threat to Settler belonging. Next, we turn to pathways in Canada that are slowly collapsing these subjectivities by absorbing Others into Settler Canadian society and driving toward complete Settler indigenization on the land.

Managing Indigenous Difference

Settler colonialism does not rely solely on the elimination of Indigenous bodies, but on the elimination of Indigenous identity and peoplehood. That is, Indigenous People can be managed within Settler Canadian society if (and only if) their connections to Nations (sovereignty) and the land are severed. A number of policies in Canadian history have pursued this end. The "enfranchisement" policy of the early twentieth century was specifically designed to draw Indigenous People into Canadian systems of work and education in the belief that this would "civilize" them out of existence as Indigenous. By withdrawing Indian Status from Indigenous People who gained university or college degrees, served in the military, or — in the case of Indigenous women — married non-Status men, it was supposed that Indigenous People could be separated from the land, reserves emptied, and that eventually Indigenous Peoples would disappear altogether into the general Canadian public. In the words of infamous Deputy Superintendent of Indian Affairs, Duncan Campbell Scott: "Our objective is to continue until there is not a single Indian in Canada that has not been absorbed into the body politic and there is no Indian question, and no Indian Department."[27] The enfranchisement policy has officially ended, but echoes of it can still be seen in the way a multicultural Canada seeks to absorb Indigenous Peoples.

The goal of the Indian Residential School (IRS) system was similar. Guided by the belief that children could be forcibly "educated" or essentially reprogrammed out of being Indigenous, official policy separated Indigenous children for long stretches of time from their families and land-based relationships in an effort to make them functionally white. We know it as the early twentieth century call to "kill the Indian to save the child." Further, relocations such as that imposed upon the Sayisi Dene mentioned earlier, or tacit removals through economic pressures or the removal of Status and therefore the right to live on reserves, are strategies often used to force Indigenous Peoples to move into urban environments, or if their cultures were traditionally nomadic or semi-nomadic, to adopt sedentary lifestyles under state surveillance. The city has often been seen as "civilized" space, incompatible with Indigenous connections to the land that were equated with "wilderness" and "nature." Indigenous People living off-reserve and especially in cities have frequently been constructed as "not really Indian," as if the exposure to urban space automatically liquidates Indigenous identity in favour of cosmopolitan multiculturalism.[28] In a practical sense, living the kind of life that settler colonialism constructs as appropriate for Indigenous Peoples — on the reserve, outside of time, poor but grateful — creates an apartheid system of both separate and unequal citizenship. However, at the same time, giving up Treaty Rights and government obligations as part of assimilating into Settler society does not necessarily remove the threat of racist dispossession and violence. As Audra Simpson has discussed with respect to Loretta Saunders, the Inuk woman murdered by her roommates in 2014, Indigenous Peoples can never safely "pass" in settler colonial society — which is to say, the fact that Loretta's features didn't stand out as Indigenous in mainstream Settler Canadian society did not save her life.[29]

Despite all these perils and antagonisms, Indigenous Peoples have found multiple, creative ways to maintain connections to land, to practice land-based cultures in urban environments, and to reaffirm urban spaces as Indigenous spaces. All of this is to say that historical attempts at assimilating Indigenous Peoples through education, removal of Status, relocation, and enforced socioeconomic change have not been successful, though the toll these imposed systems have exacted on Indigenous societies is enormous. Explicit policy aside, Canadian governments have continued to pursue, and many scholars have continued to justify, the absorption of Indigenous identities into Canadian governance and cultural traditions. Glen Coulthard, whose work we have discussed previously, has extensively documented the ways that government "recognition" of Indigenous Peoples is used to deflect from fundamental demands for decolonization. From celebrating revolutionary leaders like Louis Riel as a "founding father" of Canada and "first premier" of Manitoba, to naming Mary Simon governor general, Canadian governments and political leaders consistently bestow hollow honours on Indigenous People instead of taking real, transformative action to address settler colonial racism and dispossession.

Coulthard's concept of the colonial politics of recognition refers to a particular type of assimilationist effort by the Canadian government to circumscribe and define Indigenous Peoples in a way acceptable to Settler Canadian society. It also relies on a homogenization of the many different Indigenous Nations and cultures into "Aboriginal," the term used in section 35 of the Canadian Constitution, defined as "First Nations, Inuit and Métis" people. Even this limited differentiation is artificial, not based on fundamental differences between the cultures of Inuit and Métis nations and other Indigenous Peoples, but rather based on the legal frameworks through which the Canadian state owes obligations to these three groups: Indian Status, Inuit "N-numbers" or disk numbers, and Métis scrip. "First Nations" is a further misnomer, as at the governmental level, the term refers not to actual Indigenous Nations — the Mohawk Nation that spans from Québec to southern Ontario and into New York State, the Wetsuwet'en Nation whose huge territory lies in the Interior of British Columbia — but rather to reserve-based, government recognized bands — Wahta First Nation as separate from other Mohawk Nations, the Wetsuwet'en First Nation as an isolated community on a small reserve outside of Burns Lake. Many Settler Canadians are unaware that band council governments were imposed upon Indigenous Peoples by the Canadian government through the Indian Act in the early twentieth century. This was intended to end and replace traditional forms of governance, and create leaders and systems that could be more easily manipulated to serve state and Settler interests. However, in many cases, traditional governance structures endured alongside — and at times in competition with — band councils. The Canadian government, however, will only negotiate with, enter into agreements with, or disburse funding through band councils, creating a confusing dual system that has contributed to holding reserve communities in a position of dependency.[30] The recognition of Aboriginal rights under the Constitution flows through these legal constructs that seek to minimize collective connections to land and replace them with packages of financial and rights obligations bestowed upon recognized, officially sanctioned individuals.

This tacit, subtle form of assimilation has been generally well received by Settler Canadians, many of whom agree that Indigenous Peoples should have the rights and respect accorded to all minority cultures. Many further acknowledge that the economic and social disparities between Indigenous and Settler communities resulting from "legacies" of colonialism should be ameliorated through aid funnelled to First Nations in the form of economic development. The intent, of course, is to allow Aboriginal communities to participate in and benefit fully from "open and accepting" Canadian society. All of which reinforces the authority of Settler Canadian governments and thus Settler Canadians as the arbiters of what is fair treatment for Indigenous Peoples, and relies on notions of culture and recognition detached from land and sovereignty, or self-determination on those lands. Through aboriginalism, "Canada's Aboriginal people" are given a pride of place within the colonial system, their competing relationships to land ended. Their political relationships are oriented toward the state, and thus ultimately limited by it.[31] This is effectively an ending of Indigenous ways of life and a triumph of settler colonialism. Severed from the land and subsumed in the state, Indigenous identity can be slowly assimilated and disappeared, a form of cultural genocide through governmental "recognition" that denies the most vital parts of Indigenous lifeways.[32]

Absorbing Exogenous Others

Meanwhile, Settler Canadian society is in the constant process of managing, disciplining, and absorbing exogenous Others, perceived as outside or "not one of us," usually based on racialization or having come from somewhere else. This is to be expected, as Canada has always been about negotiating the terms under which fractured groups of often disparate peoples agree to claim land together. Settler colonialism is predicated on the movements of groups of peoples out of previous homelands and into new lands constructed as home. Many groups in Canadian history that would go on to become unquestioned members of Settler Canadian society have not had a great deal in common, openly clashed with each other, and even expressed values and practiced cultures considered incommensurate in a common society. Yet over time, many of these individuals, families, and communities have found ways to negotiate with each other, coming together to form wider Settler communities that may not always agree or even treat each other with respect but whose claims to the land are mutually reinforcing. Consider that Canada in the early nineteenth century was a motley collection of Scottish merchants, poor Irish farmers and labourers, British Loyalists recently expelled from the United States, French-Catholic residents of the former colonies of New France, Acadians, and other groups. It was, in no small part, the American declaration of war in 1812 that brought these disparate communities together in defence of the systems in which they were invested, and in defiance of American systems of governance often seen as corrupt and unwieldy even if Americans themselves were regarded kindly, as family and friends.[33] Or we could look at the way that Chinese, Sikh, and eastern European communities that flocked to the West Coast between the turn of the twentieth century and the end of the Second World War were often extremely marginalized, but have since been successful in winning governmental protection of their rights and, despite ongoing racism, often participate as "proud Canadians" in the social, cultural, and economic life of the country. Then there is the historical legacy of slavery, and contemporary reality of economic indentured servitude that has forced large populations of people from the Global South to labour in Canada. This process has continued throughout Canadian history, as new peoples and new communities have been integrated into Settler Canada, not always smoothly or immediately or to equivalent degrees of privilege, but often to at least limited degrees in the recognition that — as Settler peoples — there is common ground for mutual belonging. To be sure, racism exists in Canada, often expressed in anxieties over who can belong on the land, but so too do avenues for pursuing protection from racism. The Canadian Charter of Rights and Freedoms, for example, can be read as a settler colonial document that provides a framework for integrating new and different settler communities into the existing Settler Canadian society. That has not cured intolerance, but it has created a powerful legal and political channel for many racialized communities to seek redress within the established settler colonial framework.

The forces that compel this expansion of identity and difference in Settler Canada are important to understand because they reframe how we think about what it means to belong as a member of multicultural Canadian society. Settler identity must be understood as an *aspirational* identity. Canadians are proud and often very vocal about the benefits of being a part of Canadian society. Some of this can be measured in demographic terms: Canada is a wealthy country, a member of the G8, and boasts a relatively high quality of life. Other selling points of being Canadian are bound up with myths of peacemaking and multiculturalism, a purported moral authority and ethical freedom that come from belonging to a country with "no history of colonialism." There are many people who, for many very good reasons, want to be a part of Canadian society, and many communities have fought marginalization for years, aspiring to truly belong in Canada.

Established Settler Canadians manage difference with respect to exogenous Others by disciplining people in both official and informal ways, to ensure that newcomer or newly accepted communities buy into and reinforce the colonial systems of Settler Canadian society. The most obvious ways are the citizenship tests, which have been critiqued for reinforcing a white, settler, triumphalist version of Canadian history and almost excluding Indigenous Peoples.[34] Less obvious are the ways that newcomer peoples are recruited via particular forms of employment: many immigrant people who come to Canada have traditionally found work in resource extraction industries or sectors of the labour market related to construction and development. Forestry and logging, mining, unskilled or semi-skilled industrial labour, and construction trades are often comparatively well paid forms of employment, but are also involved in direct exploitation and destruction of Indigenous lands.

There is also what is called the "model minority syndrome," which is rooted in the internalization of social and government definitions of "good multicultural citizenship" through which "certain categories of successful immigrants are used as symbols to discipline ghettoized communities of colour, such as undocumented migrants."[35] It drives immigrant and racialized communities to over-emphasize and embellish their Canadianness, their allegiance to the Canadian system, their commitment to hard work and refusal to take assistance, regardless of whether or not they truly receive any fair or equal treatment. This aspiration to belong forces displays of conformity that overcome perceptions of difference, strengthening and expanding Settler Canadian society.

Some of the most powerful challenges to established Settler Canadian systems of oppression have come from intersectional solidarity work between Indigenous Peoples and marginalized immigrant communities and communities of colour. For example, the work of No One Is Illegal (NOII) has created significant shifts in how some marginalized communities — especially undocumented migrants and refugees — think about what it means to belong in Canada. NOII has argued for migrant rights not by demanding inclusion in and recognition from the Canadian system, but rather by arguing that the system that selectively grants citizenship, arbitrarily deports undocumented migrants and refugees (upon whom the Canadian economy at least partially depends), and disciplines difference is, itself, illegitimate. NOII tries, whenever possible, to foreground Indigenous Nations, and the rights of those Nations to determine for themselves who can live on their lands and be welcomed as guests according to their protocols. As a result, Indigenous communities have worked with NOII to oppose deportations, and undocumented workers have marched, protested, and participated in direct actions to prevent the destruction of Indigenous lands.[36] This burgeoning alliance between peoples perceived as Other by Settler Canadian society has the potential to shake the foundations of settler colonial structures of invasion, and move us away from settler colonialism and the politics of aspirationalism and assimilation.

Settler Benefits:
Mobility and Comfortable Ignorance

As we have shown, it is nearly impossible to not know something of the colonial violence and genocidal nature of settler colonial Canada, through the actions of the state to physically starve, remove, and attack Indigenous Peoples, to impose systems of institutionalized "care" through social work, education, and health provision that force assimilation and cause harm, and the narratives and myths that erase Indigenous presence and agency. Yet, frequently, Canadians seem — or claim — to "not know" about Indigenous Peoples' struggles, even those that have the potential to directly impact the lives and properties of Settler communities. Settler Canadians in Port Alberni, BC, have remained largely ignorant of the existence or implementation of the Maa-nulth Treaty that directly impacts the town and that went into effect in 2011 accompanied by large public ceremonies and celebrations.[37] Similarly, even as phrases like "land back" have come into wider usage, and Settler Canadians have been forced to grapple with the implication of Indigenous demands for the restoration of land and territory to Indigenous Nations, their full import is lost on many people. As Julie Tomiak has argued, both proponents and critics of the term and concept "land back" often equate "land" with rural or wilderness areas, ignoring that cities too are Indigenous territories.[38] Even if this were understood, Settler Canadians continue largely in ignorance of what "land back" actually means — a restoration of relationships to land and place and between the many parts that make up that place, in such a way as to not only transfer authority to Indigenous Nations but to radically reshape how land is treated. As the Land Back Editorial Collective wrote in a 2020 issue of *Briarpatch Magazine*:

> when we say "Land Back" we aren't asking for just the ground, or for a piece of paper that allows us to tear up and pollute the earth. We want the system that is land to be alive so that it can perpetuate itself, and perpetuate us as an extension of itself. That's what we want back: our place in keeping land alive and spiritually connected.[39]

Settler colonial ignorance in this case is based on not just a lack of awareness of issues, but on an inability or unwillingness to appreciate the full implications of Indigenous claims.

Likewise, despite decades of court cases, media coverage, and government apologies, many Canadians continue to deny the harms of residential schools, sparking a troubling and harmful trend that Cherokee scholar, Daniel Heath Justice, and Settler Canadian scholar, Sean Carleton, have labelled "residential school denialism."[40] Ignorance is at times intentionally performed in order to prevent Indigenous Peoples' concerns from impacting public discourses on multiculturalism and belonging, ensuring that "minority rights" eclipse Indigenous claims to land, as occurred in Québec around the Bouchard-Taylor Commission in 2007–08.[41] The mental acrobatics required to overlook oceans of evidence of systemic violence against Indigenous women, the intentional harm of the Residential School System, assimilation agendas, and the marginalization of all manner of difference, and to continue to identify with a multicultural, peacemaker nation are incredible. There is a palpable strain, at times, that results from being a Settler Canadian in the face of so much valid criticism and truth telling. So, what is it that convinces Canadians to continue to participate in settler colonialism?

It is important to recognize that there are major perceived benefits to being Settler Canadian. We prefer to discuss "benefits" but a similar concept may be more familiar. Privilege, a way of explaining how experiences of social interactions are uneven based on race, class, appearance, and other socially constructed qualities, is an increasingly common way of analyzing social inequality. Privilege tends to operate in two ways. Feminist and critical race theorist Sarah Ahmed has described privilege as an "energy-saving device" that lets one do or access something more easily (or at all) when access for perceived Others is more difficult, energy intensive, or impossible.[42] Being a white male in a corporate environment makes promotion easier when one is constantly being evaluated and judged by other white males, who often make assumptions that people who look and sound like themselves will play by the same social rules and thus not threaten their own position. The second way that privilege operates is as a buffer or crumple zone that shields the privileged from the effects of their actions. Here, class privilege provides a good example. Corporate and investment bankers may make decisions that cost hundreds and thousands of people their jobs, or their homes, or their health or educational options. However, living in gated communities or high-priced condominiums, out of the reach of the middle and lower classes, they are unlikely to have to face or be confronted by the people directly impacted by their decisions.

In Canada, two of the most powerful forms of privilege are tied to race and class. Class privilege is produced by capitalist systems that create economic inequality, privileging those higher up the wealth ladder, while white privilege is a product of white supremacy and based on the oppression of other groups. Both class inequality and whiteness are social processes born out of complex historical processes; both are reproduced through political, economic, cultural, and social institutions. There are many other types of privilege as well: patriarchy produces male privilege, heteronormativity produces straight cisgender privilege, and, as you might expect, settler colonialism produces Settler privileges.

However, while Settler privileges exist, we prefer to discuss Settler *benefits* to clarify the relationship between the expectation of advantage (benefits) and actual possession of privilege in the settler colonial context. Famed sociologist, Stuart Hall, argued that identities coalesce around layers of privilege: as people experience privileges, they come to identify with particular groups whose lives are typified by the same energy-saving devices and convenient insulators.[43] Similarly, in settler colonial societies like Canada, our ways of living on the land are supposed to produce certain benefits — the "gifts of civilization" that justify the displacement of Indigenous Peoples and ways of being from the land — and we come to identify with those benefits. However, as Beenash Jafri argues, discussed in Chapter 2, we do not all get them all the time and we do not all experience them evenly. Most importantly, some of those benefits do not actually exist: they are based on racist myths or rewritten histories and as such they only exist in the Settler Canadian imagination. When we say the "benefits" of identifying as a Settler, we are talking about both real privileges but also aspects of being a Settler Canadian that are just assumed to be better than a "nasty, brutish and short" existence in the wilderness. This is regardless of whether Settler people actually experience specific privileges or if they simply believe that they have a particularly "special" existence tied to nationalism and Canadian exceptionalism.

The first "benefit" of being Settler Canadian is mobility. In 2008, we attended a meeting of a reading group started by education scholar Trish Rosborough (Kwagiulth) to help educate provincial government personnel about Indigenous Peoples, histories, and contemporary conflicts. As part of the first meeting, Trish hung up a world map and asked attendees to put pins in the map anywhere they had family connections in living memory. As people traced their family histories, pins multiplied, filling Europe,

North America, South America, Australia, New Zealand, and parts of Asia and Africa. Then Trish stood up and placed one pin in Port Hardy, Kwakwaka'wakw territory. The Settler members of staff were suddenly confronted with a very visual explanation of their "settlerness": within their own recent family histories, they had collectively traversed almost the entire planet, and ultimately landed there, on Lekwungen territory, in Victoria, BC. The stories may have been fascinating or banal, personal or shared, but they had never before been seen as embodying a particular kind of benefit that many Indigenous Peoples might not share. Yet, this too needed further unpacking. The experiences of this group were not universal, and questions were immediately raised about how and why people moved. What started as a discussion about relationships to land became a discussion about relationships to systems of power and about how the mobility that many of us associate with our contemporary experiences is often built on deeper histories of forced relocation, diaspora, and enslavement.

This Settler mobility should not be confused with Indigenous "mobility," which we have discussed as linked to seasonal movements and cultural or religious practices, nor should it be undermined by the many Settler Canadians who have very long — sometimes multigenerational — tenure on the land or who, because of lack of socioeconomic privilege, may never leave their home community. This purported benefit inheres in the understanding that, theoretically, any Settler *could* move, *could* relocate to a different part of the country, without appealing for permission. The way that many seasonal labourers or construction and trade workers are forced to move from place to place is actually portrayed as a good thing: we are told that people are lucky to be able to chase economic benefits across the country and internationally. But it must be remembered that it is mobility only within the existing political economic system. The "benefit" of mobility is only truly a benefit if one accepts that there is no other way that we could make a material living on the land, something that Indigenous ways of being disprove. As such, Indigenous mobilities, linked to family ties, ceremonial rounds, seasonal economies, and dynamic forms of governance, are denied as the wrong kind of mobility.

Mobility, as it is conceived within Settler Canadian society, is part of what allows individuals to pursue greatness and success, to rise in terms of wealth and happiness by relocating to pursue education, employment, or the best possible environment for one's own hopes and desires. Further, while Settler peoples generally seek to connect to the land through structures such as the political and legal systems that allow individuals to claim discrete packets of property, the expansive and pervasive Settler Canadian nation and state mean that Settler Canadians can move around over huge territories and still assume that they belong wherever they go. Mobility on the land is mirrored by the myths of mobility within social structures. Canadian society is entangled with a long-standing narrative of people coming from somewhere else and becoming happier, more successful, and more "at home" here than they could ever have been "there." However, while mobility is a purported benefit of Settler Canadian society, it is also a double-edged sword.

Unstated in the benefit of Settler mobility is that Settler Canadians must also surrender attachments to other places of belonging. It might be acceptable to cheer for one's nation of origin or heritage during the World Cup, but performances of Canadianness must predominate most of the time. The ability to be mobile within Canada comes with a demand that one constantly recognize how fortunate one is to have that mobility, how happy one is to be Canadian, how much better life is here in Canada. Further, mobility is only a benefit when it is used within the established systems of power in Canadian society. Migrant farm workers are also mobile, many homeless and poor people are (precariously) mobile, and even tradespeople working on construction projects must be willing to uproot and follow new projects or have their names dropped to the bottom of employment lists. People are expected to move when and how they are told to pursue particular, often economic, opportunities. Other kinds of mobility — the mobility associated with seasonal moves between fishing camps and winter villages, for example, as was a common practice among Indigenous Nations on both the Atlantic and Pacific coasts — are instead taken as a sign of barbaric and uncivilized behaviour. These movements supported very different kinds of political economies (such as gift economies) and relationships to place than those incoming settler colonizers sought to impose. Indigenous People could not be made to labour if they were not pinned down, and the land could not be exploited while communities of people kept living on it.

The second benefit of being Settler Canadian is the benefit of not knowing, or the ability to claim a soothing ignorance about, the negative impacts of settler colonialism and the moral turpitude rightfully due to its collaborators. This ignorance is enacted in a number of ways. First and most obvious is the simple privilege of not having to encounter and internalize negative or critical histories of Canada, its peoples, and regions. When governments do make (limited) apologies, such as the one they proffered in 2008 about the legacies of the Residential School System, it is a moment of recalling in order to forget — admitting "mistakes" so that we can move on without the moral burden of rectifying past harm and more easily avoid acknowledging present problems. Of course, as discussed earlier with respect to the peacemaker myth, there is so much evidence and so many people speaking out about the harms of settler colonialism in Canada's past and present, that insisting on not knowing would require considerable effort in the absence of the systems and structures that make this selective amnesia possible.

When evidence of colonial harm is presented that cannot simply be ignored, Settler Canadians tend to reframe the discourse, admitting that the harm exists but transferring the cause — and responsibility — to other people, usually to the communities that are being harmed. Contemporary poverty, political dysfunction, substance abuse, suicide, or epidemic health issues in Indigenous communities are often reframed by Settler Canadians as being the result of Indigenous communities' poor choices, predilection to harmful behaviour, laziness, or willful backwardness. For example, when the final report of the Inquiry into Missing and Murdered Indigenous Women (MMIW) was released in 2019, it made clear that the MMIW epidemic is evidence of ongoing genocide. Further, the Inquiry released a supplementary volume on the province of Québec, citing "specific issues such as language barriers, health and social services provided by religious congregations and interaction with Indigenous and provincial police forces" as contributing factors in the epidemic. Yet despite all this evidence, traditional and social media are filled with Settler Canadians asserting that if Indigenous women are being disappeared (which they often deny), then the "obvious" reason is violence by Indigenous men. In short, they re-present the historical "Indian problem" in which Indigenous Peoples are constructed as responsible for the direct and generational harm they have suffered and endured at the hands of colonial systems and individuals.

When Chief Theresa Spence demanded attention to the housing crisis in Attawapiskat — coming to a head with her hunger strike outside the House of Commons in December 2012 — the public response was often to dismiss chronic underfunding from the federal government and instead to focus on accounting errors by the band government. This type of willful ignorance can even be dressed up in morally upright expressions of concern: Why should Aboriginal people have to suffer under these corrupt, despotic governments (regardless of the fact that they are created, mandated, and micro-/mismanaged by the federal government)? Why are their leaders not held to the same standards as ours (who are, of course, all ethically pristine public servants only ever concerned with the welfare of Canadian citizens)? The mental contortions that Settler Canadians perform to reconstruct generations of malnutrition, poor housing, insufficient or faulty infrastructure, isolation, and economic stagnation as the fault of relatively powerless band councils rather than government neglect and undermining of Indigenous political authority are staggering.

Settler people avoid questioning the centrality of settler colonialism in our lives by refusing to even consider settler colonialism as a historical and ongoing project. We also avoid talking about or pursuing in any great detail other possible ways of relating to the land or to Indigenous Peoples. Settler colonialism structures all lives in Canada, not just Indigenous ones. To be certain, the structures that Settler Canadians are made to inhabit and move within are luxurious by comparison to Indigenous Peoples' assigned spaces — the privileges and benefits that come with being a Settler Canadian are both material and conceptual and many Canadians would have trouble conceiving of life without them. But at what cost?

We cannot have an open conversation in Canada about the ethical, moral, environmental, spiritual, and cultural costs of circumscribing our entire society within settler colonial spaces, systems, and stories — yet. If we want to change the conversation, more and more Settler Canadians must come face-to-face with the fear of looking beyond the limits of settler colonialism and consider what life could look like without it.

Notes

1   Jean Barman, "Race, Greed and Something More: The Erasure of Urban Indigenous Space in Early Twentieth-Century British Columbia," in *Making Settler Colonial Space: Perspectives on Race, Place and Identity*, eds. Tracey Banivanua Mar and Penelope Edmonds, (New York: Palgrave-Macmillan, 2010), 155–75; Cole Harris, "How Did Colonialism Dispossess? Comments from an Edge of Empire," *Annals of the Association of American Geographer* 94, 1 (2004); Chris Arnett, *Terror of the Coast: Land Alienation and Colonial War on Vancouver Island and the Gulf Islands, 1849–1863* (Vancouver: Talonbooks, 1999); Howard Adams, *Prison of Grass: Canada from a Native Point of View* (Fifth House, 1999).

2   Intersectionality is a concept articulated by American legal scholar Kimberlé Crenshaw in response to the experiences of Black women in the American legal system. She argues that, by treating Black women either as Black or as women but not as both, particular challenges and realities faced by Black women were ignored,

challenges that were not faced by white women or Black men. Intersectionality has since been taken up as a highly useful framework for analyzing how multiple identities and group belongings interact and coexist and that they bring their own particular combinations of challenges and/or privileges.

3   Afua Cooper, *The Hanging of Angelique: The Untold Story of Canadian Slavery and the Burning of Old Montreal* (Athens, GA: University of Georgia Press, 2007).
4   For more on the Chinese Head Tax, see the webpage of the Chinese Canadian National Council: ccnc.ca/redress/history.html.
5   On the Komagata Maru, see komagatamarujourney.ca/.
6   For more details, see, Irving Abella and Harold Troper, *None Is Too Many: Canada and the Jews of Europe, 1933–1948* (Toronto: Lester & Orpen Dennys, 1983).
7   For an interesting examination of the overlap between Canada confronting the impacts of Japanese internment and the TRC on residential schools, see, Jennifer Matsunaga, "Carefully Considered Words: The Influence of Government on Truth Telling about Japanese Canadian Internment and Indian Residential Schools," *Canadian Ethnic Studies* 53, 2 (2021).
8   Amy Go, Dora Nipp, and Winnie Ng, "What This UNB Professor Practices Is Intolerance, Not Sociology," *Globe and Mail,* January 22, 2015, theglobeandmail.com/globe-debate/what-this-unb-professor-practices-is-intolerance-not-sociology/article22573743/.
9   Robyn Maynard, *Policing Black Lives: State Violence in Canada from Slavery to the Present* (Halifax: Fernwood Press, 2017).
10 Carol Schick, "White Resentment in Settler Society," *Race, Ethnicity & Education* 17, 1 (2014); Anne O'Connell, "An Exploration of Redneck Whiteness in Multicultural Canada," *Social Politics: International Studies in Gender, State and Society* 17, 4 (2010).
11 Dwanna Robertson, "Invisibility in the Color-Blind Era: Examining Legitimized Racism against Indigenous Peoples," *American Indian Quarterly* 39, 2 (2015).
12 Jodi Byrd, *The Transit of Empire: Indigenous Critiques of Colonialism* (Minneapolis: University of Minnesota Press, 2011).
13 Paula Madden, *African Nova Scotian–Mi'Kmaw Relations* (Halifax: Fernwood Publishing, 2009).
14 Scott Morgensen, "Queer Settler Colonialism in Canada and Israel: Articulating Two-Spirit and Palestinian Queer Critiques," *Settler Colonial Studies* 2, 2 (2012); "Settler Homonationalism: Theorizing Settler Colonialism within Queer Modernities," *glq: A Journal of Lesbian and Gay Studies* 16, 1–2 (2010).
15 See for example, Richard J.F. Day, *Multiculturalism and the History of Canadian Diversity* (University of Toronto Press, 2000); Sneja Gunew, *Haunted Nations: The Colonial Dimensions of Multiculturalisms* (New York: Routledge, 2004).
16 For more on the relationship between the Indian Act and contemporary settler colonialism, please see, Adam J. Barker, Toby Rollo, and Emma Battell Lowman, "Settler Colonialism and the Consolidation of Canada in the 20th Century," in *World History of Settler Colonialism,* eds. Edward Cavanagh and Lorenzo Veracini (London: Routledge, 2016).
17 Eva Mackey, *The House of Difference: Cultural Politics and National Identity in Canada* (University of Toronto Press, 2002).

18 Lorenzo Veracini, *Settler Colonialism: A Theoretical Overview* (London: Palgrave Macmillan, 2010), 48
19 Ivan Sablin and Maria Savelyeva, "Mapping Indigenous Siberia: Spatial Changes and Ethnic Realities, 1900–2010," *Settler Colonial Studies* 1, 1 (2011), 105.
20 Glen Coulthard, *Red Skin, White Masks: Rejecting the Colonial Politics of Recognition* (Minneapolis: University of Minnesota Press, 2014); Adam J. Barker and Jenny Pickerill, "Radicalizing Relationships to and through Shared Geography: Why Anarchists Need to Understand Indigenous Connections to Land and Place," *Antipode* 44, 5 (2012).
21 Eve Tuck and K. Wayne Yang, "Decolonization Is Not a Metaphor," *Decolonization: Indigeneity, Education & Society* 1, 1 (2012), 4.
22 Sandy Grande, "Accumulation of the Primitive: The Limits of Liberalism and the Politics of Occupy Wall Street," *Settler Colonial Studies* 3, 3–4 (2013), 370.
23 Adam J. Barker "'A Direct Act of Resurgence, a Direct Act of Sovereignty': Reflections on Idle No More, Indigenous Activism, and Canadian Settler Colonialism," *Globalizations* 12, 1 (2014).
24 Leanne Simpson, "Indigenous Perspectives on Occupation, Occupy Toronto Talks," Leanne Betasamosake Simpson, blog, February 1, 2012, leannesimpson.ca/2012/02/01/indigenous-perspectives-on-occupation-occupy-toronto-talks/.
25 Konstantin Kilibarda, "Lessons from #Occupy in Canada: Contesting Space, Settler Consciousness and Erasures within the 99%," *Journal of Critical Globalization Studies* 5 (2012), 28–30.
26 This dynamic has been well established, especially by Indigenous scholars, over many years. For example, see, Howard Adams, *Prison of Grass: Canada from a Native Point of View* (Saskatoon, SK: Fifth House Publishers, 1989), and Coulthard, *Red Skin, White Masks*.
27 J.R. Miller, *Skyscrapers Hide the Heavens: A History of Indian–White Relations in Canada* (University of Toronto Press, 1989).
28 See, for example, Paige Raibmon, *Authentic Indians: Episodes of Encounter from the Late 19th Century Northwest Coast* (Durham: Duke University Press, 2005). Alternatively, in a few cases, urban areas with high Indigenous populations become seen as "dangerous" or "wild" by mainstream Settler society, as happened with the Vancouver Downtown East Side for many years, see, Dara Culhane, "Their Spirits Live within Us: Aboriginal Women in Downtown Eastside Vancouver Emerging Into Visibility," *American Indian Quarterly* 27, 3 (2003); Amber Dean, "Space, Temporality, History: Encountering Hauntings in Vancouver's Downtown Eastside," in *The West and Beyond*, eds. Alvin Finkel, Sarah Carter, and Peter Fortna (Athabasca University Press, 2010).
29 Audra Simpson, "The Chief's Two Bodies: Theresa Spence and the Gender of Settler Sovereignty," RACE2014 Keynote: Edmonton, AB (2014), vimeo.com/110948627.
30 For more on this, see, Taiaiake Alfred, "Colonialism and State Dependency," *International Journal of Indigenous Health* 5, 2 (2009).
31 "Aboriginalism" draws from the language of "Aboriginal" in section 35 of the Canadian Constitution. The same section subdivides "Aboriginal" into "Status Indian" or "First Nations," "Métis," and "Inuit." Of course, these designations are applied to those identified as such by the Canadian state. As a result, all manner of erasures occur — some

"First Nations" cultures and social systems are radically different from each other and may be more similar to Métis or Inuit systems, but these differences are immaterial to how Canada relates to these different Peoples. This is partially why we use the term "Indigenous," which has been used and defined much more broadly and inclusively in international discourses.

32 Coulthard, "Subjects of Empire."
33 Alan Taylor, *The Civil War of 1812: American Citizens, British Subjects, Irish Rebels, & Indian Allies* (New York: Vintage Books, 2010).
34 Adele Perry and Esyllt Jones, *People's Citizenship Guide: A Response to Conservative Canada* (Winnipeg: Arbeiter Ring Press, 2011).
35 Harsha Walia, "Transient Servitude: Migrant Labour in Canada and the Apartheid of Citizenship," *Race & Class* 52, 1 (2010), 82.
36 For more on NOII and intersectional activism, see, Walia, *Undoing Border Imperialism*.
37 Vanessa Sloan Morgan and Heather Castleden, "An Exploration of Indigenous-Settler Relations in the Port Alberni Valley, British Columbia Regarding Implementation of the 2011 Maa-nulth Treaty," *The Canadian Geographer* 58, 4 (2014). doi:10.1111/cag.12120.
38 Julie Tomiak, "Land Back / Cities Back," *Urban Geography* 44, 2 (2023).
39 Nickita Longman et al., "'Land Back' is More Than the Sum of its parts," *Briarpatch Magazine,* September 2020, briarpatchmagazine.com/articles/view/land-back-is-more-than-the-sum-of-its-parts.
40 Ravi Da Costa and Tom Clark, "Testimonial Textures: Examining the Poetics of Non-Indigenous Stories about Reconciliation," In *Storytelling: Critical and Creative Approaches*, edited by Jan Shaw, Philippa Kelly, and L.E. Semler (London: Palgrave Macmillan, 2013).
41 Anne Godlewska, Laura Schaefli, and Paul Chaput, "First Nations Assimilation Through Neoliberal Educational Reform," *The Canadian Geographer* 57, 3 (2013).
42 Sarah Ahmed, "Brick Walls: Racism & Other Hard Histories," Presented at Race Conference 2014: Unsettling Conversations, Unmaking Racisms & Colonialisms, University of Alberta (2014).
43 Stuart Hall, "Cultural Identity and Cinematic Representation," in *Black British Cultural Studies: A Reader*, eds. Houston Baker, Manthia Diawara, and Ruth Lindeborg (Chicago: University of Chicago Press, 1996).

Fear, Complicity, and Productive Discomfort

UP TO NOW, WE HAVE LARGELY FOCUSED ON BELONGING in Settler Canadian society in the ways that it enhances the lives of Settler colonizers who participate in the structures of invasion foundational to Canadian society. But we would be remiss not to point out that there is both offer of reward and threat of punishment involved in Settler belonging in Canada. Scratch the surface of Settler Canadian identity, and there is a deep well of anxiety and even terror of what it might mean to be cut off from the structures of invasion that define us. Fear is a powerful disciplinary tool and also a deeply ingrained, reflexive part of the Settler Canadian identity. Fear results when we have been *unsettled*, which is to say, when Settler people are discomforted in the process of confronting how much and how profoundly our lives are structured by colonialism.

Settler Fear

Settler Canadians face the fear of losing our simultaneously free and insulated existence when we recognize our participation in settler colonialism. The realization and the associated need to respond in some way to the evidence of our colonial complicity shakes the Settler colonial identity to the core. It challenges the invisibility and taken-for-granted nature of settler colonialism, and it disrupts settler colonial indigenization and normalization.

Alongside the recognition of Settler complicity with colonialism comes the revelation — sometimes sudden — of a potential moral or ethical imperative to challenge the structures of colonialism. The jarring impact of becoming aware of settler colonialism at work in not just one place, not just one aspect of our lives, but nearly everywhere and seemingly all the time, is almost inevitably going to generate a response. However, that response runs up immediately against the same social, economic, and political structures that provide Canadians with a sense of legitimate belonging on the land, wealth and material comfort, and a strong political and cultural identity.

The fear that disciplines Settler people into continuing to support and collaborate with settler colonialism has two sources: external and internal. The first is a response to threats imposed on people when they contradict or oppose powerful institutions: it is the fear of authority, a fear that those same institutions that provide privileges might take them away.[1] Most Canadians never experience this kind of fear because they never seek to contradict powerful political and corporate elites or their vision of Canadian society. But studies of social movements have shown that there are also people who disagree with various laws, policies, or actions and would contradict government or corporate power, but do not actually become involved in organizing or participating in social mobilizations because of fear of reprisal. The massive, overwhelming deployment of police resources used against protest movements that seek to occupy and camp in public spaces — which include anti-capitalist camps, environmental campaigners disrupting logging and mineral extraction routes, and unhoused people protesting the lack of affordable housing, to name just a few — is part of recent policing tactics focused on "strategic incapacitation." This refers to the use of barricades, criminalization of public protest gatherings or marches, and constant obvious surveillance — all of which is designed to prevent protest movements from taking root in physical spaces.[2] The huge light towers and fences, reminiscent of a prison yard, assert that the police are in direct, physical control of protest spaces, and warn of impending violence should that authority be challenged. These reprisals are then paradoxically described as the "fault" of protesters or social movement actors, who are portrayed in media and police reports as inherently violent, and thus bringing the force of the police and state down on themselves.[3]

Increasingly in Canada, dissent that challenges the colonial, capitalist, racial order, is heavily policed — state surveillance is the expectation, not the exception. The overlap of policing and capitalism has led to heavy-handed tactics like those seen at the G20 summit protests in Toronto in 2010, or the RCMP attacks on Elsipogtog in 2012 during anti-fracking protests. The increased use of "kettling" to contain protesters; the use of chemical weapons, baton charges, and intimidation tactics to clear roadways for economic leaders of oil and gas exploration; and the surveillance and random arrests of community leaders and vocal opponents have all become frequent tools of police at all levels.

A prime example of this pre-emptive quashing of dissent is Bill C-51. This controversial "anti-terrorism" legislation passed into law in May 2015, essentially legalizing and formalizing many of the tactics used against protesters and activists of various kinds for many years, including unwarranted surveillance, the definition of opposition to pipeline construction and similar kinds of advocacy as "economic terrorism," and massive expansion of police powers to arrest and detain almost anyone without due process. As law professor, Pam Palmater, argued in her statement on Bill C-51 before the House of Commons, this disproportionately affects Indigenous Peoples who throughout history have had to engage in "criminal" acts because Indigenous lifestyles themselves were considered illegal. "We had to be criminal," she explains, "as in we had to break the law in order to preserve our lives, our physical security, and our identity." She further explains:

> In every single instance we have been labelled as criminals, treated as criminals, and one need only look at the current prison population to understand that this is still the case. Not just the case, but, as Howard Sapers from the Office of the Correctional Investigator has indicated, a national crisis and embarrassment. And why? Not because we're actually terrorists. Not because we're more culturally predisposed to being criminals, but as a direct result of Canada's discriminatory laws and policies. There have been endless justice inquiries which have pointed to the infection in our Canadian justice system of racism.[4]

The criminalization of Indigenous Peoples through this kind of legislation and cooperation between settler colonial and capitalist interests and elites can have a chilling effect on social movements but it also dampens broader support or potential engagement more generally. This sort of criminalization of dissent generates a pervasive sense of fear that affects individuals and social movements seeking justice at the expense of the powerful, and deters many people — of all backgrounds — from engaging with causes that they might otherwise support.

The second type of fear related to social change, however, is specific to the settler colonial situation. It is the existential fear that comes from the potential loss of belonging on the land, the return to "rootlessness," the nightmarish recollection of stories of being expelled or having to leave that lurk in the background of frontier and peacemaker narratives.[5] For the Settler colonizer, the recognition of complicity and personal benefit in a settler society based on the active oppression and dispossession of Others necessarily raises the uncertainty of what confronting colonialism might mean. Would we (Settler people) be subjected to the same treatment that was imposed on them (Indigenous Peoples)? Might we have to leave our homes, to be restricted to tiny pockets of land, or be displaced entirely? We cannot count the number of times that, while discussing colonialism and Indigenous resurgence with Settler people, the unprompted response has been a blurted and almost frantic question: "Well, what are we supposed to do? *Leave?*" More recently, discussions of decolonization through the lens of "land back" have raised accusations of ethnonationalism and the fear of racial purges should Indigenous People regain some control of their territories. This is the real root of the fear — what an end to colonial privilege might mean for the Settler. That strong, emotional, and defensive reaction shuts down conversations of how relationships on the land *could* be different and what that might mean for everybody, not just Settler people.

Settler people have a deep unspoken fear of losing privileged positions within colonial hierarchies. When we have the majority of the wealth and private property, relative freedom of movement, unstated cultural dominance, and power over many marginalized groups in society, it is nearly impossible to imagine what life on egalitarian terms would be like. Albert Memmi, writing about settler colonialism in Africa, made a perceptive observation that applies in Canada today:

> Finally [the Settler person] realizes that everything may change. He invokes the end of colonization, but refuses to conceive that this revolution can result in the overthrow of his situation and himself. For it is too much to ask one's imagination to visualize one's own end, even if it be in order to be reborn another; especially if, like the colonizer, one can hardly evaluate such a rebirth.[6]

Settler Canadians who are not motivated out of greed for an *increasing* accumulation of power, privilege, and wealth can be subdued by the threat of a *decrease* in these things. This is perhaps why so many Canadians who become aware of colonial injustices put their faith in liberal social reformism — fairer elections, economic development, cultural protection, and even the right to peacefully protest in pursuit of these things — that require little self-critical reflection, and no loss of settler benefits by Canadians.

In part the Settler's fear stems from an inability to control Indigenous relationships to the land, and resulting inability to see how those relationships might imply responsibilities for newcomers and settlers. In that incomprehension lies a fear of the unknown. Connections between Indigenous Peoples and the land itself are a source of extraordinary power and incredible responsibility — to maintain balance, to respect the agency of all elements of a place, to care for sacred sites — which contradicts the short-sighted and environmentally extractive relationships that Settler Canadians have with the land (especially at present). Simply, a serious engagement with Indigenous place-based ways of being exposes by contrast the destructive and profoundly unequal nature of Settler Canadian society. The famed environmentalist, Jerry Mander, has argued that "Western societies fear, hate, destroy, and also revere Indians, precisely because they express the parts of our personal and cultural psyches that we must suppress in order to function in the world as we do."[7] Indigenous place-based ways of being expose a particular kind of anxiety in Settler people, a concern for "settler futurity."[8] That is, Indigenous relationships to land are so fundamentally challenging to Settler Canadian claims to land that the Settler reaction to being exposed to Indigenous calls for justice is to worry almost exclusively about "rescuing a settler future" and re-establishing Settler normalcy.[9]

The existential fear of the loss of settler colonial benefits is bound up with a fear of Others. Remember the reliance of settler colonial narratives on tropes of Indigenous "savagery," and simultaneously, when settler colonialism is understood, Settler people must admit that their own history is one of violence, oppression, and injustice. In no small measure, this is anticipatory fear: a product of the expectation that Indigenous Peoples will seek revenge, the fear that what cannot or will not be "given back" will be taken by force. Settler colonizers fear Indigenous resurgence movements because the stronger those nations are, the more unavoidable their legitimate claims to land.

There is a connection to be made here to the suspicions of Indigenous claims to land that Daniel Coleman has discussed in the poetic articulations of diasporic populations (Chapter 3). For individuals and communities for whom the experience of losing a homeland or of being forced into migration is fresh, the potential threat of being made to move again has a particularly strong impact. As such, communities of dispossessed peoples can be brought into settler colonial complicity without receiving many of the purported benefits of settler colonial society because the fear of oppression within the Canadian state is less than the threat posed by a misunderstood perspective on Indigenous claims to place. Coleman explains:

> Indigeneity and diaspora are proximate cultural formations, having in common the experiences of displacement from a homeland and marginalization in the metropolitan settler state, but the differences in their histories of displacement have given them such different political trajectories that the distance between them cannot simply be got across.[10]

It is this distance on common ground that is leveraged to generate fear in communities of people with tenuous connections to the land — a fear of the unknown, which allows settler colonial elites to position Indigenous Peoples as a threat when in reality, forced mobility is far more likely to result from the neoliberal whims of state and capital power.

Fear is central to the operation and continuation of settler colonialism even for Settler people more secure in their claims to land because it can also be a reaction to being confronted with the moral repugnancy of settler colonization. This is the purpose of the "politics of embarrassment," a tactic commonly deployed by Indigenous and anti-colonial movements in Canada and globally, whereby the pernicious and inhumane actions of colonial states are revealed in media, through mass public protests, and in international forums.[11] At large scales, states and national governments have difficulty countering the charges levelled through this political tactic, while on the individual level, Settler Canadians often demonstrate instability and defensiveness in the face of these accusations. Exposure to our own settler colonial complicity, and the overwhelming uncertainty of imagining life without our settler colonial benefits, provokes an unpleasant emotional reaction that is often rooted in fear — in this case, a fear of being exposed and further illegitimated, or a fear of having to confront a painful disjuncture between our self-image and the evidence of our actions.[12] Of course, this is not a completely internalized or private reaction.

As we write, we have lived in the United Kingdom for the better part of fifteen years. We have learned during that time that it is easy to have a positive image of Canadians shown to ourselves. In the United Kingdom, the Netherlands, Belgium, France, and many other countries in Europe, the Canadian reputation of being nice, peaceful (and peacekeeping), and certainly less violent than our southern neighbour, has usually preceded us. Despite knowing this reputation is wrong, based on nationalist myths that Canada has woven together with actual histories, and based in no small part on simply not being American, we often find it hard to contradict it in the moment. In those moments, we tend to deflect with a joke about weather, politeness, or bears, which ironically usually just reinforces the image of Canadians that we project, only to have it reflected back at us. At home and abroad our self-image is connected to discourses of nationalism and patriotism, whitestream racial prejudice, and Eurocentric knowledge, just as our actions are often only revealed as destructive when they are contextualized as part of a settler colonial project of nation building. But the point remains that it is difficult to reconcile the cognitive dissonance between how we see ourselves and the harsh reality — we are discouraged from questioning too deeply the wellsprings of our national pride. This emotional disciplining is the "stick" to the "carrot" of Settler benefits. Because Settlers react with fear to being confronted with their colonial complicity, Settler people act to restore the feeling of security and exceptionalism that comes with being Settler Canadian. These actions may be rapid responses, or they may build over time and manifest quietly or as a sudden eruption. But if we slow down the playback, we can focus on that moment of seeing the indefensibility of colonialism, the dishonesty of defining national narratives, the threat of being illegitimate on the land, and the fearful reaction it provokes.

Efforts to escape from unsettling take many forms, so we have been necessarily selective in our choice of examples. The stories and experiences we share in this chapter are drawn from encounters that have left a lasting impression. We call them moves to comfort. All the stories that follow are personal, all these stories are true, and some of them are also about us.

≈

I was a passenger in a car travelling down a steep and winding road late one night on the way home after a group day out. I had been talking with the driver on and off during the few days he had been visiting about the reading I had been doing on colonialism and Canadian political theory. He was interested in what I was studying because he cared about me, and wanted to understand the work that was becoming such an important part of my life. In the car that night, he seemed thoughtful, asking questions about my understanding of colonialism in Canada and Indigenous–Settler relations. It was calm, a conversation, and I felt good that he was taking the time and effort to inquire so thoughtfully into my interests and work. I remember that he had been quiet in the car for a while, just driving. We were quiet. Suddenly, he started slamming the steering wheel with both hands. Over and over, hard. He started shouting "I didn't take land from anybody," "I've never hurt anyone," "I shouldn't have to give up what I've worked for."

It was jarring, and frightening. His response was so sudden, physical, and explosive that it overrode even his usual strong concern to keep his passengers safe when he was behind the wheel. I was scared. He was so *angry*.

≈

We gathered as a small group, no more than twenty or so people, in a mostly empty basement room in a building on campus. We were a mixed group — some Indigenous, some not, some university educated, some not, multiple genders and ages and backgrounds — and our intent was to work together as an "Indigenous solidarity" group. This was not the first meeting: we had been coming together every couple of weeks for several months. Things began with members introducing a series of points for discussion, things that were going on that we could participate in or support, some ideas for developing our own capacity. The conversations meandered, somewhat productively, for a time. But then, the mea culpas began. Someone — that night it was a white Settler woman — began crying while we were discussing a condominium development that was going to result in the destruction of a local sacred site and clear-cutting of a significant area of forest. She made a show of not making a show, dabbing her eyes and sniffling but otherwise saying nothing, until she was asked if she was okay. Then she burst forth, full of guilt and shame, at the actions of her people. She was ashamed about how ignorant and destructive white people like her could be, and it made her feel so awful.

Others jumped in; they began sharing stories of how they, too, felt *guilty*, overwhelmed by guilt, so terrifically responsible and so insufficient for the task of taking up that responsibility. Indigenous members of the group were moved to declare that they didn't "blame" her or anyone in this group, and how grateful they were that white Settler people were there, trying our best. Like too many meetings, no concrete plans for action were moved forward that night.

≈

I thought of myself as an experienced anti-colonial ally when I started working with a radical political magazine. I had the chance to work with an activist, a woman of colour with a long history of community organizing, who I knew by reputation to be extremely ethical, effective, and inspiring in social justice efforts. During our first time working together, as part of a guest editorial collective, we talked on the phone and I tried to be respectful and careful as we worked out how to bring an article together. Yet no matter what I said or suggested, she corrected me at every turn — my language, my approach, whose voices I was centring. She was polite but completely straightforward and clear about her arguments and positions. It intimidated and irritated me and I was angry. And she was *right*. Every time.

≈

It was an argument on social media, so we should have known it was not going to be productive, but we knew at least some of the folks involved in real life and so felt an obligation to intervene. It had started simply enough: with an anonymous account making critiques of right-wing politicians and their platforms, specifically Maxime Bernier and Pierre Poilievre. An Indigenous friend pointed out that, while they were right about the critiques, Liberal governments did not have a much better track record. The anonymous account demanded details; we and others chimed in: from the 1969 White Paper, through the lack of recognition of Indigenous People in the 1982 patriation of the Constitution, up to the recent "Trudeau government bought a pipeline" controversy, we provided what we thought was important evidence of deeper issues than partisan loyalties. The response was a torrent of abuse, claiming we must all love the Tories and want them elected, and calling us "useful idiots." There really wasn't anywhere for the conversation to go from there.

≈

I was at a summer-school event, a kind of "boot camp" on colonialism and Indigenous resurgence. The large gathering of students, scholars, activists, and community members was splitting into two groups, an Indigenous and a Settler "caucus," for discussions of our relationships to the project and work of decolonization. Most people moved unhesitatingly into their group, and I went with the other, mainly white, Settlers. One person, though, simply refused. Born in Canada and a person of colour, this person's parents had immigrated to Canada seeking to escape poverty and achieve a better life for their family. At first, this person tried to stay with the Indigenous caucus when the Settler people left, but was asked to go. And eventually did so, crying and visibly angered at being asked to join their "fellow" Settler Canadians. Being labelled a Settler, as they explained to the group, meant they believed they were supposed to hate their parents and grandparents, whose sacrifices had brought their family to Canada seeking a better life. They were unable to reconcile that their parents' decisions could both have been for the best for the family *and* also settler colonial. That being indigenous somewhere might not mean "not Settler" in Canada.

≈

I dreaded being asked what I was reading. Working nightshifts, I often brought books on Indigenous politics and colonial history to pass the time and keep up on my studies. I liked my coworkers in the factory, and had some good conversations about politics, economics, society, and culture with them over our boxed lunches and not-strong-enough coffee. But one man in particular, a coworker who I enjoyed most of the time as a friendly and cooperative team member with a good sense of humour and outgoing personality, was a source of dread for me. He would ask what I was reading, and I would say I was reading about the 1969 White Paper, or about Indigenous sacred places, or the creation of the reserve system. And the harangues would begin. This guy, who seemed so even-keeled and sensible so much of the time, was a tyrant whenever he spoke on Indigenous issues. His monologues on "savages" and "drunks" and how "the Indians should be grateful we give them anything at all" were energetic, assertive, and awful. Which is why I was so surprised when, after months of these sorts of encounters, he finished off one of his speeches by saying, "and I should know, because my family's Native." It turned out one, or maybe more, of his grandparents was Cayuga or Oneida, though he said he had no connection to those communities and didn't want one, for that matter.

≈

For several years, I attended the Vine Deloria, Jr. Memorial Symposium held at the Lummi Nation Tribal College, in Washington State. It was a special gathering, bringing people from all over the Pacific Northwest, from British Columbia to Oregon, and from as far away as Minnesota, Kansas, and Ontario, out to the community to talk and share ideas and work. Many of the attendees were academics, but many were elders, fishers, visitors, and students. All the talks and discussions happened in the large, wooden conference building, a single room with a high roof and rows of chairs between huge log pillars. The communal atmosphere was always a welcome relief from the stuffy, formalized academic conferences that we were used to. One year, we were very excited for one particular panel, as one of the speakers was Caleen Sisk of the Winnemem Wintu, a federally unrecognized tribe from Mount Shasta, in California.[13]

Caleen gave a great presentation; she talked about defending a river space that was used for young women's coming of age ceremonies and the Wintu decision to make a declaration of war on the United States government. Everyone cheered. Then the floor was opened to questions. A hand shot up, and a shaky voice started. It was a woman who I remembered seeing the previous day, as someone who was always smiling, but she was not smiling as she spoke. She was crying. She felt for the "Native people"; she knew their struggle was so hard. She knew from personal experience, because she — as a woman — had known the wounds of centuries of patriarchy. Her wounds were their wounds, they were both bloodied by oppression, and so on. In the end, no one knew what to say. She never asked a question. She did not return the next day.

≈

Responses vary widely when Settler Canadians come face-to-face with critiques and challenges that bring the settler colonial fear of being made illegitimate and losing privilege to the fore. For this reason, anyone who does not immediately see the consistency between the reactions above, or any others one could describe, could be forgiven for not making the connections. However, thinking through these examples in the context of settler colonialism and the Settler Canadian identity (as developed so far), we hope to make it easier to see the commonalities between these responses. When we focus on what motivates these reactions, and what the goal of such outbursts is, we see panicked efforts at disavowal in the Settler Canadian identity.

Moves to Comfort

The responses we described share a common motivation. In each, a person acted in response to a moment of confrontation or revelation centred on settler colonialism. These Settlers likely experienced fear in response to their unsettling encounters with the immoral and unethical basis of settler society. The potential for critique by others, the realization (even briefly) of personal complicity and benefit from destructive settler colonial structures, the sudden disconnect between who we think we are (good Canadians) and realization of our settler colonial identity can all be incredibly unsettling and upsetting. Fear and becoming unsettled provoke a reaction; we take them as signs of a crisis. But how we react, how we move to resolve the crisis, can take several different forms.

However, as the stories show, these strong reactions often lead to the restoration of a state of comfort, a signal that the crisis is over, meaning we can return to a normal life, one in which we can choose to not think about or engage with colonization — an option that Indigenous People and communities do not share. As we discussed in Chapter 4, a key benefit of Settler colonial identity is the convenient ignorance of the harms of colonization. This is a comfortable state in which Settlers are insulated from the impacts of their actions and their silences, and the repercussions for these choices. As a motivator, the force of the drive to re-establish Settler comfort is evident in the energy, effort, and creativity that goes into creating such varied responses to the experience of being unsettled by exposure to our own complicity.

Eve Tuck and K. Wayne Yang have developed a highly useful conceptualization of what they call "moves to innocence" — Settler intellectualizations of our relationships to settler colonialism that free us from responsibility.[14] Here, we are dealing with a somewhat different phenomenon that, influenced by Tuck and Yang, we describe as "moves to comfort." Rather than rationalizations, these are emotional shifts inspiring often irrational or illogical statements or actions designed to dispel fear and unsettling and restore the comfort of not knowing even once ignorance is not possible. As well, many of these moves to comfort do not necessarily involve an attempt to claim innocence; if anything, several of them dwell in guilt and self-punishing confession as a method of proving — if only to ourselves — that we are doing everything we can and therefore have nothing to feel bad about, really. In this, it is useful to group these moves to comfort, such as those sketched above, into two types: resolution and exception. Examining the motivations and commonalities of these responses helps clarify their often-unstated, or obfuscated, end goals.

Seeking Resolution

Settler colonial moves to comfort often rely on narratives in which settler colonialism is something that can actually be finished: Settler Canadian society can become so successful, so pervasive and all-encompassing, that it need no longer be fought for, justified, or defended against competing claims to the land. Even the status and struggles of Indigenous Peoples, when recognized, can be resolved within the given order of Settler society. The methods of addressing the obvious injustices of colonialism are, in turn, presented as evident and simple.

Consider the stories recounted here — the ill-fated online engagement and the personal story of failure during an activist encounter — both of which centre misplaced attempts to control an Indigenous anti-colonial discourse. In cases like these, settler society remains in control of addressing the problems of Indigenous Peoples. Settler people need only assume more vocal positions of leadership, or participate in the *right kind* of party politics, and Indigenous Peoples' problems will (eventually) be solved. This is because, in Settler Canadian narratives, our liberal, multicultural society always has the answers. And this assumption is so total that it is almost impossible to consider either that Indigenous Peoples might have their own answers for how to address their struggles — ones that may or may not involve Settler Canadians, or might actively displace them from positions of power — or that Settler Canadian society as such may in fact *be the problem*.

The concept of "respectability politics" is important here. There are strong social and cultural prohibitions in Canada against engaging in politics in the "wrong" way, and these judgements tend to be turned disproportionately against Indigenous, Black, LGBTQ+, and other groups seeking the redress of fundamental wrongs. There is both a valorization of "the system" as the one and only solution to the problems that the system creates, and also an ahistorical "memory" of how struggles proceeded in the past. In the first instance, any critique of governments and parties is met with admonishment to "VOTE!" as the one and only way of actually engaging in politics. As we described in the story of the encounter on social media, pointing out that the political system itself is the problem often brings assertions of partisan loyalties that distract from the very valid critique being made: as British scientist Stafford Beer articulated, "the purpose of a system is what it does."[15] When Indigenous People and others point out that the system of government in Canada, regardless of the party in power, denies Indigenous sovereignty and protects Settler Canadian claims to land, the "respectable" position arises to say it's not the system that's the problem, but the people critiquing it.

In the second instance, past struggles are reframed (or misstated) in order to make them appear somehow more moral, ethical, valorous, and effective than what is being proposed at present. For example, the long battle for equal rights regardless of race in Canada — and even more so, the American civil rights movement which holds an outsized influence over how Canadians think of social change movements — is reduced to a series of nonviolent marches and polite speeches that convinced those in power to change, with minimal disruption and certainly no bad feelings. Histories of police violence, social violence tacitly or legally sanctioned by authorities, institutional exclusion, and the use of bureaucratic mechanisms to shut down dissent are flushed down the memory hole. If and when a self-described ally is made to feel uncomfortable by harsh language, disruptive protest tactics, or the rejection of compromise positions, the ally usually moves quickly to scolding Indigenous People for apparent incivility. Often, there are "tantrums" wherein a Settler Canadian will claim that they *were* on the side of Indigenous People ... but not anymore because they were made to feel bad, and therefore Indigenous People deserve whatever they get. The feelings of Settler Canadians are to be protected at all times, even as Indigenous communities struggle for their lives. After all, can't they just resist genocide politely?

Discomforted by Indigenous Peoples taking an active role in critiquing Settler Canadian society, we tend to respond by seeking a resolution to these critiques that reinforces the absolute validity and universality of Settler spaces. These stories represent different versions of what happens when Settler people seek a resolution to the challenge of Indigenous resistance by investing in — and asserting control of — Indigenous resurgence struggles. Indigenous challenges are reconstructed as issues solvable within established Settler society through relatively simple reforms: the Settler remains superior, the system largely unaltered.

Seeking Exception

The other stories have something different in common. In each of these, the protagonist responds to the fear of being challenged by Indigenous resistance and presence by seeking exception. That is, they attempt to escape from their complicity in settler colonial harms by positioning themselves as a special case. Even in the stories in which the Settler in question recognizes the need for collective responsibility, they have somehow already escaped blame. These scenarios are closer to Tuck and Yang's moves to innocence except that, in some cases, individuals actually try to make themselves incomparable in their guilt or avoid a full penalty by pleading guilty to a "lesser charge" (i.e., an admission of responsibility for limited parts of settler colonialism). There are subtle differences in strategy among these stories, but their end goal is the same.

Let us begin with stories that centre on expressions of guilt. Feelings of guilt may seem an entirely rational response for any Settler Canadian beginning to understand their own individual and collective complicity in the sickening, pervasive, and normalized harms inflicted through settler colonialism: When they see homeless Indigenous individuals freezing in the winter. When they watch community members at Unist'ot'en or Oka or Burnaby Mountain being beaten by police, children and elders being dragged to police vans. When the national media airs yet another exposé about the lack of housing or food in northern reserves. When they have to help their children understand what residential schools are because they have not been discussed within the public school curriculum. All these situations are points at which Settler people are likely to feel guilty.

Guilt can be useful *if* it is part of a journey toward critical acceptance of responsibility, but not as an end goal in itself. Guilt is not a motivating state, but it can be used as an opportunity to identify and move toward accountability and action. However, there is a problem when a Settler person insists on centralizing feelings and expressions of guilt to the exclusion of addressing what happens next. We can get stuck on guilt.

Consider another one of the stories: a woman in the solidarity group displayed her distress at feeling guilty likely out of a very real and overwhelming sense of fear and discomfort as a result of coming to understand something of her complicity in settler colonialism in Canada. However, guilt took over the time and space set aside for organizing and planning on that occasion, as it had and did on too many others. Guilt and a public process of grieving and acknowledging responsibility displaced the actual process of sitting with discomfort and figuring out how to take productive action. Seeking to be absolved and excused from blame by other members of the group demonstrates something troubling. As historian Michel Rolph Trouillot has identified, guilt is a self-inflicted wound — evident in the amount of hurt feelings displayed, and the way that this individual centred the discussion on her feelings in response to harms being done to *other people* — that works as protection, almost a shield, from the critique or anger of others.[16] In this case, for displaying her hurt from accepting that she was part of a colonial problem, this Settler got a pass. Because she was (visibly) hurting so much already, the rest of the group moved to insist that they did not think she was part of the problem.

It also had the effect of stalling the work that had caused her to respond with feelings of guilt in the first place. Regardless of what her other actions (intentional or otherwise) may have been, reassurance is what was produced. This response is akin to someone pre-emptively claiming awareness of their status in hierarchies as a way of limiting the opportunity of others to critique them on this involvement. Declarative statements of positionality and privilege are not a substitute for engagement. Glynis Cousin terms such declarations "positional piety," whereby a person in a position of power and privilege claims "some authority (often moral) by claiming affinity with subjects, or by giving a confessional declaration of 'difference and relative privilege.'"[17] In far too many cases, Settler statements have functioned as confessions of privilege and complicity in order to give the appearance of taking responsibility while neatly avoiding actually doing so.

Seeking to associate oneself with Indigenous identity, in its multiple forms, is also a common strategy for attempting to escape implication and inclusion in Settler colonizer status: because "colonial" and "Indigenous" are constructed as binary opposites, if someone can imply that they are accepted into an Indigenous group or by an Indigenous person, they can deflect suspicions or accusations of colonialism (at least in their own minds). Whether this takes the form of the coworker whose racist comments about Indigenous Peoples were justified, in his mind, by family heritage, or the activists who justify problematic interactions with Indigenous communities by listing the names of their Indigenous friends, the end goal is the same. When a Settler explicitly attempts identification in or with a particular Indigenous group based on tenuous connections, or when a Settler individual or group seeks the approval and approbation of an Indigenous person, and uses that as justification for violating boundaries that, if others were to do so, would be considered unjust or unethical, it is clearly an attempt to distance themselves from uncomfortable accusations of colonialism and racism. Settler Canadians are taught that we are individuals, with individual rights and individual responsibilities, and when we are confronted with the fact that we collectively benefit from settler colonialism and therefore are collectively responsible for it, we tend not to reject that the problem exists, but rather that we have any hand in creating, maintaining, or confronting the problem.

Consider the New Age spiritualists who appropriate, copy, or steal Indigenous ceremonies. Often, these individuals attempt to justify their ventures by claiming the ceremony was a gift from some "Native Elder." This puts the spiritual adherent into a proximate legitimacy. They claim to be closer to an alleged source of authentic Indigenous identity than the people questioning them, which lends authority to their actions. This is an approach to legitimacy based on consumption and the logics of capitalism and ownership through which "the consumer" — the Settler person building a prefabricated sweat lodge or smudging their new home with a specially purchased kit — can gain "'the experience' of Native American ritual and wisdom through multisensory consumption. The purchaser can drink up the sacredness of Native American spirituality while creating the right ambiance with the scent of sage smudge sticks and the proper New Age music evoking the proper locale." And best of all, "the consumer can have a direct experience of Native American ritual and wisdom without ever leaving their armchair. Moreover, they are relieved of any guilt" because these practices are often wrapped in self-help tropes of enlightenment, environmental awareness, and social responsibility.[18]

Claiming exceptional status through the approval of an Indigenous individual or inclusion in an Indigenous group is akin to the awful but undying "but I can say [racial epithet], one of my best friends is [particular racial/ethnic group]." A variation of this is appropriation justified through "respect" and "admiration" for Indigenous spiritual practices, sometimes even accompanied by the recognition that appropriation occurs but a denial that what "we" are doing is appropriation because it is meant as an honouring. Perhaps worst, we have time and again seen well-meaning activist "allies" who work with Indigenous communities, but pick and choose which Indigenous individuals to respect as "leaders." In so doing, these Settler activists (be it explicitly or implicitly) deny the leadership and authority of other individuals and collectives in the community — and Indigenous communities, like any community, are not monoliths. When activists support their preferred Indigenous leader over others, they are inherently interfering in the right and necessity of the community to address their own internal disputes and conflicts. An activist's settler colonial drive to achieve the comfort of Indigenous approval and approbation or for comfortably familiar forms of authority and decision-making can result in problematic and self-defeating power dynamics.

This is what happened in the blockades at Fairy Creek, "a series of old-growth logging protests in the summer of 2021 that saw thousands of environmental activists blockade logging roads" on Vancouver Island.[19] Many of the blockade sites were organized around principles of horizontalism and anti-authoritarianism, which is to say that they were intended to be leaderless and participatory. However, many of these groups became dysfunctional in part because, as one anonymous participant relates, Settler environmental activists forced Indigenous People into positions of leadership, sometimes official and sometimes through tacit deference:

> The problem with the hierarchies at Fairy Creek that were based on deference politics was not that Indigenous People were in leadership positions. *The problem was that there were leadership positions at all,* in this case enforced by a social context that took advantage of settler guilt, transforming it into an authoritarian weapon of shame. This so-called "Indigenous Leadership" was based less on respect for the individual at the top and more on essentializing the social category they represented.[20]

The results were poor organization, knowledge transmission and communication, and collective cohesion, and many of the blockades were eventually abandoned. At Fairy Creek, Settler supporters actively undermined their own blockades by acting out of guilt rather than pursuing a deeper relationality. But this is rarely what Settler activists believe themselves to be doing; instead, they are trying to make themselves proximate to someone they see as "authentically" Indigenous. Again, this is a way to "refuse" or avoid accusations of colonial complicity by anchoring to generalized Indigenous spirituality as a defence against specific critiques. Seeking to escape settler colonial complicity, this move to comfort amounts to making Indigenous individuals or groups responsible for Settler discomfort, and using them as a tool to re-establish Settler comfort.

The attempt to escape complicity in and responsibility for settler colonial processes takes many forms. As shown in one of the stories, a common strategy is for a Settler person to use their own real or perceived oppression or marginalization as a way to claim that, as a victim themselves, they cannot be held responsible for the dispossession and oppression of Others. In this case, Settler individuals and groups use an experience (or narrative) of victimhood as a way to claim a special connection to Indigenous Peoples and to escape the possibility of censure for participation in settler colonial structures. Be it based on gender, race, economic class, or other differences, this is a move to comfort based on the assumption that all oppressions are equivalent, and all identities are defined by their accumulation of oppressions. Like guilt, in this action, the Settler uses experiences or perceptions of individual or community hurt as a shield against accusations of complicity in settler colonialism and its many harms. As we discussed in Chapter 4, however, the myriad other forms of privilege and oppression that exist in Canada as a result of hierarchical socioeconomic structures (race, class, gender, heteronormativity, etc.) do not determine Settler status. For Settlers of many types, understanding and recognizing our own oppression or marginalization can be a potential point of connection with Indigenous Peoples and struggles. For Black Canadians, settler colonialism is a root cause of both the white supremacy and racism that affects communities and daily lives, just as it has been for Indigenous folks, even if the nature of the racialization is different (exploitation for labour, removal for land), the systems of oppression are interconnected. Likewise, LGBTQ+ folks can relate to the tendencies among health care and education professionals to view them as unfit parents, resulting in interventions by systems of social care that reinforce the dominance of white, heteronormative families. However, if creating this common ground is used as justification to retreat into comfort and avoid censure for continuing to participate in and benefit from Settler Canadian status, it is dishonest.

Removal — of oneself from participation in colonialism, but more accurately from spaces where one might be *implicated* in settler colonialism — as a response is worth mentioning here. Albert Memmi developed the model of the "colonizer who refuses."[21] This describes a common way that individual colonizers openly critique and disapprove of colonial systems, and even withdraw their active participation and support, without ever realizing that withdrawal of participation is itself a privilege. One example of this is the story of the Settler who refused to leave the Indigenous space during our summer class. This person withdrew their participation in a group that would have, by its definition as Settler and "not Indigenous," shaken their self-perception as exempt from implications in settler colonization. When their attempt at removal to a more "pure" (Indigenous) space was denied, they instead removed themselves from the conversation by refusing to allow it to happen — effectively removing the offending discourse for themself and the group.

A common example of removal is the Settler who "opts out" of mainstream society: the back-to-the-earth, off-the-grid types, those who own a ranch or some other kind of private property. A current concern for many is the prevalence of "tiny homes" that are positioned as antidotes for poverty and inequality, the environmental destruction of urban and suburban sprawl, and the alienation from nature that many experience today. To the extent that tiny homes are often premised on not requiring a specific property on which to be located, one might surmise that — along with broadly anti-capitalist and environmentalist intents and impacts — tiny homes hold the potential to upset settler colonial regimes that are fundamentally rooted in dividing up the land and selling it as private property. However, Veracini sees in tiny houses the potential for new forms of settler self-displacement[22] and potential parallels between the "tiny house movement" and feminist or anarchist back-to-the-land movements, both of which have been critiqued for embedded settler colonial and racist inequalities.[23] With these advantageous privileges informing these alternative Settler lifestyles, what are they actually practicing if not the Settler benefits of mobility and ignorance? Individual moves to "opt out" of settler colonialism do nothing to address the systemic nature of settler colonization and its continuing operation. In fact, the opting out of mainstream lifestyles and pursuit of "alternative lifestyles," if not informed by anti-colonial critiques and bound up with movements explicitly contesting settler colonialism, is simply a different version of the Settler story. The story of the individual who finds themself in a hostile land but struggles to move to a more peaceful place and is rewarded in the end by a life free from (in this case) moral discomfort.

Finally, we return to the first story we told: we must deal with actions expressed as anger. As an extremely powerful emotion, moves to comfort through anger often entail elements of both resolution and exception. Anger responses insist on having the last word on the subject, achieving finality in the debate by shutting it down — that is, substituting the end for the means. Comfort is restored because the unsettling has stopped, both internally and externally, and therefore the discomforted person has been proven right (in their own mind). These responses are also about forcefully refusing implication in and responsibility for settler colonialism. The individual in the driving story worked hard to be a good citizen, a good neighbour, a good friend, a good family member; what he could not handle was the suggestion that his individual effort may not have earned him his happy life without his unearned and collective privilege, and that he, who thought of himself as a good man, might be implicated in things he found morally and ethically reprehensible. Anger in this sense is not just a cutting off, but a corrective, a forceful pushback against the disruption of our own personal Settler story.

When individuals experiencing fear as a result of encountering their own colonialism move to comfort themselves and alleviate the discomfort of fear, as in the examples above, even those actions that involve accepting settler colonial responsibility or entanglement can contribute to settler colonial power by supporting its end goals of Settler indigenization and elimination. Ultimately, the Settler who seeks comfort remains too embedded in colonial structures and practices to seriously challenge colonial power, and so contribute to it by their endorsement and acceptance of Settler benefits. The feeling of being unsettled — experiencing fear and discomfort when confronted with one's own colonial complicity, experiencing uncertainty over what to do in response to that fear — is something that runs counter to our expectations as Settler people that we will be insulated from or be able to move away from threats to our legitimacy.

Moves to comfort are just that: moves to re-establish a barrier or remove ourselves from proximity to our own colonial identities, to disavow ourselves as settler colonizers, sometimes paradoxically by admitting that we are colonizers. Our arrogance, our anger, our guilt, and our shame can all be used to rebuild the comfortable spaces of settler colonialism that we are used to residing in. But there is another way.

Beyond Settler Certainty

Our purpose in focusing on fear, on unsettling and moves to comfort, is not to minimize the emotional toll associated with the bursting of the Settler bubble. Fear is a very real and very powerful response that, from within the logic of settler colonialism, is also reasonable: all our benefits of belonging in Settler Canadian society are threatened when we are presented with the moral indefensibility of settler colonialism and our own responsibilities in and for colonization in Canada are exposed. Seeking a way back into a comfortable place, a place where either we can claim ignorance of the harms caused by our own entanglements with structures of invasion, or where we can distance ourselves from uncomfortable situations, is also an understandably attractive response. But actions in response to colonial fear and decisions to pursue comfort by reinserting ourselves into Settler structures are both clear indicators that we remain overwhelmingly defined by our attachments to settler colonialism. These are also moments that show us our settler colonial complicity. If we are unsettled by something, even if we move to restore our feelings of comfort, we can still acknowledge the pressure point, the moment at which we became aware of our choice to seek comfort. In so doing, we see the possibility of alternatives, and therefore can perceive that there is choice involved and we all can find possibilities for doing something differently.

This raises an important point: Settler people wanting to confront the colonialism pervasive in our lives and societies must accept that this process *will be* uncomfortable and unsettling. In fact, following discomfort, going further into situations and conversations that are unsettling, is a useful strategy because it helps identify points of contention in our lives where settler colonialism exerts pressure on us through our particular, personal vulnerabilities. This idea came to us originally during a conversation with Paulette Regan. We told her we felt a strong and sudden response the first time we heard her use the word "settler." She said, "What did you feel?" We could only respond, "uncomfortable." Her response was that, as a Settler person, if you feel uncomfortable, you are probably in the right place, and you are probably learning something. What we have taken from that is to sit with discomfort when it happens, to ask it questions and use it as a compass to direct us away from settler colonial security.

In 2015, the Office of Aboriginal Initiatives at Wilfrid Laurier University released *Indigenous Allyship: An Overview*. This document was produced over many years and in consultation with a variety of students (Indigenous and Settler) and Indigenous community members. Discomfort and unsettling are key components of how "good allyship" has been constructed in what is intended as a practical guide for Settler people seeking to support Indigenous Peoples' struggles. While the authors warn against reacting to Settler discomforts "that arise from confronting one's position as a settler" by seeking comfort and reassurance from "Indigenous People that one does not know, merely because they are Indigenous,"[24] they also position the discomfort that comes from deep listening and sustained engagement as crucial to ethical relationship building.[25] Likewise, scholars Sarah de Leeuw, Margo Greenwood, and Nicole Lindsay have argued that:

> Colonialism always was, and is right now, uncomfortable — particularly so for colonized subjects, but also for settler-colonial subjects. Unsettling colonialism, and indeed troubling good intentions, must similarly never be comfortable. It is, we suggest,

at the very moment when something ascends to a position of normative comfortableness that it most desperately needs troubling. It is exactly at the moment when we, especially those of us who are settler colonists, feel good about having reached a place of comfort and stabilization about unsettling colonialism that we should be feeling most troubled.[26]

It is vital that Settler Canadians remember that good intentions are not necessarily matched by happy feelings. Rather, well-intentioned Settler Canadians must be driven to engage with — despite discomfort, or risk falling into complacency and self-congratulations for hard work already done — the vast struggle that remains before us.

It is not easy for Settler Canadians to train ourselves to stop expecting comfort and to face fear as a matter of finding the path we need to walk. It is difficult to unlearn a lifetime of lessons — socializations, really — that teach us to believe that discomfort means we are doing something wrong. We must start by realizing that the instinct to pull away, or to preserve comfort, has been instilled in us, is imposed on us through our upbringing, through the culture that we have been raised in, by the dreams we have inherited from our Settler Canadian narratives that tell us we can achieve a comfortable, privileged life. Learning to face fear of uncertainty, learning to dwell in discomfort from not being in control, is an ongoing project. Repetition, experimentation, failure and reflection are all necessary. And that requires the support and help of others, a great deal of critical reflection, time and energy.

Colonialism cannot be easily expunged from our lives. Moves to innocence and comfort are bandaid measures in the sense that they rapidly restore our feelings and security, but they do little to contribute to any meaningful decolonizing efforts. Productive discomfort, too, is not a magical antidote to colonialism. Simply getting used to feeling unsettled is not the same as engaging in active struggle against colonialism. There is no magic solution that removes us as Settler Canadians from our settler colonial relationships to the land and to each other; there is only the potential for transformative change through hard work. The first step in challenging settler colonialism and the colonizer that is part of our identities as Settler Canadians is the acceptance that this is not going to be comfortable, nor will it be easy. But what comes after that first step is much bigger, broader, and, frankly, more exciting and empowering.

Notes

1. Adam J. Barker, "The Contemporary Reality of Canadian Imperialism: Settler Colonialism and the Hybrid Imperial State," *American Indian Quarterly* 33, 3 (2009).
2. Patrick Gillham, Bob Edwards, and John Noakes, "Strategic Incapacitation and the Policing of Occupy Wall Street Protests in New York City," *Policing and Society* 23, 1 (2011). See, also, Andrew Crosby and Jeffrey Monaghan, *Policing Indigenous Movements: Dissent and the Security State* (Halifax: Fernwood Publishing, 2018); Robyn Maynard, *Policing Black Lives: State Violence in Canada from Slavery to the Present* (Halifax: Fernwood Publishing, 2017).
3. Amory Starr, "'… (Excepting Barricades Erected to Prevent Us from Peacefully Assembling)': So-called 'Violence' in the Global North Alterglobalization Movement," *Social Movements Studies* 5, 1 (2006).
4. Pam Palmater "appeared before the House of Commons Standing Committee on Public Safety and National Security on the morning of March 24 as a witness to speak to her concerns about Bill C-51," The text of Pam Palmater's address can be found at globalresearch.ca/canada-anti-terrorist-bill-c-51-to-criminalize-thoughts-ofindigenous-peoples/5439608. For more on this, see, Todd Gordon, *Cops, Crime and Capitalism: The Law-and-Order Agenda in Canada* (Halifax: Fernwood Publishing, 2006); Richard J.F. Day, *Gramsci Is Dead: Anarchist Currents in the Newest Social Movements* (London: Pluto Press, 2005).
5. Many anti-colonial analyses owe a great deal to the early works of Frantz Fanon (*The Wretched of the Earth*) and Albert Memmi (*The Colonizer and the Colonized*). Both went to great lengths to expose the mental and emotional states of colonizers as a sort of pathology, a predictable set of assertions and responses required to justify dominance over a colonized people. In a more general sense, social movement scholars like Richard Day (*Gramsci Is Dead*) have traced the fear of a nomadic "war machine" — including Indigenous Peoples — as an existential threat to our settled way of life. Increasingly, settler colonial theory has shown how this functions in relation to the land in particular ways in places like Canada and Australia, for example in Daniel Salée, "Indigenous Peoples and Settler Angst in Canada: A Review Essay," *Journal of Canadian Studies* 41 (2010); Lorenzo Veracini, *Settler Colonialism: A Theoretical Overview* (London: Palgrave Macmillan, 2010); and Adam J. Barker, *Making and Breaking Settler Space: Five Centuries of Colonization in North America* (Vancouver: UBC Press, 2023).
6. Albert Memmi, *The Colonizer and the Colonized* (Boston: Beacon Press, 1965), 40-41.
7. Jerry Mander, *In the Absence of the Sacred* (San Francisco: Sierra Club Books, 1992), 213.
8. Eve Tuck and K. Wayne Yang, "Decolonization Is Not a Metaphor," *Decolonization: Indigeneity, Education & Society* 1, 1 (2012), 14, 35-36.
9. Tuck and Yang, "Decolonization Is Not a Metaphor," 35.
10. Daniel Coleman, "Indigenous Place and Diaspora Space: Of Literalism and Abstraction," *Settler Colonial Studies* 6, 1 (2016). Note here that the connecting of these positions, while not simple, is not impossible either, and that it is settler colonialism that works to prevent this.

11 Aziz Choudry, Mandisi Majavu, and Lesley Wood, "Struggles, Strategies and Analysis of Anticolonial and Postcolonial Social Movements," *Interface* 5, 1 (2013), 3.
12 This should not be read as a critique of the effectiveness of the social movements that deploy this tactic. Fear, as a reaction to the politics of embarrassment, is still an "unsettled" state that should be considered a successful impact of Indigenous mobilizations given the apathetic and under-informed status quo.
13 Caleen Sisk and the Winnemem Wintus' struggles were popularly depicted in the documentary *In The Light of Reverence*.
14 Tuck and Yang, "Decolonization Is Not a Metaphor."
15 Allenna Leonard, "The Viable System Model and Its Application to Complex Organizations," *Systemic Practice and Action Research* 22, 4 (2009), 225.
16 Michel Trouillot, *Silencing the Past: Power and the Production of History* (Boston: Beacon Press, 1997).
17 Glynis Cousin, "Positioning Positionality: The Reflexive Turn," in *New Approaches to Qualitative Research: Wisdom and Uncertainty*, eds. Maggi Savin-Baden and Claire Howell Major (London: Routledge, 2010).
18 Lisa Aldred, "Plastic Shamans and Astroturf Sun Dances: New Age Commercialization of Native American Spirituality," *American Indian Quarterly* 24, 3 (2000), 334.
19 Kieran Oudshoorn, "The Fallout of Fairy Creek," *CBC Radio*, June 1, 2023, cbc.ca/radiointeractives/features/the-fallout-of-fairy-creek.
20 Anonymous, "Water Falling on Granite: Deference Politics, Indigenous Leadership, and Anarchist Relationality," The Anarchist Library, (emphasis in original), theanarchistlibrary.org/library/anonymous-water-falling-on-granite.
21 Memmi, *The Colonizer and the Colonized*.
22 Lorenzo Veracini, *The Settler Colonial Present* (Palgrave Macmillan, 2015).
23 Adam J. Barker and Jenny Pickerill, "Radicalizing Relationships to and through Shared Geographies: Why Anarchists Need to Understand Indigenous Connections to Land and Place," *Antipode* 44, 5 (2012); Katherine Schweighofer, "A Land of One's Own: Whiteness and Indigeneity on Lesbian Land," *Settler Colonial Studies*, 8, 4 (2018).
24 Jackson Smith, Cassandra Puckett, and Wendy Simon, *Indigenous Allyship: An Overview* (Waterloo, ON: Office of Aboriginal Initiatives, Wilfrid Laurier University, 2015), 11.
25 Smith, Puckett and Simon, *Indigenous Allyship*, 8.
26 Sarah de Leeuw, Margo Greenwood, and Nicole Lindsay, "Troubling Good Intentions," *Settler Colonial Studies* 3, 3–4 (2013), 391.

Decolonization and Dangerous Freedom

SO FAR WE HAVE TRACED THE RELATIONSHIPS among settler colonialism, Settler people, and Canadian society in the twenty-first century and established why identities are necessary points of engagement. Indigenous and Settler identities are rooted in relationships to land, and divided by relationships of power and domination. As settler colonialism demands (of Settler people) and imposes (on Indigenous People) particular ways of relating to the land, our identities become bound up with the power and privilege of colonization — or the struggle against it. We have also discussed how settler colonialism is more than a legacy to be dealt with but a vital and powerful force in Canada, one with major implications for how we understand difference in our society. It affects our notions of multiculturalism and social justice, how we perceive race and class, and how we experience (or not) the various benefits of being Canadian. We have shown that the end goal of the settler colonial process is to completely normalize settler society so that colonialism "disappears" from view and being a Settler Canadian is universalized alongside the elimination of Indigenous Peoples. This drive is informed by settler colonial narratives that start with the land as a blank canvas (terra nullius) then follows the exceptional, individualized, and ultimately triumphant struggles of Settler people — pioneers, fur traders, early farmers, merchants, workers, and so on — to establish themselves in the new land. It concludes with the emergence of a progressive, successful, and coherent society, one that proceeds confidently into the future with little memory of how or at whose expense their society was established. And we have also discussed the emotional, profound, troubling, and at times hopeful ways that people respond to being confronted with their own implications in settler colonialism and their own disavowed identification with Settler Canadian status. We have drawn out how, more often than not, Settler Canadians act to restore comfort rather than engage with settler colonialism in their own lives, but also, hopefully, that Settler people can and sometimes do become and stay unsettled.

We now return to a point we raised in Chapter 1: The Settler identity, as we have constructed it throughout this book, is a way of interrogating assumptions about how we relate to the land as a collective group of people, how we relate to Indigenous Peoples including our perceptions of treaties and formalized agreements, and how we experience power and privilege in institutional or structural contexts. It asks questions that may have a vast possible array of answers. The fundamental question, always, is how do you come to be on these lands and by what right do you claim legitimate residency here? The answer for almost all Settler Canadians today is that we are here as part of the project of settler colonization that has brought so many millions of people to these lands, and our legitimacy is attached to the institutions of the Canadian state and the stories of Canadian exceptionalism. This does not need to be the only answer, though. If we can understand colonialism well enough to understand the Settler identity in the first place, then we can also understand that those forms of "legitimacy" are not justifiable ties to the land. To choose to identify as Settler Canadian today is as good as declaring, "I am aware that I am *illegitimate* on the land, and I know that I am complicit with and benefit from settler colonialism." This admission can result from a feeling of unsettlement, and provoke the same in others.

Choosing to identify as a Settler and choosing how one will act on that identity are two different concerns. As Settler Canadians, we are part of a colonizing collective, and there is no simple place we can go, or declaration we can make, that will sever us from our unearned benefits and privileges, insulate us from our fears of change, or abstract us from destructive practices on the land. It is possible, no matter how hard it may be to envision, to forge different relationships to the land that are not rooted in the displacement and genocide of Indigenous Nations, nor in fooling ourselves with the comfortable oblivion of indigenization and transcendence.

Settler, because it is a situated and process-based identity, is not foreclosed. It is not biologically determined, culturally circumscribed, or structured by a single political or economic system. It is because we, as Settler people, choose en masse to act as settler colonizers, to invest in peacemaker myths and narratives of pioneering frontiersmen and terra nullius, to believe in the multicultural promise of the Canadian identity, that settler colonizer and Settler Canadian become synonymous. From the ways that we interact with government and social systems, the training and jobs we take on, participate in patriotic events and displays, to the stories we believe and relate about the nation we belong to, we all contribute in ways big and small to ongoing colonialism. These choices are swayed by the perception of great benefits in belonging to Settler Canadian society, and great fear of what we might have to be were Settler Canadian society to cease to exist. But they remain choices. So, we have the power to choose to be something else.

Settler colonization is collective, so undoing settler colonialism will also necessarily be a collective effort. If we, as Settler-identifying people in the present, wish to be other than settler colonizers, we must undertake an archaeology of the future: an excavation of the possible. We have to challenge ourselves to imagine relationships differently and then figure out how to try and embody them. We cannot change who we are as Settler people alone, so we must work to create a broad base, to build communities — with our friends, our families, our colleagues — to undertake these efforts together. And this experimentation will run counter to everything that settler colonial Canadian society is premised on, which means it will be opposed. If we want to be different, we have to struggle to change; changing ourselves is connected to changing society around us. This means as individuals, we need to take risks to act and experiment for change alongside connecting with others to try to work together.

There is great discomfort in coming to perceive the enormity of settler colonial structures. The effort it takes to maintain critical attention to these uncomfortable issues long enough to understand our own complicity in settler colonialism is considerable. Coming to understand settler colonialism and its importance in informing almost everything we know about the Canadian state and nation — right down to our own hometowns — from politics and economics to culture and social relationships is a major task and an important step. In a society defined in part by the invisibility of systemic oppression from within, and on the disavowal of our identification with that systemic oppression, *knowing is important*. To be able to make conscious choices about how we relate to the structures, stories, and spaces that make Canada possible and real, we have to understand how those structures work and what our relationships to them are. Coming to this understanding is hard work. From history to politics to discourses of power and privilege, and perhaps most importantly, to understanding Indigenous identity and Peoples, we have a lot of (un)learning to do.

Self-education and critical self-reflection are key to the challenge currently facing Settler Canadians. However, "freeing your mind" is a step, not the destination. It is important here to note that individual acknowledgements of privilege actually do nothing to undermine the collective production of privilege, and the ritualistic confession of privilege that often accompanies social justice work ends up substituting for action. Self-education, like confessions of privilege, can become a distraction from struggle in that it allows people to feel that they are doing something revolutionary — because in identifying themselves with the problem, and learning about the extent of the challenge, their world shifts — while running the risk of substituting awareness for engagement and action. We need to create a critical mass of people not only willing to understand and admit complicity with settler colonialism but also willing to commit to doing something about it.

That "something" is decolonization. This term might be familiar; the past decade has seen its use become almost common in media, university and colleges, and corporate diversity, equity, and inclusion efforts. However, much of the use of "decolonization" seems a general reference to addressing racism or as a form of "recognition" of settler colonialism unconnected to meaningful understanding and action. Decolonization has a very different meaning for Indigenous Peoples compared to the way Settler Canadians are likely to encounter it today. To unsettle these possible understandings and demonstrate the importance to Settler Canadians of developing a critical and active understanding of this concept, we focus here on decolonization as a call to action based on relationships to land.

Decolonization: From Awareness to Responsibility

Decolonization may feel like a slippery term, and it is helpful to start with an important distinction between "anti-colonial" and "decolonizing" actions or thought. Anti-colonial acts are those that, while against colonial power in some form, often continue to follow the form of colonial narratives. For example, anti-capitalism as we discussed in Chapter 4 can be anti-colonial — against neocolonialism perpetrated by big corporations using wealth as leverage — but it is not necessarily decolonizing. Decolonizing acts, on the other hand, are "defined by the mutual sharing of place, maintenance of social-spatial organizations commensurate with their respective cultures, and mediated through respectful protocols designed to maintain alliances across, rather than in spite of, difference."[1] Decolonization is more than anti-colonialism. It is not simply opposition to colonial imposition, or even endless resistance. Decolonization as an ethic and guiding principle for collective struggle is both the ending of colonialism and also the act of *becoming something other than colonial.*

Decolonization in the twentieth century was usually a concept that referenced the dismantling of European empires after the Second World War, and the devolution of governing authority over colonial holdings in Africa, Asia, and elsewhere to local control. A branch of the United Nations was devoted to pursuing this sort of decolonization, producing new independent states where before there were foreign-governed territories or protectorates. However, as discussed in Chapter 2, this was based on a very limited definition of colonization. Indigenous scholars through the latter half of the twentieth century and into the twenty-first refused this limited use of the term, and asserted far more holistic definitions. These included the concept of "internal colonization" to refer to how Canada and the United States continued to usurp Indigenous territories within the boundaries of their respective states. The concept of the Fourth World was also deployed to refer to Indigenous and other communities alienated from territory by the global order of states. These and other articulations of colonization that included settler colonial states like Canada challenged the narrow, simple definitions of decolonization in common usage. Crucially, though, Indigenous scholars argued that decolonization was not simply about establishing "Aboriginal" states that mirror those of Canada or the United States. As Hawaiian scholar Poka Laenui argued, "True decolonization is more than simply replacing indigenous or previously colonized people into the positions held by colonizers. Decolonization includes the re-evaluation of the political, social, economic and judicial structures themselves."[2] Our use of this term follows the work of Indigenous scholars and leaders who use decolonization to describe a present-day project of rooting colonialism out of worldviews, academic knowledge and research, Indigenous self-identity, and the social and political structures that impact Indigenous life.[3]

To be clear, we use decolonization here to describe an intensely political transformative process that is intended to regenerate Indigenous nationhood and place-relationships while dismantling structures of settler colonialism that oppose or seek to eliminate Indigenous Peoples from the land. Remembering the words of Chaw-win-is — "it's always all about the land" — decolonization must be understood through references not just to how people are organized as labour, or treated as racialized or ethnic communities, but how they relate to and respond to the land as a living entity. Leanne Simpson discusses decolonization for Anishinaabe people through the lens of "biskaabiiyang," a word that roughly translates to "returning to ourselves."[4] She talks about the importance of considering sacred stories in making contemporary decisions, and the need to understand governance not in an instrumental fashion, but through the lens of responsibilities to the land that support and sustain both human and non-human communities. As outsiders, we understand this as the work of revitalizing the lessons of Indigenous knowledge systems in changing circumstances. For example, Simpson also discusses how she grappled with a traditional prohibition in her community against women wearing pants rather than skirts or dresses, especially during ceremony. Simpson shows how a return to traditional knowledge, collective decision-making processes, attention to stories and dreams, and a focus on individual responsibility and autonomy led her to a decision that she felt was both consistent with her Anishinaabe identity and reflective of her own reality. One thing this story can show us is an insight into a process of careful and caring engagement with traditional practices beyond technique or current forms, to understand the *intent* of the practice so that it can be pursued in a form appropriate to current challenges.

For Indigenous Peoples, decolonization calls for a critical return to traditional values and practices of place-thought and land-centric political economies. The scope of such a project should immediately be apparent. This is no less than a call to replace the totalizing, sovereign authority of the Canadian state with multiple, negotiated, and contingent Indigenous governance structures. It is also a call to shatter the hegemony of capitalism and established ideas of race and heritage that dictate how we understand belonging on the land today. Decolonization is a revolutionary concept in the truest sense. More than an invocation to seize political power or ownership of territory, it is rather a call to fundamentally change how we generate political power and conceive of territory. Ideally, decolonization is not simply directed against settler colonial governments and economies, but instead is embodied in the creation of social movements and communities that sustain themselves on the land, revitalize traditional trade and Treaty networks, promote Indigenous cultural expression, and challenge narrow identity binaries, all of which can combine to make the structures of settler colonialism irrelevant and impotent.

Decolonization is open-ended and multiple, creating more and more different possibilities as it is pursued. Decolonization is a transformative process, one that cannot be fully revealed or understood until it is practiced, and even then, it will comprise a shifting and moving set of goals, always responding to the needs of Indigenous communities and the ruthless re-applications of colonial power and domination. Decolonization with respect to Indigenous Nations means the replacement of colonial authority as the lodestone of settler society with responsibilities to Indigenous Peoples as articulated through treaties, confederacies, alliances, and other political arrangements. In Canada, that means an end to settler colonial relationships to land, the dismantling of the spaces, systems, and stories of invasion that root Settler people to the nation and state, and the simultaneous restoration of Indigenous ways of knowing and being on the land. Decolonization is most definitely not a metaphor.[5] It involves actual social upheaval, restitution, and political and economic struggle.

The decolonization struggle for Indigenous Peoples takes the form of resurgence (Chapter 1). For Indigenous Peoples, decolonization is concerned with regeneration of Indigenous nationhood, that is, a regeneration and re-empowerment of collective, place-based Indigenous identities, expressed through unique political formations, from clans to confederacies. This approach is not about centring colonialism, but rather about focusing on the resilience and vibrancy of Indigenous Peoples, and re-energizing Indigenous Peoples, relationships, practices, and protocols. It is about building capacity and strength within Indigenous communities so that colonial structures are neither welcome nor needed.

Leanne Simpson has discussed resurgence from her perspective as an Anishinaabe woman working to reconnect with her culture and heritage.[6] She recognizes that her struggle, while similar to those of many other Indigenous Peoples, is unique to her nation, her family's experiences of colonization, and her own personal relationships and responsibilities. As such she argues that resurgence must be different for every person, informed by common principles rooted in Indigenous knowledge and culture but also reliant on the creative capacities and personal sense of responsibility in each and every Indigenous person. That means that differentials in power must also be considered, as well as differences in cultures, specific places and histories, and the desires of individuals and communities. For some Indigenous

People, simply surviving in the face of settler colonial elimination is an act of resurgence. In some cases, learning an Indigenous language might be an act of resurgence, while for others an equivalent act of resurgence is found in the piecing together of languages once thought lost, even if they do not achieve the ability to communicate with others. Given that settler colonialism has sought to eliminate Indigenous Peoples in a wide variety of ways, so too resurgence takes on diverse practices and goals. It is defined by the struggle for decolonization that centres the lived revitalization of Indigeneity. Resurgence does not "look like" any particular action, and it is certainly not defined/definable by Settler people or society.

Resurgent Indigenous nationhood demands and requires "a massive transformation" based on revitalized Indigenous political systems based in land-relationships.[7] Resurgence articulated like this drives decolonization. Settlers need to find our own ways of building decolonizing practices, engaging in transformative struggle, and supporting the resurgence of Indigenous nationhood without claiming or pretending to possess a connection to the spiritual and material practices of Indigenous identity. There is room in Indigenous political traditions for Settlers and other outsider or newcomer peoples to participate in Indigenous societies, and decolonization is no different. Through the struggle against settler colonialism, we can start to reveal the ways that we can actually decolonize in our relationships, in ourselves, and in our society, and the material and intangible benefits it could bring.

Decolonizing Settlers

For Settler people, too, decolonization implies a deep and transformative struggle. While it is sometimes easier to assert what decolonization is not, we must remember that decolonization is difficult to picture because it is a practice rather than a goal to be achieved. The process will require different efforts and produce different outcomes for everyone. Eve Tuck and K. Wayne Yang explain that decolonization

> means repatriating land to sovereign Native tribes and nations, abolition of slavery in its contemporary forms, and the dismantling of the imperial metropole. Decolonization "here" is intimately connected to anti-imperialism elsewhere. However, decolonial struggles here/there are not parallel, not shared equally, nor do they bring neat closure to the concerns of all involved — particularly not for settlers.[8]

Decolonization is a process that affects everyone — Indigenous, Settler and Others — living on lands currently under settler colonial domination, but likely in very different ways.

Decolonization, in these terms, is not a new concept, though conversations on meaningful decolonization have tended to be confined to Indigenous communities. Settler Canadians either have not perceived decolonization as having importance for them or have been unwilling or unable to look past their own fear and discomfort to see the potential for a very different way of being on the land. Focus groups conducted in both Canada and Australia have shown that Settler people may accept that Indigenous issues are important — and some go so far as to agree that acting on them is an ethical imperative — but these same people tend to think that addressing Indigenous issues is someone else's responsibility. This is either because Settler people believe that decolonization does not actually involve them because it is solely the domain of governments and other elite actors (not true), or that they cannot possibly know enough to actually contribute (also not true).[9] Canadians, by and large, see decolonization as something that could or should happen only elsewhere, not here, not in the land of the "peacemakers." Nothing could be further from the truth. As we have shown, colonialism inheres in the very basis of how Settler Canadians think of themselves and how they belong. For Settler Canadians trying to decolonize, the fundamental, difficult, necessary, and likely life-long challenge is to figure out how to *stop colonizing*.

Decolonization requires preparation and training. Part of that is found in education, and today we have better and easier access to useful information than ever before. Settler Canadians need to start by knowing whose land they are on, knowing the histories of the treaties and agreements that predate the histories of colonialism and settlement, and knowing the land itself, understanding the features of places that make them unique. But in addition to histories, settler decolonization is about looking forward. We need to ask: What is my hope for the future? What kind of person do I want to be and what kind of life do I want to live? How will my life (and my family's lives) be made better through a difficult struggle? What am I willing to do to get there? These are big questions, but it is in the asking, the unsettling, and in the hope we generate in our efforts and answers that we find the possibilities for positive and transformative change.

Undertaking this work needs to start with us. For Settlers, decolonizing change must start with taking responsibility. Time and again, Settler

Canadians have approached Indigenous communities or individuals asking for knowledge, asking to be taught: What is colonialism? What do Indigenous People *want*? More specifically, what do Indigenous People want *from me*? While it might make sense to some that Settler people should learn about the intricacies of colonial systems that are obscured to them from Indigenous Peoples who know them well and have been in resistance to them for centuries, this expectation must be seen a different way: it is the colonizer asking the community in resistance (struggling for survival) to take time and energy out to explain how that genocidal oppression functions. In previous work, we have discussed how even seeking knowledge and asking questions can take the form of "dishonest questions" when the intent is to seek an easy answer or return to comfort — some magic wand that will make the discomfort of settler colonialism disappear.

It can be different if questions are, instead, informed and thoughtful, posed with respect, responsibility, and accountability. Questions asked this way are more honest and effective and also require Settler people to accept that the answers are not owed, that they come with an expectation of engagement and effort. They also require individuals who are grappling with their own emotional reactions to what they are learning, and communities of concerned people finding each other, to do collective work. It will require people looking long and hard at their own daily lives, their training and skills, their positions and authorities, and then asking: "how can I leverage these things, even as they are bound up with settler colonialism, in the pursuit of decolonization?" This is the process, one we need to repeat and build on — individually and together — to develop support and capacity for change as we make it.

Today, those living in Canada who are willing to discuss settler colonialism and attempt decolonizing efforts have unprecedented access to resources including videos, books, art, reports, music, dissertations, and virtual learning spaces created by Indigenous experts and some Settler and non-Indigenous People engaged in decolonizing struggles. Libraries and librarians can help find information. YouTube videos such as those produced by the Digital Wampum series are an easily accessible resource. People around us will be engaging in learning and we can, and should, ask each other for recommendations and share resources. It might be a matter of searching for quality materials that work best for how we learn, experimenting with them on our own and with communities of trust, to educate ourselves on how best to deploy them. This is challenging, but hardly impossible. There is a difference between working respectfully with or taking the lead from Indigenous People and communities, and asking them to be responsible for teaching us basic concepts and information. Taking responsibility for addressing our ignorances and biases is key.

Figuring out *how* to engage — putting understanding into action — is often a barrier to taking effective decolonizing action. At times, the most obvious methods of engagement turn out to be deeply problematic. In engaging in decolonizing efforts, we need to be careful of a particular move to comfort: claiming special status as an Indigenous "ally." There have been many discussions, both in relationship to Indigenous Peoples' struggles and in the context of other social justice movements, about the problems associated with the term "ally" and with individuals who claim that status but go on to act in deeply problematic ways. Claiming "ally" as a sort of position that one can occupy or achieve simply seems too … comfortable. We have to overcome the ally fetish, the belief that we can declare ourselves exempt from settler colonialism through some relationships or personal actions in isolation from the rest of our involvement in settler colonialism.

For us, ally is a verb, not a noun. To ally with Indigenous Peoples implies constant action — the acts that show one as moving in coordinated support of Indigenous resurgence. Ally is not a get-out-of-jail-free card or a magic shield. It describes an active process, and we need to think more carefully about how we, as Settlers, relate to this concept. Instead of seeking special status as a Settler ally, what if we seek — through actions, words, and relationships — to *be* a decolonizing Settler?

But action of what kind? Supporting in what way? The questions remain, and Settler people who would ally with Indigenous and decolonizing efforts answer it again and again as our abilities and capabilities change. We have to embrace an ethic of mutual aid that is open-ended and founded on the understanding that we will make mistakes, that we will need to ask for guidance, but that the main thrust of how we conduct ourselves has to be based on our deep engagement with respectful relationships. It is important to support Indigenous resurgence and to work with Indigenous communities. For Settler Canadians, this is new ground, and we are likely to fail as often as we succeed. We must be wary of becoming arrogant when we help Indigenous movements achieve specific strategic goals, as momentary successes do not absolve us of the responsibility for continuing to engage in other, connected struggles. Some Settler activists have been called out for holding up past successes as a badge of honour and proof of achieving a special standard or relationship that absolves them of guilt (or at least of having to feel uncomfortable about being guilty), while failing to continue the processes of self-critique and collective struggle.[10] Calling yourself ally in the absence of current collaborative decolonizing efforts is an indulgence and risks appropriating Indigenous struggles and agency.

Ally is something you do — a kind of relationship and action you practice — not something you can claim to be.

Always in Relationship

Settler colonialism is not monolithic. Rather, it is the result of a multitude of acts, from exceptional power imposed by elites to banal and everyday lived dynamics of "average" Settler people. If Canadians can see settler colonial structures as dynamic and contested, we can also begin to see that Settler people can engage in decolonizing actions by participating in struggles against the domination and elimination of Indigenous Peoples. These same struggles also are necessary for Settler people to find our own liberation from the settler colonial structures that limit and control our lives. However, it should be clear that Settler decolonization is only meaningful if it is collective.

Individual Settler people begin by questioning and interrogating our own lives, but must seek ways to link their own specific circumstances, abilities, and realities to larger movements and social mobilizations. How can Settler people relate to each other and to land as decolonizing peoples? How do we find ways to act as part of decolonizing efforts and decolonizing social change? The key guiding principle for Settler Canadians is that decolonization is and must be always in relationship. Remember that Settler and Indigenous identities relate in complex and multiple ways, and can only be fully made to make sense in relationship to each other, to settler colonialism, and to the land.

Our call to centralize the concept of being "always in relationship" in Settler decolonization struggles recognizes that Settler people and Indigenous People are *already* in relationship. However, these relationships at present are often heavily influenced by settler colonial power, resulting in colonial spaces being built around and through the act of relating. Decolonization has to be about changing relationships and making them healthy, supportive, and safe, not just in spite of colonial power, but actively against it. This is inherently a prefigurative act — an instance where the pursuit of an end goal and the actual end goal are the same.[11] That is to say, pursuing decolonizing relationship building can be a form of "direct action" against settler colonialism that prefigures whatever broad social and societal changes are being more widely envisioned. Jamie Heckert, writing on "relating differently" in the context of sexuality, explains the transformative possibilities in this type of direct action:

> [Relating differently means] meeting another — listening bodily, with empathy, to what is currently alive in them, as opposed to responding to one's own thoughts of who another is, one's image of another ... Relationship, in this sense, side-steps and undermines a moral economy of person-hood and the "the subtle ruse of power" ... on which it depends, for there is neither truth of the self nor judgment ... Relating as equals serves as a gentle form of direct action — engaging directly with others to address oppressions rather than through representation, elected or imagined.[12]

It can be an uncomfortable, emotional thing to learn to listen to people really deeply, especially when they are critiquing us or telling us that our basic process is wrong, that our assumptions are wrong, that the things that we care about and value are wrong. Not wrong in an evaluative sense, but rather wrong in that they *hurt* people. No one likes being told, "what you've done has caused harm," especially when they believe, as most Settler Canadians do, that they have been trying to help, and one of the things that we carry with us — as privileged, Settler people — is insulation from the harms we cause.

Actively pursuing different kinds of relationships starts with Settlers learning to think relationally. Thinking relationally may not come naturally, but an important first step is to begin trying to see the world as networked together, and to understand how various actions and decisions will impact the world around us. Mohawk elder Jake Swamp discusses how the Mohawk worldview can be used as a guide for thinking about how we fit into larger processes of social change. He explains that the Mohawk way of knowing is not to examine a discrete object — a tree, or a leaf, or a river — but to understand how the river, tree, and leaf are connected.[13] Part of that comes from understanding how, as a Mohawk, one might be responsible for maintaining respect and relationships with particular places. The point here is not for Settler Canadians to copy Mohawk teachings, but to first understand and then apply the principle and practice of relationality. This helps us to think through how our daily choices about speaking up or staying silent, about our assumptions and actions, affect all others in the system in which we live.

If Settler people are going to pursue decolonization and support Indigenous resurgence, we have to centre the knowledge and needs of Indigenous Nations, to view the same place that Jake Swamp described but from our own, different perspective, standing behind and to the side of the people whose land we are on. First, we must look at the web of relationships and try first to learn about what matters to Indigenous Nations to whom we are accountable without waiting to be told what to do or when to do it. We have to try to *live* our relationships even as we work toward deeper understandings of what that actually means. Second, to figure out where to contribute our time, effort, or resources so they will be welcomed in support of Indigenous efforts. And third, to organize in our own community, be it among friends, across the dinner table, with our faith groups, work colleagues, or neighbours, to support Indigenous struggles more proactively and prefiguratively. This means looking for ways to be responsible, trying to avoid mistakes knowing it is likely impossible, framing our struggles toward better living on the land through obligations under Treaty, or expectations of us as a person who intends to live on this land in a respectful way. It means looking for lessons, thinking deeply, and then trying in our own lives.

There are, thankfully, many, and increasing, examples of communities that have or are trying to do this. Following the release of the Final Report of the Truth and Reconciliation Commission (TRC), many faith communities connected to the churches that ran the residential schools took on the work of trying to reckon with their past actions (and, of course, others did not, choosing to deflect criticism and return to their comfortable positions). However, the actions of the Mennonite Church of Canada (MCC) provide an interesting extension of these works. Though the MCC did not run residential schools, members recognized that they did bear responsibility for other, related acts of settler colonization. For example, members of the MCC were active in fostering and adopting Indigenous children taken during the Sixties Scoop. Earlier, Mennonite settlers cleared and claimed large areas of land around present-day Kitchener-Waterloo from that secured for the Six Nations of the Grand River by the Haldimand Grant. Despite some internal conflict, the MCC by and large was inspired by the TRC and committed to looking for ways to signal that they understood reconciliation to be more than a box-ticking exercise, and instead, as something to be actively pursued and lived.[14] The actions taken by the Mennonites resulted from work in their own communities to raise awareness, to set priorities, to address their specific involvements and complicity with colonization, and to support Indigenous People on their own terms.[15]

Other groups organized on what might be considered "radical" principles are also pursuing decolonization, often in ways that most Settler Canadians will never hear about. In conversation with Audra and Delee, both Indigenous women and active organizers, about the disruptions that non-Indigenous anarchist activists can have on Indigenous communities, we discussed the many different groups of people who sought to assist the land reclamation at 1492 Land Back Lane. While Audra and Delee had a number of pointed — and frustratingly common — critiques of most groups, they had praise for one in particular. This group demonstrated a considered approach: they came prepared to look after themselves, took up almost no community resources, and instead worked hard to understand what the community in resistance actually needed. Then they collectively made plans to provide those things. The group's attention to sustainable action was also notable, cycling members to avoid burnout and maintaining communications with their broader network to support the provision of material resources from outside the reclamation. They struck an outstanding balance between being prepared and self-motivated, and responsive, reflective, and responsible to the Indigenous People whose territory they were on.[16]

As decolonization struggles are necessarily collective, they are often about building networks of mutual support and reliance. Since self-education is important, having a group of people who can effectively learn together is a key advantage. This is in no small part because there is always more work to do and the process of decolonial struggle changes us as we experience it, a little bit all the time. We need help to be able to reflect on what we have done, and see our own successes and our own failings. Then we need to reconstitute strategies, reconstruct relationships to people and places, and try — as Settler people — to be responsible for ourselves. Groups, self-consciously in struggle together, can be vital in providing sounding boards and caring critical perspectives on our very personal work. Further, we have to remember that the commitment that we make to be in decolonizing struggle brings with it no foreknowledge of resolution, and most certainly does not mean we always get to win. We may lose or make mistakes (*we* certainly have), and many times we lose because we did not do the right thing. From experience, we know these failures hurt. But so long as we come back and try again, these are not dead ends, just lessons on the way to more effective efforts.

Working among Settler people and in Settler communities is important for Settler Canadian decolonization, but relationships with Indigenous communities are also needed. Our Settler responsibilities lie with working for change in Settler society, but these efforts have to be constantly informed by the work of Indigenous communities and people. This is a doubly important responsibility given Settler proclivities for occupying positions of leadership and control, as we discussed in Chapter 5. As respected Māori elder, Graham Smith, stated, "Indigenous Peoples must set the agenda for change themselves, not simply react to an agenda that has been laid out for us by others."[17] How Settlers respond to Indigenous agendas determines our effectiveness in supporting decolonization and resurgence, which is not always a clear task.

In earlier chapters, we discussed the Guswenta (Two Row) Treaty, created to define the agreed relationship between the Haudenosaunee Confederacy and Settler People in their territories. Recall that it is a long belt, two rows of purple running parallel on a field of white, a symbol for the ship and the canoe travelling along the same river, forever. Based on a simplistic understanding of the Guswenta, it is possible to fall into the trap of thinking of the Treaty as representing two completely separate societies that never interact, never consider each other. In fact, objections to decolonization often rely on emotionally laden language like "segregation" or "ethnonationalism" to reject the (perceived) goals of decolonial processes. This would be a fundamental misunderstanding of how the Guswenta is constructed, as it misses that the ship and the canoe are on the same river, and that care has to be taken to keep their courses balanced. The river will twist and turn, waves will come, the unexpected will challenge everyone to keep on course. That is inevitable. And the Guswenta itself — like the relationship it expresses — is designed with this in mind.

Go back and read again the poem at the start of this book. "Forever" by Mohawk and Tuscarora poet January Rogers is among the most important and moving interpretations of what it means to think about the Guswenta today as a relational document. Rogers reminds us that it is "hard work to maintain the middle row," referring here to the three rows of white wampum beads running down the middle of the Guswenta representing peace, friendship, and respect. She tells us that this is a relationship premised on "boundaries, not borders" and boundaries are not just something drawn on the land. They are also personal boundaries, boundaries of behaviour, knowing where to "draw the line" in a relationship. "Do *not* cross that line." This requires being in relationship — respectfully — with Indigenous People and communities so we know their needs and expectations, and are aware of Indigenous relationships to the land without seeking control of them. That is how trust is built. That is how we come to know that we can be friends. That is how we achieve true and lasting peace. Forever.

This includes knowing that when respectful offers of help are respectfully refused, it is important to step away. Mohawk scholar Audra Simpson has argued that any authentic Indigenous resurgence in pursuit of decolonization requires Indigenous Nations to exercise a refusal of relations — to set boundaries of when Settler people are not welcome or should not have access to a particular knowledge or practice. Without the ability to refuse relations, Indigenous People remain subject to the "good will" of Settlers; not something with a great deal of historical success. Settler people can become very invested in particular struggles for decolonization, but we never get to own the struggles of someone else. We do not get to dictate where or how Indigenous Peoples pursue resurgence. Our role is to mitigate the harm of ongoing colonialism, support Indigenous efforts, and dismantle colonial structures of invasion. The ability to displace colonialism from our lives as Settler people only becomes possible because Indigenous Peoples, struggles, literatures, and ways of thinking become valued and understood in our ways of thinking and doing things.

Decolonization is a story. It is not one that Settler Canadians are used to telling. It is a story that is multiple, that is experimental, that has many failures but also inspirational successes. It is one that carries the weight of clear-eyed ethical foundations. Decolonization as story — with all the power and life stories hold — inspires us to challenge the very idea of what the settler colonial story is, and as we tell these stories, we have to interrogate them. We have to ask ourselves: What is my role in colonization (here and elsewhere)? How does colonialism structure my life? Can I live the life I want without contributing to the oppression, displacement, and genocide of Indigenous Peoples? Can I live a *better* life? What are my responsibilities? Whose land do I live on and what are the traditional laws and practices here? Decolonization is attempting to find an answer that addresses all of these questions simultaneously, and the only way to find that answer is to try and live it. The way we struggle will inevitably shape who we are and who we can become.

Entering the Space of Dangerous Freedom

We approach all these difficult and serious questions with critical hope. Hope must be critical. It must be rooted in the recognition of possibility despite obstacles, not the belief that a path free of obstacles exists. Taking up the Settler identity and working to create decolonization in our own lives is no simple thing. Beyond the emotional barriers of fear and discomfort, we only have the beginnings of maps, plans, or blueprints for what our futures could be. As Settler people, we are conditioned to love our triumphant stories, the kind where, if we work hard and play by the rules, we will be rewarded. The pursuit of decolonization means rejecting that story, rejecting stories of nationalism and progress, peacemaker myths and terra nullius, and the notion that Canada, as it is, is all there is. The true struggle, though, is figuring out what kind of story we intend to live in its place.

Stories make us who we are. That is why it is so important to think about and talk about *being* Settler Canadians. We have to be aware of more than just what the stories are that we currently tell about ourselves, and how they shape our lives. We also need to think about how we are changing stories for the future, trying to pursue different ways of living. Decolonization makes two demands: First, that we commit to no single method for confronting colonialism — this makes sense if we recognize that colonialism overlaps with many hierarchies of power, and so decolonization must be pursued on intersectional lines. Second, that decolonization is a transformative process, with no clear or homogenizing end goals, and in which it is the responsibility of individuals and communities of all kinds to figure out how they fit. This means that we have to accept that when Settler people pursue the transformative process of decolonization, it may mean our eventual elimination *as Settler people*.

That is the possibility that must lie at the core of Settler Canadian engagements with decolonization. Settler Canadians, aware of complicity with and benefit from settler colonialism, aware of illegitimate residency on the land, and aware of roles in the ongoing violent displacement and attempted genocide of Indigenous Peoples, must accept that among the possible endpoints of decolonization is one in which everything we know changes. We also talked about the kinds of fear Settler Canadians experience when faced with the reality of settler colonialism and their complicity in its many harms. In the context of decolonization, a process that might change so much, we have to pay special attention to Settler fears of the unknown. This fear of what life might look like must be acknowledged. This fear must be recognized, understood, and confronted lest it prevent us from following through with decolonizing efforts. It is here that the bounds of life structured by settler colonialism begin to break. That is in some senses what decolonization is offering: a different story that does not follow the expected script of Canadian national exceptionalism, banal and friendly multiculturalism, and heroics at hockey. And as much as the story of decolonization must be about Indigenous nationhood, it is not only for Indigenous Peoples. The story of decolonization is one that has room for many voices, one where many people can find ways to belong on the land without dominating, destroying, and displacing Indigenous societies. It is a story in which Settler people can become something more than merely colonizers, not by ignoring their status on the land, but by accepting, owning, and reshaping it. It is a story that may change the teller, it is a story that may change in the telling. It is not one story, but many.

If we can overcome our fear of life outside of settler colonial structures, there is a future for us — not a certain one, but certainly a possible one — in which Indigenous nationhood is resurgent and regenerated, and "Indigenous" as a collective identity falls by the wayside. All that remains are the many nations, the new and old confederacies and Treaty territories. At that point, maybe "Settler" loses any meaning too. In this future, maybe there are just the individual terms by which each Indigenous Nation or community refers to "people who come to stay."

Settler: the word itself is not important. Rather, the concept it represents today is essential and much needed at this point in history. It expresses and connects an understanding of the complex relationship between the different peoples on the land and under settler colonialism. So, if the relationships informing that concept change, the words — and our identities — will change, too. This, then, is an opportunity to re-imagine our ideas of society, nation, and belonging, and challenge ourselves to come up with better definitions that do not rely on the elimination but on the resurgence of Indigenous Peoples through an acute awareness of how settler colonialism works in our lives. It is time to step into the "space of dangerous freedom."

We were introduced to this concept through Indigenous geography. Traditionally, many Mohawk and other Haudenosaunee villages were built with a surrounding palisade wall, with a clearing between the village and any surrounding forest. No one could approach the village and cross the clearing without being seen. This can be understood as a metaphor for how we approach decolonization struggles, drawing parallels between committing to these struggles and stepping into a space "of dangerous freedom in that they undo the unequal relationship at the root of settler colonialism — a 'danger' in the sense that admitting that the settler project has failed to provide the levels of peace."[18] This space is free because we have the choice to approach the village, to return to the woods, to stay where we are and wait. All those choices have consequences. The people in the village see us, though we cannot see them. They hold the power. This is a different situation than most Settler people are accustomed to, being the one in the open, observed and vulnerable. We can choose to stay in this uncomfortable, unsettled space — a space with no guarantees, where we have to constantly learn and adapt — or we can go back to the woods. But that will be *our* choice, not one made for us by colonial elites and state authorities.

Stepping into the clearing and standing in the space of dangerous freedom is more than a metaphor. We reflect this practice in the decision to actively identify as a Settler person. When we write or speak in public, when we meet new people in Canada and abroad and they ask where we are from or how we identify, we centralize our relationships with the land, our entanglements with colonialism — our being Settler Canadian. This is a small but significant effort that permeates our lives. Owning Settler Canadian as our real identity on these lands is our first step into the clearing. When we say Settler, it is a reminder to us to rethink our own positionality, to consider what the word means and what it implies for our relationships to the land. We use it among different groups, though this is less controversial in some contexts than others. It has felt harder to say Settler at a barbeque with extended family than in a classroom, and the conversations that follow are strikingly different. This declaration, or rather, this identification is not intended as simply adversarial or to win praise. It is a reminder for us, a memento that we carry. We say Settler in part because it helps prevent our thoughts from turning toward settler colonial normalization. It reminds us that we can be coopted into settler colonialism at any point and that we remain complicit all the time. In the clearing, we are visible to each other and ourselves.

Engagement and action necessarily follow from approaching and entering the clearing and being seen. Once we step into this space and identify each other, we can then experiment with different ways of organizing ourselves or functioning as a society. We hope to invite others into these conversations by making ourselves visible by saying Settler, Settler Canadian, and Settler people. We see the impacts that speaking this word can bring — sometimes frightening, sometimes difficult, and sometimes very positive — and we believe it is worth the risk of engaging on those terms. We bring resources in terms of education, ideas for changing our actions and behaviour, and hope that claiming our Settler identities can be a part of working to address the many shortcomings of our people and (re)establishing the trust of Indigenous Nations and communities. We believe that, for everyone, active identification as a Settler Canadian can signal to others that we are ready and committed to honestly addressing settler colonialism in Canada. It is an indication that we are refusing one of the pillars of settler colonialism — the disavowal that props up invisibility and drives toward erasure and indigenization.

We say Settler because it's a place from which we can determine how we live on these lands. We say Settler to signal that we're ready to do the work. We say Settler because we believe ethical and exciting decolonial futures are possible. We say Settler because we have seen the identification shake how people feel about themselves and their belonging, and how it has been the start of decolonizing awareness and action.

We say Settler because it is who we are. We say Settler because it is not everything we could be. Now, let's get to work.

Notes

1 Adam J. Barker and Jenny Pickerill, "Radicalizing Relationships to and through Shared Geography: Why Anarchists Need to Understand Indigenous Connections to Land and Place," *Antipode* 44, 5 (2012), 1721.
2 Poka Laenui, "Processes of Decolonization," in *Reclaiming Indigenous Voice and Vision*, ed. Marie Battiste (Vancouver: UBC Press, 2000).
3 On decolonization, see, generally, Taiaiake Alfred, *Wasáse: Indigenous Pathways to Action and Freedom* (Peterborough, ON: Broadview Press, 2005); Linda Tuhiwai Smith, *Decolonizing Methodologies: Research and Indigenous Peoples* (London: Zed Books, 1999); Leanne Simpson, *Dancing on Our Turtle's Back: Stories of Nishnaabeg Re-Creation, Resurgence, and a New Emergence* (Winnipeg: ARP, 2011); Eve Tuck and K. Wayne Yang, "Decolonization Is Not a Metaphor," *Decolonization: Indigeneity, Education & Society* 1, 1 (2012), Harsha Walia, *Undoing Border Imperialism* (Oakland: AK Press, 2013), 248-276.
4 Simpson, *Dancing on Our Turtle's Back*.
5 Tuck and Yang's "Decolonization Is Not a Metaphor" has, since its publication, become a focal point for Indigenous scholarship, social movement research on anti-colonialism and decolonization, and activist practice in Canada and the United States.
6 Simpson, *Dancing on Our Turtle's Back*.
7 Naomi Klein, "Dancing the World into Being: A Conversation with Idle No More's Leanne Simpson," Yes! Magazine (March 5, 2013).
8 Tuck and Yang, "Decolonization Is Not a Metaphor," 31.
9 Ravi Da Costa and Tom Clark, "On the Responsibility to Engage: Non-Indigenous Peoples in Settler States," Settler Colonial Studies, 6, 3 (2016).
10 This is something that we have witnessed and even run afoul of ourselves. While it is not helpful to name names here, we would recommend reading the editorial by Nahnda Garlow in the *Two Row Times*: "In Defense of Myself and the Land," which discusses these sorts of problematic relationships and the impact that they have on Indigenous Peoples in struggle. See, Nahnda Garlow, "In Defense of Myself and the Land," *Two Row Times,* April 22, 2015, tworowtimes.com/opinions/columns/scone-dogs-seed-beads/ in-defense-of-myself-and-the-land/.
11 On prefiguration, see, Richard D.F. Day, *Gramsci Is Dead: Anarchist Currents in the Newest Social Movements* (London: Pluto Press, 2005); Uri Gordon, *Anarchy Alive! Anti-Authoritarian Politics from Practice to Theory* (London: Pluto Press, 2008).
12 Jamie Heckert, "Relating Differently," *Sexualities* 13, 4 (2010), 404.
13 Jake Swamp, "Kanikonriio: Power of a Good Mind," in *Alliances: Re/Envisioning Indigenous–Non-Indigenous Relationships*, ed. Lynne Davis (University of Toronto Press, 2010).
14 Dan Dyck, "Land Rights Apply to my Church and my Home," *Canadian Mennonite*. March 11, 2017, canadianmennonite.org/stories/'land-rights-apply-my-church-and-my-home'.
15 Steve Heinrich, ed, *Unsettling the Word: Biblical Experiments in Decolonization* (New York: Orbis, 2019).

16 These conversations became the basis of an episode of the *Anarchist Essays* podcast, "Episode 27: Pitfalls of Anarchist Solidarity with Indigenous Communities."
17 Graham Smith, "Protecting and Respecting Indigenous Knowledge," in *Reclaiming Indigenous Voice and Vision*, ed. Marie Battiste (Vancouver: University of British Columbia Press, 2000), 210.
18 Adam J. Barker and Emma Battell Lowman, "The Spaces of Dangerous Freedom: Disrupting Settler Colonialism," in *The Limits of Settler Colonial Reconciliation: Non-Indigenous People and the Responsibility to Engage*, eds. Sarah Maddison, Tom Clark, and Ravi de Costa (New York: Springer, 2016).

Bibliography

Abella, Irving, and Harold Troper. 1983. *None Is Too Many: Canada and the Jews of Europe, 1933–1948.* Toronto: Lester & Orpen Dennys.

Adams, Howard. 1989. *Prison of Grass: Canada from a Native Point of View.* Saskatoon, SK: Fifth House Publishers.

Absolon, Kathleen. 2022. *Kaandossiwin — How We Come to Know: Indigenous Re-Search Methodologies, 2nd Edition.* Halifax: Fernwood Publishing.

Ahmed, Sarah. 2014. "Brick Walls: Racism & Other Hard Histories." Presented at Race Conference 2014: Unsettling Conversations, Unmaking Racisms & Colonialisms, University of Alberta.

Aldred, Lisa. 2000. "Plastic Shamans and Astroturf Sun Dances: New Age Commercialization of Native American Spirituality." *American Indian Quarterly* 24, 3.

Alfred, Taiaiake. 2009. "Colonialism and State Dependency." *International Journal of Indigenous Health* 5, 2.

———. 2006. "Sovereignty — An Inappropriate Concept." In *The Indigenous Experience: Global Perspectives,* edited by Roger Maaka and Chris Anderson. Ottawa: Canadian Scholars Press.

———. 2005. *Wasase: Indigenous Pathways to Action and Freedom.* Broadview Press.

Allan, Billie and V.C. Rhonda Hackett. 2022. *Decolonizing Equity.* Halifax: Fernwood Publishing.

Allooloo, Siku. 2014. "From Outrage to Radical Love." *Indigenous Nationhood Movement* blog, March 7, 2014. nationsrising.org/from-outrage-to-radical-love/.

Anarchist Essays. 2023. "Episode 27: Pitfalls of Anarchist Solidarity with Indigenous Communities." Anarchism Research Group. Loughborough University. youtube.com/watch?v=pKqChHW4SwU.

Andersen, Chris. 2014. *Métis: Race, Recognition and the Struggle for Indigenous Peoplehood.* Vancouver: UBC Press.

Anonymous. n.d. "Water Falling on Granite: Deference Politics, Indigenous Leadership, and Anarchist Relationality." The Anarchist Library. theanarchistlibrary.org/library/anonymous-water-falling-on-granite/.

Arnett, Chris. 1999. *Terror of the Coast: Land Alienation and Colonial War on Vancouver Island and the Gulf Islands, 1849–1863*. Vancouver: Talonbooks.

Asch, Michael. 2014. *On Being Here to Stay: Treaties and Aboriginal Rights in Canada*. University of Toronto Press.

Bailey, Jane. 2021. "Confronting 'Cognitive Imperialism': What Reconstructing a Contracts Law School Course Is Teaching Me About Law." In *Royally Wronged: The Royal Society of Canada and Indigenous People*, edited by Constance Backhouse, Cynthia E. Milton, Margaret Kovach, and Adele Perry. Montreal: MQUP.

Baloy, Natalie. 2016. "Spectacles and Spectres: Settler Colonial Spaces in Vancouver." *Settler Colonial Studies* 6, 3.

Banivanua Mar, Tracey. 2010. "Carving Wilderness: Queensland's National Parks and the Unsettling of Emptied Lands, 1890–1910." In *Making Settler Colonial Space: Perspectives on Race, Place and Identity*, edited by Tracey Banivanua Mar and Penelope Edmonds. New York: Palgrave Macmillan.

Barker, Adam J. 2023. *Making and Breaking Settler Space: Five Centuries of Colonization in North America*. Vancouver: UBC Press.

———. 2014. "'A Direct Act of Resurgence, a Direct Act of Sovereignty': Reflections on Idle No More, Indigenous Activism, and Canadian Settler Colonialism." *Globalizations* 12, 1.

———. 2009. "The Contemporary Reality of Canadian Imperialism: Settler Colonialism and the Hybrid Imperial State." *American Indian Quarterly* 33, 3.

Barker, Adam J. and Emma Battell Lowman. 2024. "Indigenous Resurgence." In *The Handbook of Indigenous Public Policy*, edited by Sheryl Lightfoot and Sarah Maddison. Cheltenham: Edward Elgar Publishing.

———. 2023. "Settler Colonialism and the Criminalization of Indigenous Peoples in Canada." In *Justice, Indigenous Peoples, and Canada: A History of Courage and Resilience*, edited by Kathryn M. Campbell and Stephanie Wellman. New York: Routledge.

———. 2016. "The Spaces of Dangerous Freedom: Disrupting Settler Colonialism." In *The Limits of Settler Colonial Reconciliation: Non-Indigenous People and the Responsibility to Engage*, edited by Sarah Maddison, Tom Clark and Ravi de Costa. New York: Springer.

Barker, Adam J., and Jenny Pickerill. 2012. "Radicalizing Relationships to and through Shared Geography: Why Anarchists Need to Understand Indigenous Connections to Land and Place." *Antipode* 44, 5.

Barker, Adam J., Toby Rollo, and Emma Battell Lowman. 2016. "Settler Colonialism and the Consolidation of Canada in the 20th Century." In *World History of Settler Colonialism*, edited by Edward Cavanagh and Lorenzo Veracini. London: Routledge.

Barman, Jean. 2010. "Race, Greed and Something More: The Erasure of Urban Indigenous Space in Early Twentieth-Century British Columbia." In *Making Settler Colonial Space: Perspectives on Race, Place and Identity*, edited by Tracey Banivanua Mar and Penelope Edmonds. New York: Palgrave-Macmillan.

Barrera, Jorge. 2020. "Beyond the Barricades." *CBC News*. November 25, 2020. newsinteractives.cbc.ca/longform/1492-land-back-lane-caledonia-six-nations-protest/.

Barrera, Jorge. 2019. "National Inquiry Calls Murders and Disappearances of Indigenous Women a 'Canadian Genocide.'" *CBC News*. May 31, 2019. cbc.ca/news/indigenous/genocide-murdered-missing-indigenous-women-inquiry-report-1.5157580.
BBC News. 2022. "Dozens more graves found at former residential school sites," *BBC News*. February 16, 2022. bbc.co.uk/news/world-us-canada-60395242.
Bernstein, Jaela. 2021. "Canadians Are Among the World's Worst Carbon Emitters. Here's What We Can Do About It." *CBC News*. October 8, 2021. cbc.ca/news/science/how-canadians-can-cut-carbon-footprints-1.6202194.
Black, Conrad. 2014. *Rise to Greatness: The History of Canada From the Vikings to the Present*. Toronto: McClelland & Stewart.
Blackstock, Cindy. 2022. "The Case for an Inquiry into Canada's Treatment of First Nations Children." *Maclean's*, January 21, 2022. macleans.ca/opinion/canadian-government-first-nations-cindy-blackstock/.
———. 2004. *National Children's Alliance Policy Paper on Aboriginal Children*. Ottawa: First Nations Child and Family Caring Society of Canada.
Blomley, Nicholas. 1996. "'Shut the Province Down': First Nations Blockades in British Columbia, 1984–1995." *BC Studies* 111 (Autumn).
Borrows, John. 2010. *Canada's Indigenous Constitution*. University of Toronto Press.
———. 2002. *Recovering Canada: The Resurgence of Indigenous Law*. University of Toronto Press.
Brice, Melanie Griffith, Russell Fayant, Andrea Sterzuk, and Patrick J. Lewis. 2024. "Wena ka tapaymish ekwa kakway ka dipayhtamun? (Who Claims You and What Do You Claim?)." In *Unsettling Education: Decolonizing and Indigenizing the Land*, edited by Anna-Leah King, Kathleen O'Reilly, and Patrick J. Lewis. CSP Books.
Broome, Alice. 2023. "From the Archive: The Indian Diaspora in British Colonial Africa." *British Online Archives*. June 22, 2023. britishonlinearchives.com/posts/category/articles/629/from-the-archive-the-indian-diaspora-in-british-colonial-africa.
Bruyneel, Kevin. 2021. *Settler Memory: The Disavowal of Indigeneity and the Politics of Race in the United States*. UNC Press Books.
———. 2007. *The Third Space of Sovereignty: The Postcolonial Politics of U.S.–Indigenous Relations*. Minneapolis: University of Minnesota Press.
Budd, Brian. 2024. *News Framing of Indigenous Politics in Canada: Representation in the Era of Reconciliation*. New York: Springer.
Bulbulian, Maurice (dir.). 1987 *Dancing Around the Table, Part 1*. Documentary film. National Film Board of Canada. nfb.ca/film/dancing_around_the_table_1/.
Buchner, Katelynn, Tammy Pearson, and Susan Burke. 2022. "Indigenous Women's Experiences with Child Protection at Their Child's Birth." *Practice* 34, 4.
Byrd, Jodi. 2011. *The Transit of Empire: Indigenous Critiques of Colonialism*. Minneapolis: University of Minnesota Press.
Carleton, Sean. 2021. "'I don't Need Any More Education': Senator Lynn Beyak, Residential School Denialism, and Attacks on Truth and Reconciliation in Canada." *Settler Colonial Studies* 11, 4.
Cardinal, Harold, and Walter Hildebrandt. 2000. *Treaty Elders of Saskatchewan: Our Dream Is That Our Peoples Will One Day Be Clearly Recognized as Nations*. University of Calgary Press.

CBC News. 2022. "Indigenous Leaders Condemn Misappropriation of Orange Shirt Day by Protest Convoy." *CBC News* February 12, 2022. cbc.ca/news/canada/british-columbia/indigenous-leaders-condemn-misappropriation-of-orange-shirt-day-by-protest-convoy-1.6349344.

———. 2020."Man Who Threw Trailer Hitch at Indigenous Woman Found Guilty of Manslaughter." *CBC News*. December 14, 2020. cbc.ca/news/canada/thunder-bay/bushby-thunder-bay-trailer-hitch-ruling-1.5840583.

———. 2008. "Conservative MP Apologizes for 'Hurtful' Comments on Aboriginal People." *CBC News*. June 12, 2008. cbc.ca/news/canada/conservative-mp-apologizes-for-hurtful-comments-on-aboriginal-people-1.712106.

Cecco, Leyland. 2021. "'Dead Because She Was Indigenous': Québec Coroner Says Atikemekw Woman a Victim of Systemic Racism." *The Guardian*. October 12, 2021. theguardian.com/world/2021/oct/06/joyce-echaquan-coroner-indigenous-systemic-racism-death.

Choudry, Aziz, Mandisi Majavu, and Lesley Wood. 2013. "Struggles, Strategies and Analysis of Anticolonial and Postcolonial Social Movements." *Interface* 5, 1.

Clarkson, Adrienne. 2014. *Belonging: The Paradox of Citizenship*. Toronto: Anansi Press.

Claxton, Nicholas. 2008. "ISTÁ SĆIÁNEW, ISTÁ SXOLE 'To Fish as Formerly': The Douglas Treaties and the WSÁNEĆ Reef-Net Fisheries." In *Lighting the Eighth Fire: The Liberation, Resurgence, and Protection of Indigenous Nations*, edited by Leanne Simpson. Winnipeg: Arbeiter Ring Publishing.

Clayton, Daniel. 1999. *Islands of Truth: The Imperial Fashioning of Vancouver Island*. Vancouver: UBC Press.

Coleman, Daniel. 2016. "Indigenous Place and Diaspora Space: Of Literalism and Abstraction." *Settler Colonial Studies* 6, 1.

Cooper, Afua. 2007. *The Hanging of Angelique: The Untold Story of Canadian Slavery and the Burning of Old Montreal*. Athens, GA: University of Georgia Press.

Coulthard, Glen, 2014. *Red Skin, White Masks: Rejecting the Colonial Politics of Recognition*. Minneapolis: University of Minnesota Press.

———. 2007. "Subjects of Empire: Indigenous Peoples and the 'Politics of Recognition' in Canada." *Contemporary Political Theory* 6, 4.

Cousin, Glynis. 2010. "Positioning Positionality: The Reflexive Turn." In *New Approaches to Qualitative Research: Wisdom and Uncertainty*, edited by Maggi Savin-Baden and Claire Howell Major. London: Routledge.

Cresswell, Tim. 2004. *Place: A Short Introduction*. Oxford: Blackwell Publishing.

Crosby, Andrew, and Jeffrey Monaghan, 2018. *Policing Indigenous Movements: Dissent and the Security State*. Fernwood Publishing.

Culhane, Dara. 2003. "Their Spirits Live within Us: Aboriginal Women in Downtown Eastside Vancouver Emerging into Visibility." *American Indian Quarterly* 27, 3.

D'Arcy, Paul. 1998. "No Empty Ocean: Trade and Interaction Across the Pacific Ocean in the Middle of the Eighteenth Century." In *Studies in the Economic History of the Pacific Rim*, edited by Sally Miller, A.J.H. Latham, and Dennis Flynn. London: Routledge.

Da Costa, Ravi, and Tom Clark. 2016. "On the Responsibility to Engage: Non-Indigenous Peoples in Settler States." *Settler Colonial Studies*, 6, 3.

———. 2013. "Testimonial Textures: Examining the Poetics of Non-Indigenous Stories about Reconciliation." In *Storytelling: Critical and Creative Approaches*, edited by Jan Shaw, Philippa Kelly, and L.E. Semler. London, UK: Palgrave Macmillan.

Daschuk, James. 2013. *Clearing the Plains: Disease, Politics of Starvation, and the Loss of Aboriginal Life*. Regina, SK: University of Regina Press.

Day, Richard J.F. 2005. *Gramsci Is Dead: Anarchist Currents in the Newest Social Movements*. London: Pluto Press.

———. 2000. *Multiculturalism and the History of Canadian Diversity*. University of Toronto Press.

Day, Iyko. 2015. "Being or Nothingness: Indigeneity, Antiblackness, and Settler Colonial Critique." *Critical Ethnic Studies* 1, 2.

Dean, Amber. 2010. "Space, Temporality, History: Encountering Hauntings in Vancouver's Downtown Eastside." In *The West and Beyond*, edited by Alvin Finkel, Sarah Carter, and Peter Fortna. Athabasca University Press.

de Leeuw, Sarah, Margo Greenwood, and Nicole Lindsay. 2013. "Troubling Good Intentions." *Settler Colonial Studies* 3, 3–4.

Deloria, Vine, Jr. 2006. *The World We Used to Live In: Remembering the Powers of the Medicine Men*. Golden, CO: Fulcrum Publishing.

———. 2004. "Philosophy and the Tribal Peoples." In *American Indian Thought*, edited by Anne Waters. Malden, MA: Blackwell Publishing.

———. 2003 (1973). *God Is Red: A Native View of Religion*, 30th anniversary edition. Golden, CO: Fulcrum Publishing.

———. 1997. *Red Earth, White Lies: Native Americans and the Myth of Scientific Fact*. Golden, CO: Fulcrum Publishing.

Deloria, Vine, Jr., and Daniel P. Wildcat. 2001. *Power and Place: Indian Education in America*. Golden, CO: Fulcrum Resources.

Derworiz, Colette. 2024 "Woman Pleads Guilty in Inuit Identity Fraud Case, Charges Dropped Against Daughters." *CTV News* February 10, 2024. ottawa.ctvnews.ca/woman-pleads-guilty-in-inuit-identity-fraud-case-charges-dropped-against-daughters-1.6763947.

Dhillon, Jaskiran and Will Parrish. 2019. "Canada Police Prepared to Shoot Indigenous Activists, Documents Show." *The Guardian*. December 20, 2019. theguardian.com/world/2019/dec/20/canada-indigenous-land-defenders-police-documents.

Denis, Jeff. 2015. "A Four Directions Model: Understanding the Rise and Resonance of an Indigenous Self-Determination Movement." In *More Will Sing Their Way to Freedom: Indigenous Resistance and Resurgence*, edited by Elaine Coburn. Halifax: Fernwood Publishing.

———. 2012. "Transforming Meanings and Group Positions: Tactics and Framing in Anishinaabe–White Relations in Northwestern Ontario, Canada." *Ethnic and Racial Studies* 35, 3.

DeVries, Laura. 2011.*Conflict in Caledonia: Aboriginal Land Rights and the Rule of Law*. Vancouver: UBC Press.

Diptee, Audra. 2002. "Black and Indigenous Protesters Are Treated Differently Than the 'Convoy' Because of Canada's Ongoing Racism." *The Conversation*. February

17, 2002. theconversation.com/black-and-indigenous-protesters-are-treated-differently-than-the-convoy-because-of-canadas-ongoing-racism-176653.

Donovan, Moira. 2023. "Why Are Indigenous Fisheries Still Drawing Anger and Violence?" *The Tyee*. October 27, 2023. thetyee.ca/News/2023/10/27/Canada-Ignoring-Supreme-Court-Indigenous-Fisheries-Violence/.

Dunbar-Ortiz, Roxanne. 2014. *An Indigenous Peoples' History of the United States*. Boston: Beacon Press.

Dyck, Dan. 2017. "Land Rights Apply to my Church and my Home." *Canadian Mennonite*. March 11, 2017). canadianmennonite.org/stories/'land-rights-apply-my-church-and-my-home'.

Ede, Amy. 2022. "The Convoy's Appropriations Are an Attack on Indigenous People," *The Tyee*, February 18, 2022. thetyee.ca/Opinion/2022/02/18/Convoy-Appropriations-Attack-Indigenous-People/.

Edmonds, Penelope. 2016. "'Polishing the Chain of Friendship': Two Row Wampum Renewal Celebrations and Matters of History." In *Settler Colonialism and (Re)conciliation*, edited by Penelope Edmonds. London: Palgrave Macmillan.

Edwards, Peter. 2011. *One Dead Indian: The Premier, the Police, and the Ipperwash Crisis*. Vancouver: Stoddart Publishing.

Evri, Yuval, and Hagar Kotef. 2022. "When Does a Native Become a Settler? (With Apologies to Zreik and Mamdani)." *Constellations: An International Journal of Critical and Democratic Theory* 29, 1.

Ewen, Alex. 2014. "Bering Strait Theory, Pt. 1: How Dogma Trumped Science." *Indian Country Today*. indiancountrytodaymedianetwork.com/2014/06/13/bering-strait-theory-pt-1-how-dogma-trumped-science-155284.

Fanon, Frantz. 1963. *The Wretched of the Earth*. New York: Grove Press.

Faragher, John Mack. 2014. "Commentary: Settler Colonial Studies and the North American Frontier." *Settler Colonial Studies* 4, 2.

Fine, Sean. 2015"Chief Justice says Canada attempted 'cultural genocide' on Aboriginals." *The Globe and Mail*. May 28, 2015. theglobeandmail.com/news/national/chief-justice-says-canada-attempted-cultural-genocide-on-aboriginals/article24688854/.

Flanagan, Tom. 2000. *First Nations? Second Thoughts*. Kingston: McGill-Queens Press.

Forester, Brett. 2023. "Grassy Narrows Chief Questions Federal Commitment to Mercury Care Home Amid Delays, Soaring Costs." *CBC News*. June 20, 2023. cbc.ca/news/indigenous/grassy-narrows-delays-mercury-care-home-1.6882699#:~:text=The%20federal%20government%20and%20Grassy,centre%20to%20nearly%20%2490%20million.

Fournier, Emelia. 2023. "Federal Government Needs to Counter Rise in Residential School Denialism Says Kimberly Murray." *APTN News*. September 28, 2023. aptnnews.ca/national-news/federal-government-needs-counter-rise-in-residential-school-denialism-says-kimberly-murray/.

Frank, Gloria Jean. 2000. "'That's My Dinner on Display': A First Nations Reflection on Museum Culture." *BC Studies* 125/126 (Spring/Summer).

Fraser, Crystal Gail. 2024. "Residential School Denialism Is an Attack on the Truth." *The Conversation*. July 3, 2024. theconversation.com/residential-school-denialism-is-an-attack-on-the-truth-233318.

Freeman, Victoria, 2010. "'Toronto Has No History!': Indigeneity, Settler Colonialism, and Historical Memory in Canada's Largest City." *Urban History Review* 38, 2.
Garba, Tapji, and Sara-Maria Sorentino. 2020. "Slavery Is a Metaphor: A Critical Commentary on Eve Tuck and K. Wayne Yang's 'Decolonization Is Not a Metaphor.'" *Antipode* 52, 3.
Garlow, Nahnda. 2015. "In Defense of Myself and the Land." *Two Row Times* online newspaper. April 22, 2015. tworowtimes.com/opinions/columns/scone-dogs-seed-beads/in-defense-of-myself-and-the-land/.
Greenwood, Margo. 2021. "An Open Invitation to Address Anti-Indigenous Systemic Racism." *The Lancet* 397, 10293.
Gaudry, Adam. 2018. "Communing with the Dead: The 'New Métis,' Métis Identity Appropriation, and the Displacement of Living Métis Culture." *American Indian Quarterly* 42, 2.
Gaudry, Adam and Darryl Leroux. 2017. "White Settler Revisionism and Making Métis Everywhere: The Evocation Of Métissage in Québec and Nova Scotia." *Critical Ethnic Studies*, 3, 1.
Gillham, Patrick, Bob Edwards, and John Noakes. 2011. "Strategic Incapacitation and the Policing of Occupy Wall Street Protests in New York City." *Policing and Society* 23, 1.
Go, Amy, Dora Nipp and Winnie Ng. 2015. "What This UNB Professor Practices Is Intolerance, Not Sociology." *Globe and Mail*. January 22, 2015. theglobeandmail.com/globe-debate/what-this-unb-professor-practices-is-intolerance-not-sociology/article22573743/.
Godlewska, Anne, Laura Schaefli, and Paul Chaput. 2013. "First Nations Assimilation Through Neoliberal Educational Reform." *The Canadian Geographer* 57, 3.
Gordon, Todd. 2006. *Cops, Crime and Capitalism: The Law-and-Order Agenda in Canada*. Halifax: Fernwood Publishing.
Gordon, Uri. 2008. *Anarchy Alive! Anti-Authoritarian Politics from Practice to Theory*. London: Pluto Press.
Goulding, Warren. 2001. *Just Another Indian: A Serial Killer and Canada's Indifference*. Calgary: Fifth House Publishers.
Grande, Sandy. 2013. "Accumulation of the Primitive: The Limits of Liberalism and the Politics of Occupy Wall Street." *Settler Colonial Studies* 3, 3–4.
Green, Adam J. 2006. "Telling 1922s Story of National Crime: Canada's First Chief Medical Officer and the Aborted Fight for Aboriginal Health Care." *Canadian Journal of Native Studies* XXVI, 2.
Green, Joyce. 2017. *Making Space for Indigenous Feminisms, 2nd edition*. Halifax: Fernwood Press.
Greenwood, Margo. 2021"An Open Invitation to Address Anti-Indigenous Systemic Racism." *The Lancet* 397, 10293.
Gunew, Sneja. 2004. *Haunted Nations: The Colonial Dimensions of Multiculturalisms*. New York: Routledge.
Haig-Brown, Celia. 2010. "Indigenous Thought, Appropriation, and Non-Aboriginal People." *Canadian Journal of Education* 33, 4.
Hall, Anthony. 2003. *American Empire and the Fourth World: The Bowl with One Spoon, Part 1*. Montréal: McGill-Queens University Press.

Hall, Stuart. 1996. "Cultural Identity and Cinematic Representation." In *Black British Cultural Studies: A Reader*, edited by Houston Baker, Manthia Diawara, and Ruth Lindeborg. Chicago: University of Chicago Press.

Hamilton, A.C. 2001. *A Feather Not a Gavel: Working Towards Aboriginal Justice*. Winnipeg: Great Plains Publications.

Harris, Cole. 2004. "How Did Colonialism Dispossess? Comments from an Edge of Empire." *Annals of the Association of American Geographer* 94, 1.

Heckert, Jamie. 2010. "Relating Differently." *Sexualities* 13, 4.

Hebert, Joel. 2019. "'Sacred Trust': Rethinking Late British Decolonization in Indigenous Canada." *Journal of British Studies* 58 (July). doi:10.1017/jbr.2019.3

Heinrich, Steve (ed.). 2019. *Unsettling the Word: Biblical Experiments in Decolonization*. New York: Orbis.

Howe, Miles. 2015. *Debriefing Elsipogtog*. Halifax: Fernwood Publishing.

Human Rights Watch. 2013. *Those Who Take Us Away: Abusive Policing and Failures in Protection of Indigenous Women and Girls in Northern British Columbia, Canada*. Research report. hrw.org/reports/2013/02/13/those-who-take-us-away-0.

Hunt, Sarah. 2013. "Ontologies of Indigeneity: The Politics of Embodying a Concept." *Cultural Geographies* 21, 1.

———. 2011. "An Open Letter to My Local Hipsters." *Media Indigena*. September 20, 2011. mediaindigena.com/sarah-hunt/issues-and-politics/ an-open-letter-to-my-local-hipsters.

Indigenous Saskatchewan Encyclopedia. "Mistusinne." University of Saskatchewan (ND). teaching.usask.ca/indigenoussk/import/mistusinne.php.

Jafri, Beenash. 2012. "Privilege vs. Complicity: People of Colour and Settler Colonialism." *Equity Matters*, blog, March 21, 2012. ideas-idees.ca/blog/privilege-vs-complicity-people-colour-and-settler-colonialism.

Jewell, Eva and Ian Mosby. 2023. *Call to Action Accountability: A 2023 Status Update on Reconciliation*. Toronto: Yellowhead Institute. yellowheadinstitute.org/trc/.

Johnson, Daniel M. 2011. "From the Tomahawk Chop to the Road Block: Discourses of Savagism in Whitestream Media." *American Indian Quarterly* 35, 1.

Kanu, Yatta. 2011. *Integrating Aboriginal Perspectives into the Curriculum: Purposes, Possibilities, and Challenges*. University of Toronto Press.

Khasnabish, Alex, and Max Haiven. 2014. *The Radical Imagination: Social Movement Research in the Age of Austerity*. Halifax: Zed Books and Fernwood Publishing.

Kilibarda, Konstantin. 2012. "Lessons from #Occupy in Canada: Contesting Space, Settler Consciousness and Erasures within the 99%." *Journal of Critical Globalization Studies* 5.

Kino-nda-niimi Collective (eds.). 2014. *The Winter We Danced: Voices from the Past, the Future, and the Idle No More Movement*. Winnipeg: ARP Books.

Klein, Naomi. 2013. "Dancing the World into Being: A Conversation with Idle No More's Leanne Simpson." *Yes! Magazine*. March 5, 2013. yesmagazine.org/peace-justice/ dancing-the-world-into-being-a-conversation-with-idle-no-more-leanne-simpson.

Kovach, Margaret. 2009. *Indigenous Methodologies — Characteristics, Conversations, and Contexts* University of Toronto Press.

Kupperman, Karen. 2000. *Indians and English: Facing Off in Early America*. London: Cornell University Press.
Kymlicka, Will. 2001. *Politics in the Vernacular*. Oxford: Oxford University Press.
Laenui, Poka. 2000. "Processes of Decolonization." In *Reclaiming Indigenous Voice and Vision*, edited by Marie Battiste. Vancouver: UBC Press.
Leonard, Allenna. 2009. "The Viable System Model and Its Application to Complex Organizations." *Systemic Practice and Action Research* 22, 4.
Leroux, Darryl. 2019. *Distorted Descent: White Claims to Indigenous Identity*. Winnipeg: University of Manitoba Press.
Leroy, Justin. 2016. "Black History in Occupied Territory: On the Entanglements of Slavery and Settler Colonialism." *Theory & Event* 19, 4.
Lindeman, Tracey. 2023. "Quebecers Take Legal Route to Remove Indigenous Governor General Over Lack of French." *The Guardian*, August 10, 2023. theguardian.com/world/2023/aug/10/quebec-mary-simon-indigenous-governor-general-removed-canada-french.
Little Bear, Leroy. 2004. "Land: The Blackfoot Source of Identity." Presented at Beyond Race and Citizenship: Indigeneity in the 21st Century Conference. University of California.
Longman, Nickita, Emily Riddle, Alex Wilson, and Saima Desai. 2020. "'Land Back' is More Than the Sum of Its Parts." *Briarpatch Magazine*. September 2020. briarpatchmagazine.com/articles/view/land-back-is-more-than-the-sum-of-its-parts.
MacDonald, David. 2021. "Settler Silencing and the Killing of Colten Boushie: Naturalizing Colonialism in the Trial of Gerald Stanley." *Settler Colonial Studies*, 11, 1.
Mackey, Eva. 2016. *Unsettled Expectations: Uncertainty, Land and Settler Decolonization*. Halifax: Fernwood Press.
———. 2002. *The House of Difference: Cultural Politics and National Identity in Canada*. University of Toronto Press.
MacLeod, Alec (dir.). 1992. "Acts of Defiance." National Film Board of Canada. Documentary film. nfb.ca/film/acts_of_defiance.
Macoun, Alissa, and Elizabeth Strakosch. 2013. "The Ethical Demands of Settler Colonial Theory." *Settler Colonial Studies* 3, 3–4.
Madden, Paula C. 2009. *African Nova Scotian–Mi'Kmaw Relations*. Halifax: Fernwood Publishing.
Magnusson, Warren, and Karena Shaw (eds.). 2002. *A Political Space: Reading the Global Through Clayquot Sound*. Minneapolis: University of Minnesota Press.
Mamdani, Mahmood. 2020. *Neither Settler Nor Native: The Making and Unmaking of Permanent Minorities*. Cambridge, MA: Belknap Press.
Mander, Jerry. 1992. *In the Absence of the Sacred*. San Francisco: Sierra Club Books.
Mann, Charles. 2006. *1491: New Revelations of the Americas Before Columbus*. New York: Vintage Books.
Mashford-Pringle, Angela, and Angela Nardozi. 2013. "Aboriginal Knowledge Infusion in Initial Teacher Education at the Ontario Institute for Studies in Education at the University of Toronto." *International Indigenous Policy Journal* 4, 4.
Matsunaga, Jennifer. 2021. "Carefully Considered Words: The Influence of Government on Truth Telling about Japanese Canadian Internment and Indian Residential Schools." *Canadian Ethnic Studies* 53, 2.

Mawani, Renisa. 2010. *Colonial Proximities: Crossracial Encounters and Juridical Truths in British Columbia, 1871–1921.* Vancouver: UBC Press.
Maynard, Robyn. 2017. *Policing Black Lives: State Violence in Canada from Slavery to the Present.* Halifax: Fernwood Press.
McCarthy, Theresa. 2017. *In Divided Unity: Haudenosaunee Reclamation at Grand River.* Phoenix: University of Arizona Press.
McGuire, Mollie C., and Jeffrey S. Denis. 2019. "Unsettling Pathways: How Some Settlers Come to Seek Reconciliation with Indigenous Peoples." *Settler Colonial Studies* 9, 4.
McLeod, Christopher (dir.). 2002. *In the Light of Reverence.* Bullfrog Films. Documentary film.
Memmi, Albert. 1965. *The Colonizer and the Colonized.* Boston: Beacon Press.
Miheshua, Devon, and Angela Cavander-Wilson. 2004. *Indigenizing the Academy: Transforming Scholarship and Empowering Communities.* Lincoln, NE: University of Nebraska Press.
Miller, J.R. 2004. "'I Will Accept the Queen's Hand': First Nations Leaders and the Image of the Crown in the Prairie Treaties." In *Reflections on Native-Newcomer Relations: Selected Essays,* edited by James Miller. University of Toronto Press.
———. 1996. *Shingwauk's Vision.* University of Toronto Press.
———. 1989. *Skyscrapers Hide the Heavens: A History of Indian–White Relations in Canada.* University of Toronto Press.
Milloy, John. 1999. *A National Crime: The Canadian Government and the Residential School System, 1879–1986.* Winnipeg: University of Manitoba Press.
Moradi, Fazil. 2023. "In Search of Decolonised Political Futures: Engaging Mahmood Mamdani's Neither Settler Nor Native." *Anthropological Theory* 23, 4.
Moreton-Robinson, Aileen. 2015. *The White Possessive: Property, Power, and Indigenous Sovereignty.* Minneapolis: University of Minnesota Press.
Morgensen, Scott Lauria. 2012. "Queer Settler Colonialism in Canada and Israel: Articulating Two-Spirit and Palestinian Queer Critiques." *Settler Colonial Studies* 2, 2.
———. 2011. "The Biopolitics of Settler Colonialism: Right Here, Right Now." *Settler Colonial Studies* 1, 1.
———. 2010. "Settler Homonationalism: Theorizing Settler Colonialism within Queer Modernities." *glq: A Journal of Lesbian and Gay Studies* 16, 1–2.
Nakamura, Naohiro. 2012. "The Representation of First Nations Art at the Art Gallery of Ontario." *International Journal of Canadian Studies* 45–46.
Niezen, Ronald. 2003. *The Origins of Indigenism: Human Rights and the Politics of Identity.* Berkeley: University of California Press.
Noxolo, Pat, Parvati Raghuram and Clare Madge. 2012. "Unsettling Responsibility: Postcolonial Interventions." *Transactions of the Institute of British Geographers* 37, 3.
O'Connell. Anne. 2010. "An Exploration of Redneck Whiteness in Multicultural Canada." *Social Politics: International Studies in Gender, State and Society* 17, 4.
Obomsawin, Alanis (dir.). 2000. *Rocks at Whiskey Trench.* National Film Board of Canada. Documentary film. nfb.ca/film/rocks_at_whiskey_trench/
———. 1993. *Kanehsatake: 270 Years of Resistance.* National Film Board of Canada. Documentary film. nfb.ca/film/kanehsatake_270_years_of_resistance.

———. 1984. *Incident at Restigouche*. National Film Board of Canada. Documentary film.
Oudshoorn, Kieran. "The Fallout of Fairy Creek." *CBC Radio* June 1, 2023. cbc.ca/radiointeractives/features/the-fallout-of-fairy-creek.
Palmater, Pamela, 2016. "Shining Light on the Dark Places: Addressing Police Racism and Sexualized Violence Against Indigenous Women and Girls in the National Inquiry." *Canadian Journal of Women and the Law* 28, 2.
Parmenter, Jon. 2014. *The Edge of the Woods: Iroquoia, 1534–1701*. Lansing, MI: Michigan State University Press.
Perry, Adele, and Esyllt Jones. 2011. *People's Citizenship Guide: A Response to Conservative Canada*. Winnipeg: Arbeiter Ring Press.
Pertusati, Linda. 1996. "The 1990 Mohawk-Oka Conflict: The Importance of Culture in Social Movement Mobilization." *Race, Gender & Class* 3, 3.
Phillips, Ruth. 2005. "Re-Placing Objects: Historical Practices for the Second Museum Age." *Canadian Historical Review* 86, 1 (March).
Post Media. 2014. "In 1966, a Sacred Aboriginal Rock Was Blown Up to Make Way for a Man-Made Lake. Now Divers Search For Remnants." *The National Post*. August 27, 2014. nationalpost.com/news/canada/in-1966-a-sacred-aboriginal-rock-was-blown-up-to-make-way-for-a-man-made-lake-now-divers-search-for-remnants.
Prashad, Vijay. 2000. *The Karma of Brown Folk*. Minneapolis: University of Minnesota Press.
Preston, Kayla. 2022. "'Freedom Convoy' Rolls Through Ottawa Encouraging the Participation of Canada's Far-Right." *The Conversation*, February 1, 2022. theconversation.com/freedom-convoy-rolls-through-ottawa-encouraging-the-participation-of-canadas-far-right-175902.
Raibmon, Paige. 2005. *Authentic Indians: Episodes of Encounter from the Late 19th Century Northwest Coast*. Durham: Duke University Press.
Razavi, Kamyar. 2023. "Indigenous Rights Collide With $35B Western Canada Pipeline Expansion." *Global News*, November 22, 2023. globalnews.ca/news/10103531/indigenous-rights-collide-with-35b-western-canada-pipeline-expansion/.
Regan, Paulette. 2010. *Unsettling the Settler Within: Indian Residential Schools, Truth Telling, and Reconciliation in Canada*. Vancouver: UBC Press.
Renaud, Rob, and Susanne Reber. 2005. *Starlight Tour: The Last, Lonely Night of Neil Stonechild*. Toronto: Random House Canada.
Rifkin, Mark. 2013. "Settler Common Sense." *Settler Colonial Studies* 3, 3–4.
Robertson, Dwanna. 2015. "Invisibility in the Color-Blind Era: Examining Legitimized Racism against Indigenous Peoples." *American Indian Quarterly* 39, 2.
Rodríguez, Clelia O. 2018. *Decolonizing Academia: Poverty, Oppression and Pain*. Halifax: Fernwood Publishing.
Rogers, January. 2014. *Peace in Duress*. Vancouver: Talon Books.
Rossiter, David and Patricia Burke Wood. 2022. *Unstable Properties: Aboriginal Title and the Claim of British Columbia*. Vancouver: UBC Press.
Sablin, Ivan, and Maria Savelyeva. 2011. "Mapping Indigenous Siberia: Spatial Changes and Ethnic Realities, 1900–2010." *Settler Colonial Studies* 1, 1.

Salée, Daniel. 2010. "Indigenous Peoples and Settler Angst in Canada: A Review Essay." *Journal of Canadian Studies* 41.

Saul, John Ralston. 2008. *A Fair Country: Telling Truths About Canada*. Toronto: Penguin Books.

Schick, Carol. 2014. "White Resentment in Settler Society." *Race, Ethnicity & Education* 17, 1.

Schweighofer, Katherine. 2018. "A Land of One's Own: Whiteness and Indigeneity on Lesbian Land." *Settler Colonial Studies*, 8, 4.

Simpson, Audra. 2014. "The Chief's Two Bodies: Theresa Spence and the Gender of Settler Sovereignty." RACE2014 Keynote: Edmonton, Alberta. vimeo.com/110948627.

Simpson, Leanne. 2017. *As We Have Always Done: Indigenous Freedom Through Radical Resistance*. Minneapolis: University of Minnesota Press.

———. 2012. "Indigenous Perspectives on Occupation, Occupy Toronto Talks." Leanne Betasamosake Simpson blog. February 1, 2012). leannesimpson.ca/2012/02/01/indigenous-perspectives-on-occupation-occupy-toronto-talks/.

———. 2011. *Dancing on Our Turtle's Back: Stories of Nishnaabeg Re-Creation, Resurgence, and a New Emergence*. Winnipeg: Arbeiter Ring Press.

Simpson, Leanne, and Kiera Ladner (eds.). 2010. *This Is an Honour Song: Twenty Years Since the Blockades*. Winnipeg: Arbeiter Ring Press.

Sloan Morgan, Vanessa, and Heather Castleden. 2014. "An Exploration of Indigenous-Settler Relations in the Port Alberni Valley, British Columbia Regarding Implementation of the 2011 Maa-nulth Treaty." *The Canadian Geographer*. DOI:10.1111/cag.12120.

Smith, Graham. 2000. "Protecting and Respecting Indigenous Knowledge." In *Reclaiming Indigenous Voice and Vision*, edited by Marie Battiste. Vancouver: University of British Columbia Press.

Smith, Jackson, Cassandra Puckett and Wendy Simon. 2015. *Indigenous Allyship: An Overview*. Waterloo: Office of Aboriginal Initiatives, Wilfrid Laurier University.

Smith, Kevin. 2009. *Liberalism, Surveillance, and Resistance: Indigenous Communities in Western Canada, 1877-1927*. Athabasca, AB: AU Press.

Smith, Linda Tuhiwai. 1999. *Decolonizing Methodologies: Research and Indigenous Peoples*. London, UK: Zed Books.

SpearChief-Morris, Joy. "Pierre Poilievre Sharply Criticized After Speech to First Nations: 'You Have a Lot of Education to Do'." *Toronto Star*. July 11, 2024. thestar.com/politics/federal/pierre-poilievre-sharply-criticized-after-speech-to-first-nations-you-have-a-lot-of-education/article_c1869ba6-3e1e-11ef-8112-2ba3b757030b.html.

Spiceland, Erin, and Rachel Byington. 2015. "'Fact Check: Is Vanilla Ice Really Native?' Choctaw Researchers Investigate." *Indian Country Today*. April 28, 2015. indiancountrytodaymedianetwork.com.

Starblanket, Gina and Dallas Hunt. 2020. *Storying Violence: Unravelling Colonial Narratives in the Stanley Trial*. Winnipeg: ARP Books.

Starr, Amory. 2006. "'... (Excepting Barricades Erected to Prevent Us from Peacefully Assembling)': So-called 'Violence' in the Global North Alterglobalization Movement." *Social Movements Studies* 5, 1.

Stavans, Ilan (ed.). 2014. *Becoming Americans: Immigrants Tell Their Stories from Jamestown to Today*. Washington: Library of Congress.

Steacy, Lisa. 2022. "Man Who Allegedly Drove Truck into B.C. Residential School March Charged." *CTV News*. November 24, 2022. bc.ctvnews.ca/man-who-allegedly-drove-truck-into-b-c-residential-school-march-charged-1.6166606.

———. 2022. "'He Ran Me Over': Attendees of B.C. Residential School Memorial March Hit by Truck." *CTV News*. June 5, 2022. bc.ctvnews.ca/he-ran-me-over-attendees-of-b-c-residential-school-memorial-march-hit-by-truck-1.5933849.

Swamp, Jake. 2010. "Kanikonriio: Power of a Good Mind." In *Alliances: Re/Envisioning Indigenous-non-Indigenous Relationships*, edited by Lynne Davis. University of Toronto Press.

Tannock, Stuart. 2011. "Points of Prejudice: Education-Based Discrimination in Canada's Immigration System." *Antipode* 43, 4.

Taylor, Alan. 2010. *The Civil War of 1812: American Citizens, British Subjects, Irish Rebels, & Indian Allies*. New York: Vintage Books.

Teillet, Jean. 2022. "Indigenous Identity Fraud: A Report for the University of Saskatchewan." Saskatoon: University of Saskatchewan.

The Canadian Press. 2015. "Trudeau's 'Because it's 2015' Retort Draws International Attention." *Globe and Mail*. November 5, 2015. theglobeandmail.com/news/politics/trudeaus-because-its-2015-retort-draws-international-cheers/article27119856/.

———. 2022. "Meeting between B.C. RCMP, Indigenous Group Got 'Out of Hand' After Hit-and-Run at Memorial March." *CTV News*. June 9, 2022. bc.ctvnews.ca/indigenous-group-meets-with-rcmp-after-memorial-marchers-allegedly-hit-by-truck-driver.

Titley, Brian. 1992. *A Narrow Vision: Duncan Campbell Scott and the Administration of Indian Affairs in Canada*. Vancouver: UBC Press.

Tomiak, Julie. 2023. "Land Back/Cities Back." *Urban Geography* 44, 2.

Trouillot, Michel Rolph. 1997. *Silencing the Past: Power and the Production of History*. Boston: Beacon Press.

Tuck, Eve, and K. Wayne Yang. 2012. "Decolonization Is Not a Metaphor." *Decolonization: Indigeneity, Education & Society* 1, 1.

Tully, James. 2005. "The Struggles of Indigenous Peoples For and of Freedom." In *Political Theory and the Rights of Indigenous Peoples*, edited by Duncan Ivison, Paul Patton and Will Sanders. Cambridge University Press.

———. 1995. *Strange Multiplicity: Constitutionalism in an Age of Diversity*. Cambridge University Press.

Tunney, Catharine and Quenneville, Guy. 2002. "RCMP Feared That Mounties Might Leak Operational Plans to Convoy Protesters: Documents." *CBC News*, November 16, 2002. cbc.ca/news/politics/rcmp-insider-threats-convoy-covid-pandemic-ottawa-1.6569502.

Turner, Dale. 2006. *This Is Not a Peace Pipe: Towards a Critical Indigenous Philosophy*. University of Toronto Press.

Turner, Nancy, Marianne Ignace, and Ronald Ignace. 2000, "Traditional Ecological Knowledge and Wisdom of Aboriginal Peoples in British Columbia." *Ecological Applications* 10, 5.

Veracini, Lorenzo. 2015. *The Settler Colonial Present*. London: Palgrave Macmillan.
———. 2011. "Isopolitics, Deep Colonizing, Settler Colonialism." *Interventions* 13, 2.
———. 2010. *Settler Colonialism: A Theoretical Overview*. London: Palgrave Macmillan.
———. 2010. "The Imagined Geographies of Settler Colonialism." In *Making Settler Colonial Space: Perspectives on Race, Place and Identity*, edited by Tracy Banivanua Mar and Penelope Edmonds. Hampsire, UK: Palgrave Macmillan.
Vowel, Chelsea and Darryl Leroux. 2016. "White Settler Antipathy and the Daniels Decision." *TOPIA: Canadian Journal of Cultural Studies*, 36.
Walia, Harsha. 2021. *Border and Rule*. Chicago: Haymarket Books.
———. 2013. *Undoing Border Imperialism*. Oakland: AK Press.
———. 2010. "Transient Servitude: Migrant Labour in Canada and the Apartheid of Citizenship." *Race & Class* 52, 1.
Waters, Anne. 2004. "Language Matters: Non-discrete, Non-binary Dualism." In *Native American Thought*, edited by Anne Waters. Malden: Blackwell Press.
———. 2004. "Introduction." In *Native American Thought*, edited by Anne Waters. Malden: Blackwell Press.
Watts, Vanessa. 2013. "Indigenous Place-Thought & Agency Amongst Humans and Non-Humans (First Woman and Sky Woman go on a European World Tour!)." *Decolonization: Indigeneity, Education & Society* 2, 1.
Whynacht, Ardath. 2021. *Insurgent Love: Abolition and Domestic Homicide*. Halifax: Fernwood Publishing.
Williams, Nia and Rod Nickel. 2024. "Trans Mountain Oil Pipeline Change Approved by Canadian Regulator." *Reuters*, January 12, 2024. reuters.com/world/americas/canada-regulator-wraps-up-trans-mountain-pipeline-variance-hearing-2024-01-12/.
Willmott, Kyle, and Alec Skillings. 2021. "Anti-Indigenous Policy Formation: Settler Colonialism and Neoliberal Political Advocacy." *Canadian Review of Sociology/Revue canadienne de sociologie* 58, 4.
Willow, Anna J. 2012. *Strong Hearts, Native Lands: The Cultural and Political Landscape of Anishinaabe Anti-Clearcutting Activism*. Albany: State University of New York Press.
Wilson, Shawn. 2008. *Research Is Ceremony: Indigenous Research Methods*. Winnipeg: Fernwood Publishing.
Wolfe, Patrick. 2013. "Recuperating Binarism: A Heretical Introduction." *Settler Colonial Studies* 3, 3–4.
———. 2011. "After the Frontier: Separation and Absorption in U.S. Indian Policy." *Settler Colonial Studies* 1, 1.
———. 2006. "Settler Colonialism and the Elimination of the Native." *Journal of Genocide Research* 8, 4.
Yerxa, Jana-Rae. 2014 "Refuse to Live Quietly!" *Indigenous Nationhood Movement* blog. March 12, 2014. nationsrising.org/refuse-to-live-quietly.
Yesno, Riley. 2002. "Fake Indigenous Art Is the Tip of the Iceberg of Cultural Appropriation." *CBC News*. October 5, 2002. cbc.ca/documentaries/the-passionate-eye/fake-indigenous-art-is-the-tip-of-the-iceberg-of-cultural-appropriation-1.6606937.

York, Geoffrey, and Loreen Pindera. 1991. *People of the Pines: The Warriors and the Legacy of Oka.* Toronto: Little Brown.

Zinger, Ivan. 2023. *Office of the Correctional Investigator Annual Report 2022-2023* Office of the Correctional Investigator. oci-bec.gc.ca/en/content/office-correctional-investigator-annual-report-2022-2023#s9.

Zreik, Raef. 2016. "When Does a Settler Become a Native? (With Apologies to Mamdani)." *Constellations: An International Journal of Critical & Democratic Theory* 23, 3.

Index

Aboriginal title, 17–18, 113–114, 123n31
ally/allyship, 43–44, 161–162, 167, 175–176, 189–190
anger (emotion), 16, 21, 41, 162–163, 168–169, 173–174
appropriation (of culture), 12–13, 62, 76–80, 133, 170
assimilation, 8–9, 16, 34, 67
    and residential schools, 26, 46n21, 86, 138
    law and policy, 131
    as elimination, 60, 139–141
    in Russia, 134
Australia: 52–54, 75, 187

Bering Strait Theory, 55–56, 88n7
British Empire
    in North America, 23–26, 55, 57, 110, 117, 128
    in Africa and Asia, 27–28, 55, 128
Bryce, Dr. P.H., 85
Byrd, Jodi, 35, 129

Canadian Broadcasting Corporation (CBC), 68
capitalism, 126, 129, 170
    and the politics of recognition, 46n19,
    and privilege, 59, 146

and whiteness, 70–73
and policing, 155–156
anti-capitalism, 133–135, 173
children in care, 66, 81–82, 192
citizenship, 101, 113, 139, 141–142
    and multiculturalism, 15, 130
    and political identity, 41–43, 84, 120
    and socialization, 66–67, 131
colonization
    colonialism (concept), 10, 13, 19, 27–28, 52–53, 80, 183
    historical, 8, 11–12, 22–27, 85, 110, 183
    ongoing, vii, 8–9, 18, 70–71
    resistance to, 10, 21, 64
comfort, 41, 170, 179–180, 186–190
    and identity, 30–31, 86–88
    and ignorance, 71,
    moves to, 160, 164–165, 171–175, 180, 188–189
    see also discomfort
complicity, 7, 9, 71, 74–75, 125–127
    and exceptionalism, 167–169
    and fear, 154–155, 157–160, 174
    and responsibility, 37
    awareness of, 33, 41, 69, 165, 174–175, 180–182, 196
    denial of, 32, 171–172

Constitution (of Canada), 14, 20, 45n13, 113–115, 139–140, 152–153n31
convoy protest, 12–13, 17–18
COVID-19 pandemic, 11, 17

decolonization, viii, 28, 182, 184–185, 193–198, 200n3
   and resurgence, 185–186
   and Settler people, 186–191
   definition of, 182–183
Deloria, Vine Jr., 88n6, 98, 106, 121n7
diaspora, 102–104, 158–159
discomfort, 18, 30, 41–42, 127, 190–191
   and unsettling, 154, 168, 169, 173, 198
   importance of, 175–176, 181
   with being called Settler, 7
   with Indigenous resistance, 22, 167
   see also comfort
discrimination, *see* racism
dualism (non-discrete, non-binary), 33–36, 59

Eastern Métis, *see* identity fraud
education, 10–11, 66–67, 81, 181–182, 187
elimination (of Indigenous peoples), 19, 60–62, 89n19, 94n77, 138
enfranchisement, 16, 46n20, 138
epistemology, 38–39, 96–97

Fairy Creek, 171
fear (emotion), 41, 165, 167–168, 177n5
   and decolonization, 196–197
   and moves to comfort, 174, 176
   of immigrants, 128,
   of losing privilege, 154–155, 157–160, 164, 180–181
   of reprisal by authorities, 155–156
   see also discomfort
fisheries conflicts, 64–65, 89–90n24
frontier (narrative), 68–69, 75, 157, 181
futurity, 158

genocide, vii, 7, 9, 60–61, 86, 89n19, 140–141, 149
   see also elimination

Grassy Narrows, 14
guilt (emotion), 41, 161, 165, 168–172, 189–190

Haldimand Grant, 26, 64, 107, 192
Haudenosaunee Confederacy, 48n31, 194–195, 197–198
   relationships with other nations, 114, 116–117, 119
   land reclamations, 106–107, 122n23, 133–134
   Six Nations of the Grand River, 23–24
Hunt, Sarah, 39

identity
   Canadian, ix, 6, 49n40, 52, 57–58, 60, 109–110, 158–159
   concept of, 13, 27–30, 34, 58
   identity fraud, 62, 79–80, 92n56
   Settler, 7–8, 30–33, 141–142, 178–180, 195–198
   Indigenous, *see* Indigenous Identity
   questioning, 37
Idle No More, 6, 21, 47n29, 76
ignorance, 9, 15, 70–71, 86–87, 145–150, 165, 175
Indian Act, 26–27, 62, 131–132, 140, 151n16
Indigenous
   identity, 27, 99, 138–139, 184, 197
   international politics, 29, 48n32, 130
   place-thought, 96–99
   relationship to Settler identity, 33–35
   ways of knowing, 38–39, 96–98, 182–183
Ipperwash, 3, 82, 106–107, 122n23
intersectionality, 150–151n2, 196

Kovach, Margaret, 38–39, 98–99

labour and work, 35, 111, 123n27, 146–147
   and immigration, 71–73, 142–143
   and mobility, 147–148
   Indigenous labourers, 23, 55
   unfree labour, 26–28, 58–60, 75, 110

land and place, 6, 33, 95–96, 183–184
  and identity, 32, 69, 99–100, 105–106, 108–109, 178–179
  and knowledge, 38–39, 96–99
  colonial claims, 10, 24–26, 63, 67–68, 73, 157
  destruction of, 61–62, 158
  land acknowledgements, 8
  Land Back movements, 63–64, 143, 185, 192
  personality of, 99
  sharing, 8, 23

Macdonald, John A. (PM), 60, 111, 127
Mamdani, Mahmood, 27–28, 49n39
Memmi, Albert, 49n42, 157, 172, 177n5
Memorial to Laurier (1910), 40–41, 50n54
Mennonite Church of Canada (MCC), 192–193
Métis, 9, 13, 26, 34, 79, 82, 140, 154n31
migration, *see* mobility
Missing and Murdered Indigenous Women (MMIW), vii, 8–9, 44n1, 60–61, 83, 149
mobility, 103, 133–134
  as benefit, 146–148, 173
  as threat, 157–159
  Indigenous, 147
  stories of, 68
  to colonies, 52–53
  varying experiences of, 36, 104–105, 127–128
Mohawk (Nation), 20–21, 191
multiculturalism, 104, 137, 179
  and assimilation, 15, 133, 138–139, 145
  and immigration, 68, 103
  and model minorities, 143
  and nationalism, 74, 84, 142
  Canadian culture, 14, 18, 57, 59, 131–132, 197

nativism, 102–3
New Age spiritualism, 78, 170
No One Is Illegal, 70, 143

Northwest Mounted Police, *see* policing
Nunavut, Territory of, 80, 120–121

Occupy movements, 134–136
Oka standoff (1990), 20–21, 47n27, 63–64, 106–107, 122n23
ontology, 38–39, 96–97

Pacific Northwest, colonization of, 25, 117
Palmater, Pam, 156, 177n4
patriarchy, 54, 146, 164
peacemaker myth, 55, 84–87, 157, 187
policing, 6, 10, 44n6, 82, 155–156
  incarceration, 67, 107, 155–156
  Royal Canadian Mounted Police (RCMP), 11, 17–18, 82, 85, 93n65, 107–108
  police violence, 17–18, 26, 82, 85, 93n65, 128–129, 155–156
Poilievre, Pierre, 12, 17, 162
privilege, 72, 75, 125–126, 142, 145–146, 169, 172–173, 182
  and mobility, 36, 147
  and race, 59, 73
  loss of, 155–157,
  of ignorance, 86, 148, 191
  of inaction, 83
property (territorial), 16, 54, 63–64, 68, 99–101, 132, 147–148, 173

Québec, ix, 24, 45–46n13, 64, 83, 89–90n24, 103, 130, 145, 149
Québecois identity, 74, 109, 126

racism, 61–2, 72–73, 98–100, 102–4, 125–126, 172
  and Blackness, 36, 127
  and exogenous Others, 35, 71–72
  institutional, 10, 44–5n6, 81–83
  racial violence and genocide, 9 26, 80–81
  whiteness, 75–76, 103–105, 125, 127–8, 146
recognition, politics of, 15–16, 22, 29, 46n19, 62, 78–79, 138–141, 182
reconciliation, 8, 192–193

Regan, Paulette, 31–32, 85, 90–91n38, 94n77, 175
relationships, 1–4, 7–8, 22, 33–34, 42, 58–59, 105–106, 108–109
  and decolonization, 144, 185, 189–194, 197
  and claiming land, 32–33, 61–62
  and conflict, 36–37, 96, 111–112
  theories of, 96–99
  refusal of, 194
  to land and more-than-human world, 38–39, 95–96, 100, 132, 157, 179
  through treaty, 112, 114–121, 184, 191, 193–4
reserves, 9, 11, 16, 25–26, 46n20, 62, 67, 107, 111, 138–140
residential schools, 6, 22, 26, 44n4, 46n21, 65–66, 85
  and genocide, 60, 138
  denialism, 11–12, 86–87, 145
  graves, 10
  see also Truth and Reconciliation Commission (TRC)
resource extraction, 8, 54, 67, 76–77, 107, 133, 142–143
  pipelines, 14, 18, 82, 93n65, 107, 156, 162
  see also, capitalism
respectability politics, 166
responsibility, 40, 90n38, 160, 170, 174, 188, 196
  and identity, 28, 184–185
  denial of, 86, 105, 149, 167–169, 171, 173, 187
  for self-critique, 42, 189, 192–193
  to care for land, 41, 63, 106, 158
resurgence, 40, 185–186, 195
  and Settler responsibility, 41, 186, 189
  definition, 19
  Settler fear of, 157–158
Rogers, January, 1–5
  Forever (poem), 1–4, 116, 194–195
Royal Canadian Mounted Police (RCMP), *see* policing
Royal Commission on Aboriginal Peoples 1996 (RCAP), 8–9, 117

Royal Proclamation (1763), 23

Scott, Duncan Campbell, 46n21, 138
settler colonialism (concept), 37, 41–43, 52–62, 176n5
  and founding empires, 56–58
  debates about, 7, 27–28, 49n39
  goals of, 60–62
  spatial divisions, 63–64
  structures of, 33, 53–54, 64–67, 108–109, 126–129
  violence of, 9, 20–21, 61–62, 82–84
Simon, Mary (GG), 14, 45n13
Simpson, Leanne Betasamosake, 40, 76, 184–185
socialism, 73, 133–134
social movements, 38, 167, 178n12, 189
  policing of, 155–156
  reinforcing settler colonialism, 129–130, 137
sovereignty, 19, 21, 89–90n24, 105, 113, 122n19
  Settler Canadian, 14, 25, 60–62, 64, 114–115, 117, 132, 184
  Indigenous, 20, 22, 65, 107, 109, 166, 186
  and settler collectives, 53–54, 57, 74, 101
Spence, Chief Theresa, 149–150
subjectivity, 28–30, 33–34, 137
  exogenous Others, 58–60
  triangular relations, 35, 58–60

Tecumseh and the Shawnee Confederacy, 24
terra nullius, 111–113, 179–181
tiny homes, 173
transcendence (concept), 53–55, 62
treaties, 19–20, 24–26, 85, 113–121
  Douglas Treaties, 117, 120
  Numbered Treaties, 26, 118
  Two Row Treaty, 116–117, 194–195
trucker convoy, *see* Convoy protest
Truth and Reconciliation Commission (TRC), vii, 7–10, 14–15, 31, 60, 65, 151n7, 192–193

Unist'ot'en, *see* Wet'suwet'en
United States of America, 23–26, 57, 84–85, 103–104, 141, 167

Veracini, Lorenzo, 53–54, 58, 173
victimhood, 13, 71–72, 110, 171–172

Walia, Harsha, 70–71, 104–105
War of 1812–13, 24, 101
Watts, Vanessa, 38, 96–98
Wet'suwet'en (nation), vii, 7, 11, 17–18, 82, 107–108, 122n23
White Paper (1969), 20, 130, 162
white supremacy - see "racism"
Wolfe, Patrick, 49n43, 53–54, 94n77